WATERFOWL

WATERFOWL
Care, Breeding and Conservation

Simon Tarsnane
Photographs by Frank Todd

hancock
house

ISBN 0-88839-391-1
Copyright © 1996 Simon Tarsnane

Cataloging in Publication Data
Tarsnane, Simon, 1953-
   Waterfowl
   Includes bibliographical references
   ISBN 0-88839-391-1

1. Waterfowl culture. 2. Waterfowl—Breeding. I. Title.
SF510.W3T37 1996   636.6'8   C96-910395-6

Production: Lorna Brown
Editing: Nancy Miller
Cover photo: Frank Todd
Back cover photo: Sandy Smith

Published simultaneously in Canada and the United States by

HANCOCK HOUSE PUBLISHERS LTD.
19313 Zero Avenue, Surrey, B.C. V4P 1M7
(604) 538-1114   Fax (604) 538-2262

HANCOCK HOUSE PUBLISHERS
1431 Harrison Avenue, Blaine, WA 98230-5005
(604) 538-1114   Fax (604) 538-2262

Contents

The Photographer
Frank S. Todd

Almost all of the waterfowl photographs in this book are the work of Frank Todd.

Frank has been a friend of mine for more than twenty years, and when it came time to assemble photographs for this book, I could think of no single source better than Frank's enormous library of photographic work from which to extract the necessary slides. True to his usual complete unselfishness when it comes to helping a fellow aviculturist, Frank gave me everything I needed. Indeed, when it came to photographs of birds that number only fifty to one hundred survivors in the wild, Frank literally hauled out sheets of slides, asking, "How many do you want?"

Frank Todd is a well-known figure in aviculture. He built up the finest collection of waterfowl in America (at the time), at Sea World, San Diego, where he was first, Corporate Curator of Birds and later Corporate Vice-President of Aviculture and Research. His love of Arctic and Antarctic birds and mammals led to decades of research in these regions (a work still ongoing), and he ultimately brought to fruition the design and operation of the Penguin Encounters at Sea Worlds in San Diego, Ohio, Texas and Florida, some of the most sophisticated zoological exhibits ever.

Frank is also credited with successes in many other fields of aviculture including the raising and management of the only Californian Condor in captivity in the 1960s. Since then, he has had many first breeding successes with a vast array of different birds such as ramphastids, birds of prey, lorikeets, tinamous, ibis, penguins, alcids and so on.

His vast knowledge of animal life is well known to those in the zoological business, but still his favorites remain the aviformes of the world. Apart from being a world-class photographer,

Frank Todd and Cereopsis Goose.   *Photo: M. Lubbock*

he is also a distinguished lecturer and author of many books and articles, and is a tireless worker in the field and at his home which he shares with his wife Sherlyn and their two dogs, in San Diego, California. He is currently the Executive Director of Eco-Cepts International.

I once described Frank (to a friend of mine), as a rare cross between a tiger and an Indian guru. You don't know what you've got, but when it speaks, shut up and listen!

Frank, for all your help and advice, a giant "*Gracias, amigo.*"

Dedication

To Warren Hancock (1914-1981)—A Gentleman

Although I hardly knew him, he was something of a legend in waterfowl circles. He was a true gentleman, and a man gifted with the art of stockmanship. His studies (mostly committed to paper) of the Arctic birds which he so dearly loved are classics in detail and intimate observation. His many trips to Alaska enabled him to collect, photograph and study birds in the wild, and this knowledge helped him in his captive endeavors. I dedicate this book to him and his work.

His son Bill carries on the good work in a way that would make Warren very proud.

Thanks Warren, for your inestimable contribution to us.

Foreword

In this impressive single-volume treatise, Simon Tarsnane has promulgated something entirely uncommon in the annals of waterfowl literature—a concise and informative blend of the captive management and natural history of virtually all genera in the waterfowl family, together with photographs of exceptional quality that are probably unequalled in any other book on the subject.

While it is geared primarily to the waterfowl breeder, the book surveys aspects of the natural history, ecology and conservation of many species, and contains some heretofore unpublished wild observations of the behavior and biology of certain waterfowl, and these may be helpful to those working with some of the species which have proven more difficult to propagate.

As was the case with his first publication, *A Manual of Ornamental Waterfowl Management*, the text of this book is of high quality and should prove extremely helpful to both the novice and more experienced aviculturist and Simon's hypotheses on some of the lesser understood aspects of waterfowl culture will prove stimulating and thought provoking to the more serious students in this field. His grasp of the subject matter is superb and is undoubtedly the result of his many years of propagational experience with waterfowl both in England and America.

Whether an aviculturist, zoo curator, biologist or simply a person interested in the propagation and conservation of waterfowl, you will find this book an invaluable addition to the store of knowledge on waterfowl breeding and management.

GEORGE A. ALLEN, JR.
GAMEBIRD RESEARCH AND PRESERVATION CENTER
SALT LAKE CITY, UTAH

Introduction
and
Acknowledgments

As mankind's relentless colonization of new land continues, more animals than ever face the threat of extinction. Waterfowl are certainly not immune to the effects of man, although some are well able to adapt. Growing human populations need space to live, farm, fish and recreate. As a result some animal species, already threatened, will be extirpated.

Developing countries and developed ones must put the needs of their peoples first. The consequence is habitat loss at a staggering daily rate. As deltas and marshlands are drained, both waterfowl and their habitats disappear. The millions of acres of trees leveled to put a highway through the South American rain forests has already altered local climates. What is the answer? Do we deny ourselves progress or do we exterminate species? The only answer to this immense problem is management. Sensible management is a process of give and take. In order to save a particular piece of wetland habitat, it might become necessary to financially compensate those who would despoil it. Personally, I feel the cost may be worthwhile. On the other hand, holding up the construction of projects large or small, because a tiny, isolated vernal pool is discovered with the "possibility" that it "could" house a Tiger Salamander or a lone Fairy Shrimp, is sheer lunacy.

Many wildlife groups have banded together to force governments to pay attention to the serious plight of some of the world's disappearing habitats and the flora and fauna that inhabit them. Some countries have embraced the ideas of conservation and management, others merely pay lip service to the intent. Still others would like to help preserve lands and species but can't get the cooperation of their own people. It is a never-ending exasperation which I believe will only ever be realized financially. If a poacher or an industrialist can be shown that an animal or a piece of land, preserved now, can be worth more over time than just the one time pay off they normally expect, we have some hope. A live animal can be photographed many thousands of times by eager tourists bringing with them their dollars, thus an animal's capital potential can be huge. A dead elephant is only worth the price of its tusks.

The politics of the wild are mirrored by the politics of captive propagation. Traditionally, it was the zoological parks which had the most access to species because of the financial and influential backing of their patrons. The species that were collected from around the world were rarely or never shared with the private breeder. On the other hand, it was the private breeders who made immense contributions to the successful propagation of various species when allowed to participate in the sharing of a particular species with a zoological institute. Most of the certificates for first breeding of waterfowl hang on the walls of private breeders, not in the offices of zoo curators.

I am glad to see the situation changing. Information and species are being farmed out more and more to those who can do the best job with them, be it in the zoological or private sector. There are many things both parties can learn from each other, and indeed, should learn. Between the two sides exists a vast amount of knowledge and practical expertise. We must ensure that our prejudices do not become a gravestone for any species and that, in part, is the reason for this book.

There are many books covering waterfowl and their habitats in the wild. Among my favorites are the works of Delacour, Scott and especially Frank Todd. These works are incredibly detailed and researched and beautifully photographed. This book concentrates on waterfowl and their successful propagation and management in captivity. I originally compiled it in 1985. This will be a second edition, updated substantially, as much has changed in the propagation and management of waterfowl in ten years. It remains my intention to provide a working book for those enthusiasts who keep and breed waterfowl. Many well-known species may seem to have been glossed over. This is simply because many breeders keep and propagate these species without difficulty.

The book has been laid out with chapters relating to captive management, propagation and disease control followed by chapters describing the behavior and idiosyncrasies of the various forms of ducks, geese and swans in captivity. Most of the information, observations and suggestions are drawn from personal experience. I do not expect people to agree with some topics: this in itself being a good thing. Through making suggestions or observations about a topic, ideas evolve—and the more productive ideas available to propagators, the better the end results and standards in aviculture will be.

I would like to express my thanks to the many people who have helped me compile this book. Firstly, I owe a great debt of gratitude to Walt Sturgeon and Melissa Miller for Americanizing an otherwise English book! Also between them they edited, corrected and rewrote some sections and provided additional data. Also, I thank Betty Bottom who typed the original draft copy, and Bob Elgas for supplying a most interesting section on the discovery of the Tule Goose. I would also like to thank some people who have had a major influence on my career in waterfowl, and whom I consider friends and mentors. They are Frank and Sherlyn Todd, Mike and Ali Lubbock, Chris Marler, George Allen, Bill Hancock, Gus and Karen Hebb, Dick and Dart Matice, Isolee and Sandy Smith, Walt Sturgeon and Bob Elgas. There are many, many more friends that I have been lucky enough to meet and get to know over the years, and you all know who you are. My thanks and best wishes to each and every one of you.

Finally, I would like to thank my wife Ellen for her ever-present help and support.

1

Stockmanship

"Stockmanship" and "stockmen" are terms normally associated with agricultural enterprises. The swineherds, shepherds and herdsmen are all stockmen, as are cowboys and poultrymen. They all have one thing in common; a good stockman is a good planner. He knows everything about his charges before his season begins. He knows when a particular cow or sheep will be giving birth, or that grazing in a certain field is coming to an end and plans for new grass areas. He is a vet, biologist, countryman, manager, woodsman, carpenter and handyman, but most importantly a good stockman cares deeply about his animals. He knows by the color of the sky and the direction of the wind that tomorrow will be bitterly cold and moves extra food and protection for his beasts—instinctive behavior.

It is important to realize that keeping waterfowl is an avocation, not an occupation, and attention to the flock is often necessary twenty-four hours a day, seven days a week, and it is carried out on the birds' schedule, not yours. With waterfowl, there are literally millions of dos and don'ts that can only be taught by experience and lots of dedication. Some of us are lucky enough to be full-time waterfowl breeders and keepers, but most waterfowl enthusiasts have other jobs (in order to support their expensive hobby) and simply cannot be around their ducks all the time. In short, in order to be a good stockman it is often necessary to sacrifice sleep and other activities to meet the demands of the birds, and success seems to be directly proportional to the time devoted to them.

A good waterfowl keeper not only needs to be a caring stockman, he also needs to be a good observer and be acquainted with duck psychology. He should know how his birds behave, what they do and don't like and what they hate. He may be able to induce an unproductive pair to breed by many diverse and subtle ways. It may be that the area they are in is to blame or that their pen mates are unsuitable companions. They may need a certain type of nest box or an addition to their diet at a specific time of year. There are thousands of important little things of which to take notice. At feeding time, he doesn't rush through the pens spewing out a hail of grain and pellets from the feed bucket. Taking his time, he empties away spilt food and cleans the feeding area, so as not to encourage mold build up or allow bacteria to flourish. He looks for potentially lethal things in the pen, such as bits of wire, hog rings, nylon bristles from a scrub brush, plastic bags, ring pulls, even the fork of a branch with which a bird may be able to hang itself. The birds are also individually scrutinized for signs of stress disease or injury. He thinks something like this...

That limp. How did the bird get it? Does the foot look infected? Has it been attacked or did the bird damage it on the side of the pond or catch it in the wire mesh.... How about that old Rosybill? She's looking a bit hunched up and that normally bright red eye looks a bit pale. Maybe I need to catch him and take some fecal or blood samples or a throat culture.... These geese look a little thin and they don't seem to have eaten much. Maybe there's an internal parasite to blame—better get a fecal sample to identify the culprit so I can treat it specifically.... How about these breeding areas? What about that mixing of Wood Ducks, Hooded Mergansers and Goldeneye?

On and on this thought process goes, all of it vital to good management. Let us run through the months of the year to see which topics and hazards arise and when we can expect them.

July through August see most waterfowl flightless and in

eclipse plumage. Instinctively, the birds are nervous. This is the time of year in the wild that predation occurs so easily because they are flightless. They spend more time on water. Can they get out all right or will they beat their pin feathers on the side of the pond and bleed? They need protein and fiber in order to harden those new quills, some grain mixed with the pellets will help. Give them enough areas of shade and hiding cover. Make certain no one is getting bullied by already molted birds. If the weather is wet—are those eclipse feathers getting soaked? If it's not wet, have the birds got enough cool shade?

Coming into September the birds are almost fully feathered. The Hoodies are already displaying; the Wood Ducks and Mandarins are back in color. The days are shorter and it's colder in the early morning. Add a little more wheat to the diet to develop more of a fat layer to combat oncoming winter. Are those big trees outside the fence safe or will they come crashing down on the fence in a gale? The predators are moving more, sensing hard weather ahead. Put out some traps. The leaves need cleaning up. Put back feeding time an hour in the morning and advance it an hour in the evening so during the ducks' most active periods they have privacy and food. If you have a stream or river supplying your ponds, keep an eye on the weather; there may be flooding. Check indoor quarters for your birds if you live in an area that gets cold during winter. Disinfect bowls and drinking equipment, and check heat lights. If your birds winter outside, start to erect shelters for them and make sure they have clean, mold-free bedding.

November sees the days shortening even more. Winds and the first snows can be expected this month in some northern areas. Check aviary roofs for strength. Be ready to get out of bed at three in the morning to push snow off netting. Check water pumps if you use them to make sure they are okay for the next month or so. Maybe heat tape the inlet and outlet pipes to prevent freezing. Check aerators and bubblers. Now is the time to bring in some of the smaller or tropical species such as Ringed Teal, Orinoco Geese, Magpie Geese and Tree Ducks. Also now is the time to bring in nest boxes to dry; ready to be cleaned and repainted.

December, January and February are the coldest months. In the cold northern areas, all but the hardiest birds are inside. Those outside have bedding, shelter and heat. Ponds have bubblers, heat bars or aerators to maintain some open water. Pumps are turned off before they freeze solid. The indoor birds must not be crowded. Stress-induced maladies rear their ugly heads. Make sure you have fresh supplies of vitamins and antibiotics. Birds that don't see sunlight for a while may need vitamin supplements in their feed. Watch out for those little things such as a bird that starts paddling when it is in the water, not wanting to settle in as normal. You catch the bird and a check reveals its breast feathers are starting to deteriorate. A check on the preen gland indicates a lack of oil suggesting a blockage. A Smew breaks a leg high up at the hip jumping into an empty pond during cleaning. The vet says it won't mend—it's too high a break to be able to splint. An hour's thought comes up with a tape splint. A little improvisation pays off and two months later he is walking with barely a trace of a limp.

Birds indoors don't like to be on concrete floors. Bumblefoot develops quite quickly under these conditions. There are many good rubber and vinyl matting products available today and they are lightweight and easy to hose down. One I like is called Neo-Tex and is used in the food service industry. Avoid using artificial turf products, as geese love to rip it up and try to eat the fibers.

Indoor lighting must be turned off at night otherwise birds may start molting and Arctic birds start to think it must be summer. Heat fans set at 50°F are used and the fan blades suitably wired over to prevent teal flying in and being chopped to pieces.

Cleaning is a daily job, done slowly and quietly to avoid stressing the birds. All standing water puddles are dispersed so that a dry surround to the pool is maintained. Remember, a warm, wet duck is as dead as a cold, wet duck. The fans move air so no

damp, still pockets form, bringing bronchial or aspergillosis outbreaks.

The sides of the outside ponds are kept ice free so birds can
get out. Empty pens have their ponds chlorinated, soaked and
rinsed thoroughly ready for spring.

March can bring bad weather, but is generally warmer. Birds
indoors have their heat reduced gradually so that they acclimatize
to outdoor temperatures, two weeks should be enough. Nest
boxes are put out, ponds filled and more breeders pellets are
added to the diet. Grit is changed from granite chip to oyster shell
to help egg formation. Incubators are checked, fumigated and
tested. Brooders and infrared lights are checked and feeding
bowls and drinkers for young birds are sterilized.

A breeding pen plan is made. Why didn't the Smew breed
well last year? Was it because the Hooded Mergansers kept flying
from the bottom pond and using the Smew boxes? A partition
will prevent this. Were the Ross' Geese upset because of the
Ruddyheads next door continually mock charging the fence?
Some fiberglass sheeting between the two pens will settle them.
Why was the Black-necked Swan clutch infertile? Too small a
pond or too shallow so they couldn't copulate properly? Deepen
and enlarge the pond or switch them to a more suitable pen. Was
the reason that the Barrow's Goldeneye didn't lay (when you
were certain that they would) because of the Eiders in the same
pen pushing them around? Were the boxes properly positioned?
Check it!

Finally the birds are put outside. As they are released, check
their wing bands or leg bands. Replace old worn ones. Color band
females individually so you can see who is laying and who isn't.
Keep a record of all your birds' ages, origins, whether they are
pinioned or full winged, past breeding performance, parents, etc.
The diet should lean heavily toward a breeder ration now as the
birds settle into a new season. Eggs are picked up and recorded
daily when the bird is off the nest. Keep an eye open for egg-
bound birds. Predators are really moving now—more traps. The
weather can be uncertain—bring in clutches from low-lying,
flood-affected areas just in case. Test the incubator and get that

generator installed in case of spring power failures. Eggs are set and candled, with the infertile and dead ones disposed of.

April–July sees all the usual laying, hatching and rearing activity—sitting up nights helping weak birds out of eggs— swearing to improve the blood lines next season! And so on and so on....

All of these points are a mere handful of the sort of things a conscientious waterfowl keeper will be thinking and doing.

Weather varies up and down the hemispheres, thus it is safe to say if you are in Florida your birds may never have to be indoors, whereas in North Dakota and Montana they may be.

Those points are just a few of the basics of good waterfowl maintenance, and if an individual hasn't the time, then stamp collecting is a far better pastime!

In early summer your friends might phone you and say "Can we come and see the birds?" They more than likely possess a horde of small, rampaging hooligans who have no idea of how to behave around your stock. Explain to them nicely that the birds are laying and are very vulnerable to being upset and deserting nests because of ill-mannered behavior. Tell them to come in October when all the birds are back in color again. "Oh, no—it's too cold then."—Well, you didn't really want to see them anyway did you?

2

Facilities

Planning suitable facilities for the various waterfowl can at first seem an impossible task. How does one mimic the Brazilian jungle, the high Andean plateau or the sea shore? Luckily one trait of waterfowl under captive conditions is their adaptability. Essentially, a pen need only provide shelter, nesting facilities, grazing and a watering and bathing area. Different species utilize any one of these commodities to a greater or lesser extent. One important aspect of a pen is cosmetic value. A collection ought to be a special place for its owner—somewhere where birds and their surroundings blend and harmonize. This takes hard work and dedication. Keeping a large collection tidy or a small one clean can be quite a headache, but with thought many problems are overcome.

Water Supply

Before fences are erected or plants installed, water supply has to be considered. Three sources of water are utilized in collections and in most cases a hybrid including two or three sources will provide the best year-round system.

First is a natural stream, pond or river water supply. In many respects this can be the most hazardous—great attention must be paid to the following points.

Rivers or streams are always susceptible to pollution. Chemical spills can be disastrous and can come at any time. Farmers are using pesticide sprays more and more. In areas of high rainfall, this accumulates in streams or rivers, altering pH values, killing plant and insect life and affecting your birds. Second, high and low flow rates must be carefully considered. A pretty little stream in spring can become a raging destructive torrent in winter or during a quick rainstorm. In summer, the same stream may become a mere trickle leaving pools stagnant and susceptible to disease outbreaks. Also, debris washed downstream can clog grids and block pipes. Predators use water courses while hunting; raccoons, mink, rats and others can enter a collection this way and kill many birds. Pumping water from a stream for use in your ponds also causes problems. Filters must be regularly checked as well as the mechanics of the pump itself. Electrical outlets may be some distance away, so gasoline or diesel fuel stored at the pump site can result in accidental pollution. If the intake pipe derives its water from another duck pond, the end must be screened to stop birds being sucked in head first. Also, there are legal implications involved in water rights, amounts allowed to be pumped and, of course, discharge of used water back into the river or stream.

Artesian, or well water, is a better proposition as generally the water is of good quality and if the well is drilled to a sensible depth, seasonal water-table variations will not affect your water availability. There is no debris or pollution to worry about and no vermin intrusions should occur. This water is generally clean and cold, a valuable asset to any waterfowl enterprise. It is always a sensible idea to get the water tested for acidity or alkali levels as this may affect varieties of water plant and insect life in your pond.

City water is the third type normally used. Its huge disadvantage is one of cost unless only a few small ponds are used. However it is clean, dependable, and with its small amounts of chlorine, fairly pure. The chlorine content can help delay algae buildup on concrete ponds during warmer months. One method to delay this further on small ponds (6' x 4' x 2') is to immerse a salt lick block (the kind used for cattle or sheep) in the water.

".Seconds," blocks that are delivered chipped or broken, can be bought very cheaply and will dissolve overnight. Small ponds can be treated in this fashion once every five or six weeks and algae buildup can be controlled fairly effectively. Of course, the other benefit is to the birds themselves—especially sea ducks. Most sea-dwelling waterfowl are equipped with salt extraction glands. In fresh water, these glands become flaccid and are subject to viral attacks. Keeping these glands at least partially active by the addition of salt, either in their pond water or in a food bowl, may be beneficial to the birds' overall health. It has to be noted however, that many successful propagators of sea ducks never use salt at all.

Another advantage of city water is it does not have to be pumped; it can be delivered via a hose pipe under relatively good pressure in most areas. This helps keep water open and ice free in winter.

Recycling Water

A lot of attention is paid today to water conservation. While this is sensible, it will also help cut down on water bills. Recycling water via a pump can be a very effective and economical choice. This may require the construction of a filter to take out bio-mass such as leaves, feathers, floating grain, small rock or sand particles, and the like. In my own experiments in California where water is at a premium, I have found that sand filters tend to become clogged too quickly in a system that has even a small bird population. There is simply too much bio-mass. My friend Dick Matice designed a system that worked very well and kept the water beautifully clear, however the population of waterfowl in this aviary was tiny. Under lightly to normally stocked conditions there is too much bio-mass to filter out. My aviaries were run with recycled water and after a week or so in the hot summer months, algae would start to green the water and they were emptied and cleaned. All had large drains in the bottom and so were easily emptied and cleaned with a high pressure hose that stripped the algae off the cement. Stubborn areas were sprinkled with pool chlorine, allowed to "soak," and then hosed off. Make certain the birds cannot access a pond being treated in this way.

The filter system I used comprised of a tub of 100 gallon capacity (a stock watering tub would also work; make sure the capacity is larger than needed), which had a back flush system installed in the bottom. The filter material was pea gravel filling the tub to three-quarter capacity and having a double-folded fitted screen of shade cloth on the top. The shade cloth lasted very well and caught all the initial bio-mass in the out flowing water, while the pea gravel trapped a lot more. Periodically the whole thing was backwashed by a 2-h.p. pump and the system worked as well as could be expected. (There is a product currently being tested at golf courses that introduces a bacteria into the water that specifically attacks the tiny algae organisms that cause water to "green." It is said to be harmless to fish life and all other water life. If it proves harmless to waterfowl, it may well be worth investigating.)

Pumps and Hydrodynamics

Most modern, high-output centrifugal pumps work well in aviaries. These pumps are available in a variety of horsepowers and inlet/outlet sizes from industrial supply outlets or even large department stores. All we have to do is figure out what we need from a pump in terms of volume and voltage (220 can be cheaper than 110) and order it! As an example of effectiveness, let me use my aviary experiences to outline some good and bad points.

My original aviary consisted of seven ponds connected by channels or "spillways." The water was delivered into the top three ponds (which were quite small), flowed out down the spillways to two further ponds of larger size that flowed into the sixth and finally the last pond. The aviary was constructed on land that had a seven-foot gradient difference over 120 feet. I chose a 1-h.p. pump that could be wired to 115 or 230 volts (I used 115), and which had 1½ inch inlet and discharge ports. It was rated as giving 4860 gallons per hour at 10 feet of head. The system was designed to recycle the water from its point of entry, through the ponds, into and through a filter and finally into a large tank (700 gallon capacity). As the tank collected water, a mercury float switch inside the tank (wired to the pump) would float up until the tank was nearly full, at which point it would automatically turn the pump on and water would again be recycled through the ponds. As the level fell in the tank, the switch would fall until it turned the pump off and so the cycle continued. The pump was fitted with a back flow check valve at the outlet port to stop the pump losing its prime and the delivery pipes to the top three ponds were reduced in size from 1½ inch to 1 inch to improve pressure. Furthermore, the delivery pipes all had independent valves that could be used to turn down or stop water for each pond, for the purpose of pond cleaning or repair. When the time came to replace the supply with fresh water, ponds were drained into the tank which was subsequently drained and the water used to irrigate trees on the property outside the pens.

The whole system worked well but did have some time-consuming design flaws that I vowed never to incorporate into the next aviaries I would build. One problem was that I had not installed drains in the ponds, figuring that they were small enough to clean by hand, and another was that I had not brought in an outside water source to refill them or clean them with. This meant dragging hoses into the pens in order to clean out the ponds. Cleaning days were dreaded! I had to use a small, portable submersible pump to pump out the ponds, then brush them to scrub off the algae, then spray them with a high pressure hose and pump out that waste water again before refilling them. It became a chore I hated.

My second aviary design got rid of a lot of these problems. I had made a study of pond systems from Koi carp ponds to sewage ponds. This new aviary had a main supply of water on hand within the aviary. All ponds had drains and I installed "bottom squirters." These were ¼-inch pipes fitted strategically into the bottom of each pond and supplied with water from the pump. The new pump was a 2-h.p. model wired to 220 volts, with 2-inch ports and narrowing down the flow into ¼-inch pipes gave very good pressure to the water at the bottom of the ponds, allowing the warmer surface water to mix with the cooler, bottom layer, which helped to prevent algae build up, and thus lengthy cleaning sessions! This new complex had four large ponds incorporating two waterfall inlets and a purely cosmetic "spring" and gave me a flow of nearly 8,000 gallons per hour which fairly flew the water around the system and made for a really impressive waterfall. I designed a larger filter of the same materials as previously mentioned and used the bottom half of a 1,200 gallon septic tank as the catchment receptacle. Otherwise the whole system was much the same as the original design (just larger), and worked flawlessly. Furthermore, one comment I got from visitors was always how pretty everything was inside the aviary and how lovely the sound of flowing water was. This was all down to design esthetics, about which, more later.

Ponds

Ponds fall into two categories; ponds with a natural bottom, and those with an artificial structure, i.e., concrete or fiberglass.

To maintain waterfowl on large ponds a "natural" bottom is your best option. However, there are several points that need attention with this type of environment. Assuming that the pond bed holds water, the amount and delivery of water must be considered.

If you have a stream filling your pond remember that possible winter flooding or summer "dry ups" can be serious problems for your birds. If ponds are susceptible to seasonal water variations, make sure the banks slope very gently to allow easy access and exit for your birds or have suitable spots built in for this purpose.

Water and ducks erode bank sides very efficiently. With a good volume of moving water some thought must be given to where the stream flows into the pond and out. Water entering a pond from a channel starts up a gentle whirlpool effect. Banks either side of an entry point can be eaten away quite quickly. At the exit point water converges from two sides. Make sure both areas have a concrete "apron" or some fabrication of rocks or large stones to prevent erosion.

In pondside low spots, where water occasionally breaches the

26

bank, birds will quickly dabble and uproot grass and surrounding vegetation. Fine mesh, plastic wire laid from 2 feet back from a bank to 2 feet into the water prevents busy beaks doing their work. Make sure the mesh is well seated or birds may get their heads caught under it. The alternative to an anti-erosion mesh system is to use rocks or boulders. If you use these materials to help preserve your pond sides try as much as possible to get material of roughly the same size. Large holes between stones can trap feet, beaks and heads—leading to inevitable consequences.

Ponds are usually connected by pipes or channels. Cater for at least four times the volume of moving water generally encountered. Thus pipes will be large enough to handle this extra volume during winter flooding. Channels should have high enough sides to prevent excess water from spilling onto the surrounding ground and flooding it. Pipes also have to be duckproof. Of course, none of these systems are completely foolproof. A sudden downpour can cause puddles anywhere, and once standing water is encountered by ducks, they start dabbling away!

In many ways, small pens and concrete ponds are easier to look after. Concrete ponds only need cleaning and draining occasionally but problems can arise.

Most of the plumbing in today's ponds is of plastic origin. It is important not to skimp in this area by using cheaper, thin-walled pipe. Remember that the pipe will be in the ground covered over for many years and once laid, may not be accessible again. Use good quality PVC schedule 40 or ABS. Make sure to use the correct glue for the pipe as well. Take the time to clean all joints before they are glued and leave the pipe exposed if possible until all has been laid so you can pressure test it for leaks or bad joints. Nothing is more frustrating than to have to dig a pipe back up to repair it. Don't encourage blockages by using different sizes of pipe. I like to use 4-inch piping as this diameter will take a lot to clog. When laying cement around drain pipe collars, make sure that the cement is tightly bonded to the drain collar so it will not leak. Don't use 90° "Ls"; these become bottlenecks for debris. Use 22° or 45° turns that will allow exiting water to carry debris away. If you are not using spillways to deliver water between ponds and are using a piped delivery, you may wish to incorporate a stand pipe as both drainer and overflow pipe for emergencies. Ducks like to investigate holes that water flows into and sometimes will lounge against an exit pipe causing an overflow. A stand pipe needs to be situated above the normal level of the pond and at the same level as the middle of the exit pipe. As the water rises in the pond because of "fowl blockage"(!), it will be able to flow down the stand pipe into the drain before the water crests the pond's banks and produces a muddy mess around the side of the pond. Finally, make sure birds can not access the top of the stand pipe. Because they are curious by nature, ducks could get heads or bodies trapped, so use a wire cover. The only drawback to using stand pipes is one of cosmetics, it is not the nicest thing to see sticking out above the water line. This is why I prefer to use spillways. In cases where water is delivered between pens and where you do not wish the birds to commingle, a grid can be constructed to keep apart the web-footed menace!

Cement ponds are prone to cracking during settlement but attention to the pond's construction before any cement is poured will pay dividends. In the initial excavation of the pond area, make the size of the pond wider and deeper by at least 8 inches. This will allow you to put in a 4-inch layer of fill gravel to act as a blanket for the curing cement. Always use wire to reinforce the pond and allow for a degree of movement during hardening. This will offset cracking and lengthy and costly repair work. You may still get a few surface cracks but if you use 4 inches of thickness to the cement, the cracking will only occur at the cement's surface, not all the way through. Finally, in hotter locales, wet the cement down every hour during the curing process with a fine misting spray; this helps to minimize cracking and facilitates the curing process.

When it becomes necessary to clean or scrub out cement ponds, make sure any bristles from the brush are washed away or picked up. The old wire brushes were very effective cement cleaners but their shed bristles were a death trap to waterfowl when picked up and ingested. Nylon brushes are potentially as lethal, but their bristles clean away easier in the stream of a good powerful hose.

The use of rocks to line ponds or to give cosmetic value to a pond can be a double-edged sword. The worst way of doing this is to position the rocks and then pour the pond, hoping the cement will seal to the rocks. It won't, and over time the rocks will settle causing leaks and cracks. If you wish to use rocks around the edge of your pond or to break up the water flow in a spillway, put the rocks in after the cement has been poured. It is easy to design a pond to facilitate this eye-pleasing concept. Simply build a shelf into the cement where the desired rock is to go, or widen out the top of the pond and leave a little wall to the edge creating a "shelf" all around the pond. Then you can hand place the rock and back fill to the wall, giving the appearance of the rock in the water. When pouring spillways, make ledges about a foot wide like a staircase all along the length of the channel. When the cement has hardened, you can place rocks at different positions to trap, tumble or swirl the water which will assist in the aeration of the flow, and give that lovely "babbling brook" sound.

Some pond designers have sought to incorporate plants into their cement designs. While this can be done, you will get more debris in the water, so one has to weigh the pros and cons. Also some water supplies may not be conducive to plant life because of high mineral or chlorine content. But if you still have the urge to try it, go ahead. Where done successfully, the effect is beautiful. One design I saw had individual pockets laid into the cement to take a plant in its container. Another was planned like the rock-shelf technique, but had a second internal wall. The rocks had a ledge to sit in and a wall behind them to maintain the water level and made it appear that they rose up out of the water naturally. The plant design had a second wall on the inner side of the pond and just below water level. This created a trough of sorts, into which the plants were put. The plant's root system was therefore in two or three inches of water and had been covered just below the water line with thick, plastic netting to stop probing beaks from doing their damage. The mesh was anchored into the cement wall on both sides with masonry screws. The effect was exquisite. It looked like plants growing around the sides of a natural pond and had lilies, flowering sedges and mares tail reeds planted into it. Cosmetics play an important part in aviary design both for your birds and for your own pleasure. Be creative!

Freeze Protection

Keeping water open is quite a problem in northern American states and in parts of Europe. In Montana, temperatures of -50°F during winter can freeze slow-moving water in hose pipes, let alone pond water. However there are ways to combat this as one has to ensure the water supply is ice free.

If city water is used, in conjunction with hose-pipe delivery, the faucet should be located inside a building and the delivery pipe lagged with insulation material or heat tapes. Similarly, lengths of pipe outside can be heat taped to help prevent freezing. Heat tape is merely a heating element inside a plastic, protective cover which can be wound around piping and connected to an electric supply to prevent icing. Metal and plastic pipes can be protected in this fashion.

Artesian water that has to be pumped to the surface is not immune to freezing during exceptionally cold weather. Electric pumps located outside can actually freeze solid, so a few precautions should be taken.

First, a small house should be constructed around the pump and lined with insulation to take advantage of the pump's own heat output and to keep at least a portion of the input and output pipes warm. Second, heat tapes can keep further lengths of piping warmer. Pump house heaters with low-temperature thermostats are also available.

Of course, water does not necessarily have to be supplied to keep a pond ice free. There are a number of electric aerators currently available. These can be divided into three types. One variety uses a small propeller to keep water moving. Care must be taken to ensure ducks cannot become decapitated while diving. The simplest way to do this is to construct a small wire screen around the propeller. The second variety is a small submersible pump (or "sump" pump) that acts as a sort of underwater fountain. The third type is commonly referred to as a "bubbler." These machines compress air which is delivered via piping into a pond. The delivery end is plugged, and the last few feet of piping drilled to provide air-delivery holes.

These machines can easily be made at home. They work best on large, deep ponds. The size of the holes should vary with the power of the pump. The distance between holes needs to be about the same as the depth of your pond, i.e., 6 feet apart if the pond is 6 feet deep. With small compressors ($\frac{1}{2}$-h.p.), use a No. 64 drill. No more than 15 or 16 holes need to be drilled.

Bubblers will work in shallow water. The secret is to keep the bubbles small and the air supply to a minimum so there is a slow circulation of water. If violent bubbling action is used it tends to make the pond freeze all the way through instead of slowly bringing warm water to the surface and allowing the water which replaces it to warm up.

If you don't want to use machines (and they are not always necessary, especially on small ponds) electric heat lamps can be provided. Very small ponds can be kept clear using two or more heat lights suspended 2 feet above the water. Modern Pyrex heat lights will not shatter if water comes in contact with them. It is best to provide a roof over these small ponds to help keep the heat in and weather out, therefore allowing maximum use. One big drawback to electric heaters is their ability to shatter (if glass or "quartz") or short out (if they are the core resistor variety) when splashed with water. The other problem is one of light output, especially at night. Birds can be induced to molt completely out of season as they perceive "daylight" during the dark hours and thus their molting mechanics are thrown out of synch. Breeding seasons can be totally upset because of this prolonged light in winter. Only use high light output heaters sparingly or in the severest of conditions to keep water open.

One final pond management tip. In a small collection, chlorinating concrete ponds is a good idea (once the birds have been moved out). This will effectively kill any remaining algae and provide a measure of disinfecting to the surrounding concrete. Care must be taken to ensure chlorine levels are not excessive. Ponds, once soaked for 48 hours in a chlorine-water solution, must be washed out at least three or four times with water before the birds are put back into their pens for the new season. (Chlorine or pH testing kits are available in pet stores specializing in fish and also from swimming pool supply outlets.)

Fencing and Top Netting

Once the ponds and water supply have been designed, a security fence and/or a roof for the aviary should be considered. It is quite obvious that waterfowl have many predators and steps need to be taken to ensure their safety. These measures will depend on how the individual breeder wants to keep his birds. If all are to be pinioned, the need for a roof may not exist. However, while a fence will keep out land-based predators, nothing will stop a hawk or an owl from dining on your precious charges. The cost of top netting has come down significantly in the last ten years and is now very affordable. I couldn't conceive of building an aviary without one. The cost of replacing valuable birds lost to aerial predators, more than offsets the cost of the netting. The other benefit to having a roof, is that you can keep full-winged stock and have the joy of watching them in flight. The birds themselves are calmer when they know they can fly and I think they make better breeders. However...catching them?... Well if you plan your aviary sensibly, and rear all young outside the facility, there is almost no need ever to have to catch a bird up except when it is ill. At any rate, we are all agreed that we need a good fence around our aviaries.

A good perimeter fence should be 6½ to 7 feet tall with 1 or 2 feet of fencing buried in the ground and turned outward to prevent predators from digging into your enclosures. The top should have an outward overhang set between 45° and 90° to the vertical. Electric wires should be positioned (if legal in your area) at heights according to the variety of predators you expect. A cat for instance is likely to jump to a height of 4 or 5 feet, as is a dog, so a wire positioned accordingly will repel these. Rac-

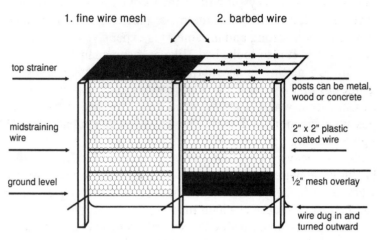

Diagram 1: An example of perimeter fencing.

coons tend to stand on their hind legs to survey surroundings. Wire should be positioned at about the height of the front paws. Mink pose a difficult problem, but if the bottom 2 feet of fencing is overlaid with ¾-inch mesh chicken wire, mink often can't be bothered to scale this smaller mesh. If they do, wire positioned at the top will "zap" them when they get there. Three-foot fiberglass sheeting at the bottom of the fence line prevents predators from seeing the collection. If they happen to hear the birds when passing and stand up to get a better look—put an electric wire along the top. This will take their minds off fresh duck!

A good predator-proof perimeter fence is an excellent investment that allows the use of less secure but more artistic interior partitioning. Chain-link fencing is one of the longest lasting varieties and can be obtained with a plastic or galvanized metal coating. Chain link comes in various mesh sizes, the most popular of which is the 2-inch size. This size is usually free of "blobs" of galvanized zinc coating that congeals on quickly dipped wire and which birds can easily pull off. Deaths from metal poisoning occur very swiftly when this happens. When selecting chain link watch for this condition and avoid it or buy plastic-coated fencing instead. As always, it will be the most expensive birds which seem impelled to nibble at the metal particles. Although chainlink fencing is strong and durable, it is expensive and sometimes unnecessary. It also looks bad...like a prison camp.

Poultry netting is an alternative. There are many types and gauges of poultry netting available today and even in areas such as California where I experienced cats, coyotes, dogs, skunks, possums, raccoons and more, I never had an unwanted entry. This lighter netting can have many advantages. It is easier to work with than heavy chain link and very durable. It blends into the background better and is thus less of an eyesore. It is cheaper and when used in conjunction with an appropriate electric fence, it can be just as secure as chain link.

Pens constructed inside the security fence need to match the needs of the birds kept within them. For example, pens for sheldgeese need not be large, 20 x 20 ft. is sufficient for one pair. However, it is best to go slightly larger on size so a portion of the pen can be divided and rested part of the year, providing fresh grazing later.

Internal fencing should provide a barrier between species that do not mix well, such as shelducks, sheldgeese and swans. Also, fences need to be high enough to prevent birds from climbing over. If swans are kept next to geese, make sure that they can't reach over and maul their neighbors. Don't forget to allow sufficient height for snow buildup in winter. Rough board fencing between pens provides a visual barrier and discourages birds from pacing the fence or trying to get into the next pen. This also eliminates fighting through the fence while still allowing vocal stimulation. If wire is used between pens, mesh sizes need be small enough so that birds cannot get their heads or beaks stuck. It is always a good idea to bury the bottom of the fence a few inches into the ground so birds cannot get stuck and so parent-reared youngsters cannot stray into neighboring pen and be beaten or killed.

In a pen where 5 or 6 pairs of geese are kept, there should be sufficient grazing for them all year, a larger water area, and enough land so that pairs can set up territories during the breeding season without overlapping their neighbors.

Fencing across ponds or strips of water is a potential death trap for waterfowl. Wire rusts in time, and developing holes can trap birds underwater as effectively as a fish net. Wooden bulkheads used to divide water areas should periodically be inspected for underwater gaps which trap birds' heads and drown them.

Many breeders like to keep stock full winged and construct aviaries to contain them. There are no hard and fast rules governing sizes of these pens; different species require differing amounts of flying space. However, there are one or two points to look out for: first, don't crowd the birds and make sure species are compatible. Try not to use posts or supports with sharp sides and pay careful attention to plants in and around the aviary. A newly constructed pen, freshly planted, can look ideal—but in three or four years time, the small trees could grow through the sides or top of the pen, straining and breaking wire or netting and creating holes for birds to escape. Holes also let other birds in, and sparrows quickly foul aviaries by eating and contaminating food intended for your waterfowl.

In certain areas snow can pile up on an aviary roof and collapse it. There are two solutions to this problem: one is to construct a flat-topped aviary reinforced every two feet or so with substantial joists or beams. This is not very pretty but can in time be hidden by climbing plants, although again steps must be taken to ensure their growth does not block out the light. The second alternative is a roof that "gives" with the snow's weight. These are best made in a tent style: two main posts support a wire cable between them and the roof slopes down either side to the top of the side fencing. Additional side braces can be put in for added support. Snow will pile up on any aviary eventually, and there really is no alternative except to get out there and knock it through with a long-handled brush or other instrument—making sure that you don't put any rips in the roof while you do it! One of the great delights of keeping waterfowl in a flight aviary, is to watch them fly. Some are so beautiful and agile, others just seem programmed to rush from point A to point B as quickly as possible. This aspect of waterfowl keeping also has its price. Birds can injure themselves flying into posts or crash landing on the edges of ponds. You simply can't avoid an occasional injury but with a little thought you can reduce their occurrence dramatically.

Firstly and most simply, make the aviary large enough to fly in. Think about what sort of birds you want to keep and build for them. For instance, Ringed Teal can flitter around a small area as they are such agile flyers and seem to be able to land on a postage stamp. Other agile flyers, such as Pygmy Geese and Green-winged Teal need more landing area. Buffleheads and Ruddy Ducks need a veritable runway to take off and land on, so these species will need lots of water surface and not much in the way when they are flying as they are not very agile pilots! Give the birds plenty of flying room and turning space and large landing areas. Don't have lots of roof support posts littering their flight path. Make sure that when you are landscaping the aviary that you don't put in shrubs or trees or pampas grass that can grow to enormous widths or heights quickly thereby robbing your birds of yet more flying space. Attention to these small details are vital.

Aviary roofing material can be chain-link fencing, chicken wire or nylon netting. They all have advantages and disadvantages. Chain-link netting is tough and heavy duty but needs substantial support. Chicken wire easily bellies in with snow, and can easily bend out of shape. Just about everybody uses nylon roof netting these days. It may not actually be "nylon," but it is a synthetic of some sort. Many companies make this netting now, and it is long lasting in all sorts of weather, has UV protection and better bursting characteristics than the product of ten years ago. It is light, easy to work with and highly flexible as well as being relatively cheap. Choose the "weight" of netting you want and the mesh size carefully. Heavier weight netting is useful in cold winter areas but is not necessary in California. Make sure your birds can't get their heads stuck in the mesh. I have seen only a few accidents involving this and normally they occurred when the mesh size was too large (about 2 inches). I have always used 1-inch mesh and had no problems with it. Birds colliding with it tend to bounce off better, despite the fact that the mesh size is large enough for smaller ducks to get their heads through. One freak fatality occurred that is worth mentioning.

During a morning feeding, I found a Cinnamon Teal lying dead on the path inside my aviary. I examined it carefully and noticed what appeared to be puncture marks about its breast and head. Looking up, I saw some feathers stuck in the top net. Then it became obvious. Once owls learn that they can't get through an aviary roof, they still like to perch on the roof support posts in order to spy out the land better. An owl had swooped in for a landing on one of the support posts and had spooked the Cinnamon Teal into the air, where it got tangled in the net. The alert owl saw its chance and pounced on its helpless victim impaling it with its claws. After a while, the owl realized that it could not pull the teal through the net and let it drop. As I said, this was a freak occurrence.

Top netting is normally attached to the fencing with hog rings. This process can be laborious although the end result is a good one. One other way that seems to work well involves threading plastic "weed eater" line between the fence wire and top net. In effect, you are sewing the two together. This process speeds up the work markedly and is a lot cheaper and just as secure as using hog rings. Additionally, there are no metal rings to drop that your birds can pick up later and one spool of line goes a long way!

Gates leading in and out of an aviary or an unroofed collection need to be secure and fitted with a return spring in case they are left open. They need to sit flush with the ground so nothing can crawl in underneath. In areas of high traffic or where machinery has access, the ground can become trodden down or rutted. When installing the gate, build a cement sill under it. If you are not anticipating the need to drive equipment into your aviaries, make sure the gate is wide enough for the largest thing that will need access, for example, a backhoe.

Grazing and Plant Selection

Having provided ponds and fencing, what about surroundings?

Grazing and vegetation are both very important to the welfare and breeding success of your birds. However, not all birds need grazing vegetation and some need little nesting cover. Which varieties of plants and grasses can we use here?

Swans and geese are great grazers. They can quickly graze down and foul small areas of land. In these cases a fast-growing grass with a good root structure should be planted. When constructing the pen make the area large enough to fence off and rest a piece of it. This is especially important in areas where parasitic worms are a threat, and where pairs of swans or geese are allowed to rear their young. An area fenced off in autumn, limed (to kill the worm eggs) and rested until the following year when the young are hatched will produce good quality grazing. Most importantly, young birds will not be infested with parasites during their first few meals. Where this procedure is difficult to carry out, birds will have to be wormed at least twice a year (see Disease Control and Remedies chapter).

Grass need not be of good nutritional value—although it helps if it is. Nutrition can be balanced by the daily food ration. Some soils simply will not grow grass with good food value but it will provide fiber—a very important part of their diet.

The following grasses can be used in a variety of locations and temperature ranges:

- For hot areas: turf-type fescues, rye grasses and Bermuda.
- For shady areas: Carefree tall, Falcon tall, Titan tall are all good fescues. Gulf annual rye is good too.
- For a strong type of grass that is resilient: Conestoga tall, Wrangler tall and Falcon tall fescues are good.
- For heavy traffic areas: Accolade perennial rye, Achiever perennial rye and Kentucky bluegrass are all good bets.

Remember that birds graze a great deal and need adequate areas. Brents, sheldgeese and most of Grey Geese happily eat grass to the almost total exclusion of other food. These birds will need close watching in areas of high parasite density. Routine fecal exams should be performed on regular basis (see Disease Control and Remedies chapter).

Trees and shrubs are an important part of your enclosure too. The major rule is to think of your birds' needs first, then do your own thing. You will probably find that your likes are also those of your birds. A sensibly planted enclosure should provide shelter in every month, grow its own nesting material and be economically laid out to provide easy management.

Think about the type and purpose of plants in the aviary. Big broad-leaf, deciduous trees can mean a lot of autumn raking while dwarf varieties are better, as are conifers and bamboo—the latter providing excellent cover and nest material.

Consult your local university for a list of hardy species for your area. They are also a great resource in analyzing soil types and matching them to vegetation that grows well in your area. They generally do this service at little or no cost. The U.S. Soil Conservation Service is another important source of information. The local agent is usually more than glad to come to your facility and offer advice, again at no expense to you. Maximum use should be made of local vegetation which can be dug and moved to desired sites, the only cost is a little physical exertion.

Plant species that should be considered by function are:

Nesting cover	Ornamental	Hedges & Windbreaks	Marginal Plants
Pampas Grass*	Yew	Box	Juncus Reed
Juncus Reed	Poplar	Lonicera nitida	Bulrush
Gorse	Willow	Yew	Cattail
Heather	Rowan	Cupressus	Phragmites
Mares Tail	Reed*	Bamboo	Lily
any long grass	Eucalyptus	Beech	Watercress
Low growing	Manzanita	Dogwood	Bamboo
Willow Herb	Silver Birch	Barberry	Wild Rice
Bamboo*	any Conifer	Olive (Russian)	
Sedges	Photinia	Blueberry	
Vinca	Cotoneaster	High Bush Cranberry	
Juniper	Ornamental	Wild Rose	
Bronze Flax	and low		
	growing or		
	clumping		
	Bamboo		
	Ornamental		
	flowering		
	cherry		

---

* These plants can grow very fast and/or attract rats and voles.

Trees as windbreaks or for ornamental value can be your own choice. Willows combine quick waterside growth with beauty and autumnal color, but plant sensibly to allow for those shed leaves in autumn clogging your pipes and grids and silting up ponds over time. *Cupressus* types can form effective windbreaks to deflect biting winter gales. Poplars are fast growers and certain varieties are used for windbreaks in many parts of the country. Don't plant trees too close to your perimeter in case they come down in a storm and also so they don't become an avenue for predators. Don't plant them too close to small concrete ponds as their root structure can raise and crack concrete.

Remember there are many types of bamboo, some very hardy, and you need not live in the tropics to propagate it. Remember also that the majestic Maple outside the aviary that shades it in summer will shed its leaves all over the roof of the pen in autumn. (One small tip is to wait until the leaves have dried out and use a portable electric leaf blower to blow them off the roof.)

Many varieties of shrubs exist. Simply choose what you want, and if it grows fairly readily for your area, plant it.

Rowan and Elderberry provide ornate autumn sights, and food for wild birds. Pampas grass, bamboos and Juncus Reed also have good cover value and make ideal nest material for waterfowl. They can harbor rats, a possible disadvantage, but as with all vermin, diligence and observation are necessary to stay on top. Sedges, flags, bulrushes, watercress and lilies are all good water plants, providing ideal habitat for ducks and their insect food. Make sure this latter category of plants are well established before introducing ducks. There are one or two tricks to get around this. You can cover the planted roots with fine mesh wire. Do the same with pond banks to stop natural (and avian) erosion. If you decide to use concrete ponds you can construct a ledge just below the water line and fill this with earth in which to establish marginal plants in their pots. Make sure the roots are protected.

Swans are probably the most destructive to waterside plants, with geese a close second. Only you can gauge the population-to-planting ratio. I have found on planting a small bay and erecting a protective fence around it, that the plants become established. When the fence is removed swans don't seem to worry the area too much—but swans are individuals, so only you can tell. Snow Geese and Bean Geese, occasionally Pink-footed Geese, can all be good uprooters; if you are unsure simply don't plant the pond margins. Ducks can dabble away water plants given time, but on a big lake with a sensible duck population there should be enough space so that no one spot is badly affected. Stifftails love to hide in reeds and under overhanging bushes, and will nest in reed clumps with little encouragement.

Vegetation and pond variety are just as important as good fencing. Plants provide the duck pen with cover both in and out of the water, windbreaks, natural fences and great beauty to complement your waterfowl. Plants can include your favorites, giving you an ideal retreat—your own little Garden of Eden. As far as your waterfowl are concerned it should do the same for them—remember they have to live and breed there.

Watering Systems

Once an aviary has been landscaped, plants need water to survive in hot, dry weather. Providing them with food and water so they will grow and flourish is as important to the plant as food is to your birds. Modern technology has bombarded us with a wide range of irrigation choices. Here are two of my favorites.

Above-ground watering can be easily accomplished by using rotating sprinkler heads. Most modern designs allow you to cut down the normal 360° watering circle to water any part of that circle. All sorts of heads are available to work under various pressures and their spray distance is adjustable. I have mounted these types of heads in pairs just below the top of roof support poles to give maximum coverage. (A single 360°-arc sprinkler mounted on top of the pole can work too but if it needs maintenance, this will have to be done through the netting.)

As good as these sprinklers are, they can still waste precious water and in hot climates such as California, a good system to use is an "on-ground" system catering to individual plants.

On-ground systems deliver water to plants via an astonishing

41

array of emitters. A long length of ½-inch PVC hose is laid among your plantings and different volume emitters are punched into it at each plant location. Heads include drip emitters at rates of ½ a gallon per hour up to 15 gallons per hour. Forty-five degree, 90°, 180° and 360° fine-spray heads cover larger areas. Then, small rotating-head sprinklers can cover up to a 15-foot radius. This type of irrigation saves money and delivers exactly the right amount of water to your plants. The system also caters for feeding the plants and has fittings that compensate for varying water pressures. The only problem I have encountered in hot climates is that pipe exposed to the hot sun tends to heat up the water it is delivering to your plants, so you may want to cover it. Also, when it gets hot, the plastic expands a little and even with pressure regulators, can blow apart at joints. Some of these small emitters get blocked occasionally so a periodic check is needed to ensure proper function. Finally, remember that your new plants are going to grow at differing rates, possibly blocking irrigation to others later on...plan sensibly in advance. One good thing about the PVC system is that it allows for a great deal of flexibility as plants mature and spread.

3

Acquiring Your Stock

Regardless of the type of waterfowl you intend to keep, you will want fit, healthy birds. Getting such stock is not easy. Good stock is dependent on two very closely related issues. The first is bloodlines; the second is management expertise. Poor bloodlines—birds inbred for generation after generation, produce in waterfowl the same symptoms as can be found in other animals suffering from inbreeding; notably poor fertility closely linked with weak young, inherited afflictions and poor disease resistance. It is of no earthly good to buy such stock. You will saddle yourself with a lot of unnecessary heartbreak, so forget it.

Some birds are, to the aviculturist, expensive items and the problems that can arise by swapping young at the season's end make most breeders think very hard about whether it is worth it. Personally I feel it is. In England, where distances are much smaller, outcrossed bloodlines are hardy and produce breeding adults in the end. Getting someone to be a party to a swap of this type in America, is difficult, not surprisingly, as longer distances and cost involved can lead to birds being delayed in subzero conditions at airports en route to their destination. It is better to wait and make the swap in the spring, and this patience will normally pay off in the end.

To get good stock you must buy from a reputable breeder. There are quite a few around, and for those of you new to the game, the thing to do is to talk to other waterfowl breeders and keepers. Generally speaking, the better-known breeders are the ones to go to. Those who have been trading in waterfowl for ten or more years invariably have a reputation to keep, and in your inquiries you will find the same names popping up time after time. The breeder who says "come and see" generally has nothing to hide and even if he hasn't got what you want, he will have been in the business long enough to know where the best bloodlines are to be obtained and can help accordingly. If you buy cut-rate stock you will get "cut-rate birds." The best stock to buy should be either as closely related to wild stock as possible, or from stock lines that have been outcrossed to maintain sturdiness. You will find some breeders have very good male strains, whereas others have good laying female strains. In these cases buy one bird from each and use them as your "pair." Keep a good record of your birds' performance over the seasons and after some time you will see how much good stock profits you.

A good records system is very important. Establish it when you are just getting started and the flock is small. It is quite easy to keep track of the lineage of your stock when you only have a few birds and you haven't had them very long, but as you add to your stock it isn't long before you become hopelessly lost. At this point only bands and records will give you good information on your flock. An adequate record system can be developed using a 5 x 7-inch file card for each bird. Include information on origin, age, sex, band number, breeding record, medical history and eventual cause of death. With this type of system a daily log can be used to record information which can then be transferred to the cards on a batch basis. The advent of the modem PC computer has made this task almost pleasurable. If we are to continue to maintain some of the rarer species in captivity those records become very important in mating young birds so they are as distantly related as possible.

When buying your stock, ask to see the breeder's records. He will be delighted to show them, especially if they are well kept and you will know instantly that the man not only is a good stockman but more than likely produces good birds as well.

Some waterfowl that have been bred in captivity for years may now be impossible to import for political reasons, or because they are protected in their country of origin. If you want these types of birds (which may not have had wild blood introduced for many years), find a strain which has been outcrossed vigorously. A reputable breeder will be a good stockman and will be able to tell you his stock's origin.

The next phase in stock acquisition will revolve around what mixes well together. Here are a few general guidelines to avoid bloodshed. Keep sheldgeese, Abyssinian Blue-winged Geese, Egyptian, Cereopsis and Spurwinged Geese, swans and shelduck (except the European Shelduck) in their own separate pens. Some other geese (seemingly very much dependent on their various strains) can be aggressive. Ask when you purchase about habits, diet, breeding season and so on. In this way you will be able to get a good idea of who is compatible with whom. Permanent squabbling in pens can lead to poor egg laying (if any) and eventual death. Consult the last few chapters of this book on specific bird groups to gain further information on their adaptation to captivity.

New birds should be isolated for a period of time until parasites and disease checks can be done. Virtually all birds carry the odd internal and external parasite, virus or particular disease susceptibility and before the birds are introduced to your collection these should be tended to. Birds introduced to a collection will be under a great deal of stress as new pecking orders are established. They must be in top physical condition to endure. Plan your bird moves well so you are not continuously rushing about with a net catching birds and stressing them. In a small enclosure catch them without the net if possible.

Herein lies another very important lesson in waterfowl management: stress kills birds. Stress through harassment lowers the physical strength of a bird, allowing other ailments to prevail, gradually wearing down and eventually killing the bird of a cause brought on by the initial stress.

During their molt, most waterfowl undergo another rather delicate period. Most assume a cryptic, or camouflage plumage while they are flightless. They molt their primaries at one go and so, in the wild at any rate, leave themselves easy victims to predators should they be surprised on land. They seek safety on water and islands while their new feathers grow. During this time birds should never be caught for fear of damaging the delicate blood feathers which bleed easily and lengthily. You will be able to see the stubby new feathers encased in their shiny sheaths, appearing blue in color. Never move, acquire or try to introduce birds during this period.

Settling of new stock can be hazardous and stress inducing. There are, however, ways of coping with this problem. First, having decided on the pair of birds you want, find out about them before they arrive—preferably before you order them. The sort of things you need to know are: where do they come from, what is their diet, are they aggressive, do they suffer from cold or frostbite in winter, do they need deep or shallow water, what are their nesting requirements, how quickly do they breed and at what time of year? Do your homework. There are many people to ask so get one or two opinions if possible.

Never try to introduce new birds at night. This is often fatal. Birds cannot settle in their new environment properly in the dark. They are easy prey for night predators such as rats or owls and are often attacked by other inhabitants of the pen. Introduce them in the morning at feeding time. This is the time when most of your stock is milling about close to you waiting to be fed and so less likely to worry new birds because their minds are on food. Check that your new birds are a true pair (if you have bought a pair) and are pinioned correctly. Show them the pond for a few minutes before gently releasing them onto the water to one side of the crowd awaiting breakfast. Now feed the other birds and your new arrivals should be able to see where the food is.

Ponds with lots of bank cover are best for ducks of all sorts. New birds can retreat to a quiet spot and watch things from a distance, gradually becoming integrated with the others. Watch your new birds closely for the next few days to make sure they are settled in and feeding well.

When it becomes necessary to introduce a new mate to an

established bird it is a good idea to move the established bird to another area at the same time the new mate is introduced. This puts them on more equal footing while they get used to each other. The established bird feels less secure and consequently will be less aggressive. Once the matchmaking is complete the pair can be moved back to their permanent home.

The question often comes up about introducing new birds to a large, unfenced area such as swans to a large lake or river. The person introducing the birds obviously wants them to stay nearby. One technique used is to build a temporary holding pen which extends into the water. The birds are held there for a few weeks while they get their bearings and get used to being fed. When the time for release comes, the water end of the pen is opened and the birds are allowed to swim out. Feed the birds inside the pen for a while and they will learn to go in and out. At this point the pen can be removed or if there is some desire to catch the birds later, leave it to serve as a trap.

New birds, while exploring their new surroundings, are particularly prone to sampling bits and pieces around the pen. String, wire, nails, staples and glass are all killers. Some birds are particularly bad in this respect, notably mergansers and goosanders who love to play with anything shiny. Even sticks and feathers can cause impacted gizzards. Keep in mind that once you have released these sorts of birds onto a large stretch of water they are virtually impossible to catch again. So make sure that before releasing new stock they will not have to be caught later.

Finally, if you work on the principle that if there is a way to injure or kill themselves, birds will find it, then you have time before birds go into a pen or indoors to scrutinize surroundings for any possible death traps and in so doing save yourself a lot of heartbreak and money!

4

Diet and Nutrition

In the wild, waterfowl vary their diets seasonally, some markedly, some more subtly. This is done to take advantage of differing foodstuffs available and because of certain biological needs.
For instance, many waterfowl will start to eat a lot of insects,
crustacean or other animal life in the period just before nesting.
Some species not even considered to eat animal life change to
this diet. I have seen Ruddy Ducks hauling rafts of weed to the
surface and picking out the shrimp and snails hiding within. To
the casual observer, the bird is doing no more than grazing on
water weed, but if you look closely, this totally different dietary
need is being fulfilled. The added proteins and calcium are going
toward the formation of eggs. In winter, waterfowl find themselves in areas where the vegetation is totally different than at
their breeding grounds. Having converted a lot of their summer
grazing into energy for migration, they arrive at their wintering
areas ready to "stock up" for winter. This is when geese especially like to raid farmers' bean fields or carrot fields. Snow
Geese grub up tubers in the osier beds. Again, the diet has
changed, just as it has for the wild birds, and we must pay
attention to our birds' needs seasonally.

Formulating correct diets for your waterfowl is an important
part of waterfowl management. Everyone asks "What protein
percent do you feed your birds?" as if this is the only factor that

merits particular attention in the makeup of the diet. If you believe this, then I'm afraid you are kidding yourself. Equally important are fat, carbohydrates, fiber, trace elements, minerals and vitamins.

Proteins are simply amino acid chains which vary in their efficiency within a bird, depending on its natural diet. The commonly held myth that sea ducks need be stuffed full of high-protein food ultimately damages more birds than it provides with a healthy productive life. Birds that live on animal protein rather than synthetic proteins or plant and cereal proteins have a system adapted for different proteins or amino acids which in turn work differently within the bird.

Small sea fish such as sprats or herrings contain about 10 to 15 percent animal protein. It does seem that in order to mimic this with synthetic protein foods, protein content in the manufactured food needs to be higher—around 30 percent. However, this sort of food (dog chow) need only be given as an additive and not as a major part of the diet, to sea ducks or fish eaters. Generally, the protein source used in most dog chow is soya. There are lower protein (27 percent) foods based on animal protein only made by some firms. These are the types I prefer: some of the newer dog chows are being made from grass fed lamb and rice. The fact that the meat (lamb) has been naturally fed is a positive step forward. This means that no growth hormones or steroids in the flesh will be handed on to your birds in the chow. Also, one or two manufacturers are using lamb which has never been injected, even with a worming solution.

Obviously, the reason most breeders use dog chow or trout chow for fish eaters is because of ease of availability. One cannot always get fresh mussels, crayfish, etc. and they are very expensive. Some breeders supplement with fish. When deep frozen and then thawed, it is next to useless as a food item. Thiamine (Vitamin B) is completely destroyed during freezing and the effectiveness of other minerals and vitamins are diminished, some to the point of being useless. Some really incredible breeding results have been achieved (notably Chuck Pilling, Paul Dye, Steve Putchel, Mike Lubbock, Frank Todd and Bill Hancock) using dog chow and pellet-based foods, but as that intelligent author Dr. Anderson Brown relates in his incubation book "...these men are superb stockmen..." and having read the stockmanship chapter in this book I think you will realize this "feel" for birds is probably your most precious asset.

In order to understand the dietary needs of our birds, let's look at the ingredients most commonly found in their manufactured rations and see how they benefit the bird.

Vitamins

Vitamin A is found only in animal tissues and constitutes a major part of fish.

However, plants contain a substance known as carotene which birds can convert into vitamin A internally. It is an unstable vitamin, that is, it breaks down rapidly when exposed to heat and light—but is needed in a diet to produce good hatches.

Vitamin D is also present in fish. Direct sunlight helps convert sterols into vitamin D, but in cold northern areas where birds are wintered inside, vitamin D must be part of a supplement feed to keep birds healthy as they are not in direct sunlight while indoors. Growing birds need it to offset the occurrence of rickets and other skeletal deformities, possibly including "angel wing," or "flip wing." Vitamin D is needed to absorb calcium and phosphorous and is therefore an important ingredient in a diet.

Vitamin K helps stop excessive bleeding during injury, as it helps the blood to clot.

B_1 or Thiamine is found in all cereals and, as mentioned, is easily destroyed in the freezing process of fish. It is a useful vitamin in any diet.

Riboflavin is probably the most important vitamin influencing hatching success. Egg white has great quantities of it and deficiencies cause many hatching problems. Layer-pellet rations usually have less riboflavin present than do breeder rations. The production of fertile eggs and good embryonic formation is of no concern to the commercial egg producer, as his interests are the production of edible eggs only. Waterfowl breeders need to use breeder, rather than layer rations.

A lack of vitamin B1 affects chick growth—its absence is a major contributor to dead-in-shells. It breaks down proteins. Therefore, birds on high-protein diets (sea duck and chicks) need added quantities.

Folic acid has properties involving the formation of red blood cells. It is naturally synthesized by bacteria in the gut and those people advocating antibiotic treatment for their birds on a regular basis, destroy this much needed element.

Vitamin B is another much needed vitamin. A minor lack of it can reduce hatch success substantially as it is the major contributor to blood formation.

Minerals

Salt—not particularly important in diets—is present in most made up foods. It is important to sea ducks however, to maintain function of the salt extraction glands. The advantage of having this organ working, and not flaccid and shrunken, is obvious. Feeding them in salt water will help.

Calcium and calcium phosphate are known as the bone builders and eggshell formers. Oyster shell is high in calcium and is normally given during the breeding season to allow an adult female to form good eggs without draining her own calcium reserves. Interestingly, too much fat on your bird will have a blocking effect on the dispersion of calcium through the system—that is why experienced breeders advocate fit, not fat, birds. Also fat insulates sexual organs, producing infertility.

A lack of manganese will effect eggshell and tendon formation and decrease hatchability. Manganese is normally incorporated in most diets in adequate levels. Alfalfa sprouts provide manganese for winter-hatched geese such as Ne-Ne when no natural source is available. Trace elements present in rations include iron, copper, zinc and cobalt. Iron and copper play important roles in red blood cell formation and in the building of healthy blood vessels. Aneurysms can be the result of a copper deficiency. All these are normally present in most made up foods in adequate levels. Iodine is also present in most prepared foods but may be further supplemented for sea ducks and geese (Em-

51

perors, Brents, Kelp Geese) whose natural vegetation (kelp and other sea vegetation) is very high in iodine. Iodized salt is one way of providing this—feed dog chow, or greens in iodized salt water.

Crude fiber is normally present in pelleted foods at a rate of 3 to 5 percent which appears to be adequate, especially when supplemented with grit. Grit constitutes an important addition to diet. It is amazing how few people provide their waterfowl with grit outside of the laying season. Granite grit (#2 size) should be available during nonlaying periods and birds wintering indoors should be provided with a tray of grit.

Many sea ducks use shell to grind up food. Mussels and other shellfish, crustaceans and mollusks are often swallowed whole. Their shells aid the grinding action of the gizzard. Eiders and Scoters are often seen swallowing large pebbles. These are ground down and used as abrasives for other food items. The gizzard muscle size difference between wild Eiders and captive ones is substantial and a healthy, well-worked gizzard will offset minor stomach impactions.

Poultry pellets are designed primarily for hens but do well for waterfowl. However, it should be noted that waterfowl have a higher requirement of vitamins and minerals than do domestic fowl, and so additives made up with the vitamins and minerals discussed should be added.

Pelleted and Crumble Rations

Most commercially available rations for poultry and game birds come in a pellet or crumble form. Obviously, young birds find the crumble easier to swallow but there are crumble rations made for adults too. If you can, feed your waterfowl on a game-bird diet rather than a poultry ration. Game-bird diets are formulated slightly differently from poultry diets, and with good reason. After all, a duck is not a chicken. You wouldn't feed your cat on parrot food would you? There are also many types of diet that take into account the seasonal variations in diet that we discussed earlier. For example, there are, rearer, grower, maintenance, breeder and layer rations. Find the one you need to fit the occasion and maybe add a little wheat or millet to it for variance. Mazuri foods have a very good line of rations created specifically for waterfowl. For more information write to: PMI Feeds Inc., 1401 S. Hanley Rd., St. Louis, MO, 63144.

Supplemental Greens

In some areas, especially the cold northern states, some breeders like to supplement waterfowl diets with greens of some type. All waterfowl can benefit from this practice, even those in warmer climates. There's nothing better to ducks and geese than a good chew on some greens. Most greens provide little more than iron and fibre but are a useful supplement. Lettuce, cabbage and spinach are all good, as are sprouted soy beans or alfalfa (rich in Vitamins E and K). Some hydroponic concerns are doing this very effectively now and may be worth a visit. Naturally occurring greens such as watercress or duckweed (*Lemma minor*) are also good to use. One word of caution about any naturally growing weed bought in for food. A lot of these water plants harbor their own microsystems and shrimp, water snails and other insects live in it. A few of these insects can carry internal parasites that are passed onto your birds when eaten. Make sure this sort of weed is washed thoroughly and agitated to separate out the insects and crustaceans. (See instructions for use in How To Feed section.)

Supplemental Live Food

Crickets and mealworms have proved to be very effective and well-accepted supplements to waterfowl diets for both young and adult birds. These are fed as not only a dietary change, but also to stimulate certain types of young waterfowl to start feeding. However, some breeders like to provide these to adult birds as a treat now and then. Once a week, I would go over to the marina at our local lake and buy some live minnows. I had a tank and a small pump set up at home so I could keep them for a few days. When the birds saw me coming with the fish bucket, there was great excitement. The minnows hardly had a chance once in the water. Smew, Buffleheads, Hooded Mergansers, American Mergansers, they all went crazy, diving, twisting, intercepting and trapping the fleeing minnows. Others got in the act too. The Orinoco Geese loved live fish and I had to stun the fish a little because the Orinoco's couldn't move as fast as the other fish eaters. The little African Pygmy Geese loved them too. Interestingly, years ago when my friend Mike Lubbock had returned from Africa, he told me that he had seen Pygmy Geese regurgitating guppies. They obviously eat a few fish in the wild, maybe for the sorts of reasons we have already discussed, so it came as no surprise to me to see them mirror this behavior in captivity. In America, minnows or shad are raised commercially for anglers. In Europe and England, minnows and sticklebacks (having had the spines removed) are sometimes fed to waterfowl having been netted or trapped out of a stream. Unfortunately, these little fish carry tape worms and other internal parasites similar to the occupants of the water weed.

Supplemental Vitamins

Occasionally it may be necessary to supplement your birds' diets with extra vitamins and/or electrolytes. This is a good practice for birds indoors during winter time as well as for those outside braving the blast! Newly hatched and growing birds can also be fed this way. As mentioned earlier, most rations contain sufficient vitamins in them, but in older (more than 6 months), or poorly stored food, vitamin breakdown is fast and your stock may benefit by its addition. There are many brand names available through pet store outlets, veterinary hospitals and feed stores. Two of the best that I have used are, Salisbury's Vitamins and Electrolytes and Vionate.

The only requirement for dog food usage is your potential diners should be able to eat it without choking. Most dog foods range between 20 to 40 percent protein and should only be used as a supplement. Avoid oily varieties, these form a slick on the water surface and can adversely affect plumage waterproofing. Trout pellets can be mixed with dog chow. They are liver-based, a more natural protein for sea ducks, as are the lamb and rice-based foods.

Grains

Most breeders add a cereal grain to pelleted rations from molt onwards through winter, decreasing it again as spring arrives.

My own experience indicates wheat is the best grain—its high starch content helps birds put on an insulating fat layer for winter. It is a relatively high-protein grain, and has good fiber. Sprouted wheat is probably the best way to give wheat to birds, but is very time consuming and likely not worth the effort. Millet is a good grain which is extremely nutritious and palatable, especially to teal and stifftails. Make sure when buying that it has not been treated with chemicals.

How to Feed

This process starts in the feed room. The room should be airy, clean and free of vermin. Feed bags should be stacked on a pallet off the ground allowing passage of air under them. A dark room is better as certain vitamins break down quickly under light conditions. The date the food is manufactured should be noted, as well as its longevity or shelf life. This affects its usefulness as a source of nourishment. Some foods state they should be used by a certain time. If you halve the period stated, you benefit greatly as will your birds.

Frequency of feeding is also an important factor and depends greatly on the size of your collection and the time involved in feeding. There are also pros and cons to be considered.

If you have a small collection and also have to go to work every day you can easily get by feeding once—either morning or evening. You need only use a bowl or feeder which contains a suitable amount for one day's ration to the inhabitants of the pens. During the breeding season it will probably be better to feed (and collect eggs if you are artificially raising young) at evening time, thereby reducing the disturbance to laying stock which normally lay in the early morning.

If you have the same work situation with a large collection, some people prefer to feed once or twice a week, using large containers for food. In areas of high humidity and warmth, pellets and grains can quickly dampen, mold and become hazardous to your birds' health. Also, quite a mess of spilled food can accumulate around a feeder as can droppings. One way to offset this is to use a large tray on which the feeder is situated and tip away all the spilled food and the droppings when you do your feed round. In both situations however, and especially in winter, an evening feed is important as it allows you to observe your stock for signs of disease or other ailments and allows you to check heat lights, heat bars, shelters, aerators and pumps for any problems which may arise overnight.

If you can spend all day with the birds (as some of us are fortunate enough to do), then you can create your own agenda, but always remember not to disturb laying birds during their season or unduly stress more timid varieties with your presence.

A lot of breeders swear by wearing virtually the same sort of clothing every time they appear in the pens. I think it is undeniable that birds recognize their keeper(s) and are certainly alarmed by very bright colors, noise or deviations from the normal feeding routine. Some people who I know also dress differently to catch birds—reckoning that the birds identify the "catching man" and the "feeding man" separately and therefore don't panic when the same person (dressed differently again) comes out to feed them.

Finally, you may notice in areas where winter cold spells set in for a week or ten days that birds feed frantically before and after the cold weather, but not during. It is senseless to disturb birds under these conditions as getting up, walking away and settling in a colder spot uses up precious energy needed to keep the body warm. Just make sure that they have shelter from the wind, some heat if possible and that longer-legged species such as Whistling Duck, Spurwings, tropical geese and ducks have dry straw or some other insulative material on which to sit thereby offsetting the incidence of frostbite. (Delicate species should be indoors.) Open water and dry feed should be provided even if it appears to be a waste of time.

If you feed your birds correctly, you will not waste food every day; that is to say bowls will be empty or almost so. Feed slightly heavier during laying periods. A cold spell may demand more food, a mild one demands less. Ducks are in fact very good at telling weather (or seem to be!) and many times in winter on mild evenings I have seen them feed frantically. This can indicate a cold night or a storm next day. Make sure feeding bowls are waterproof as pellets quickly turn to mush in water. Old food must be picked up and disposed of immediately.

If you have fifty birds in a pen don't use one trough—use six or seven. Smaller, more timid birds will be bullied out of the way. During breeding season, this is especially relevant when dealing with geese. Feed pairs in the territories which they appear to be defending so fighting is avoided.

Keep to the same route when feeding and birds will get used to your movements.

A seasonal wheat/pellet ratio for your birds can be as follows:

July-September	1 measure wheat	2 measures maintenance pellets
September-October	2 measures wheat	2 measures maintenance pellets
November-February	3 measures wheat	2 measures maintenance pellets
February-March	1 measure wheat	2 measures breeder pellets or crumble
March-July	phase out wheat	breeder pellets, crumble and/or dog chow. Supplement greens if needed

Variations due to geographical location need to be considered in this schedule.

One variety of waterfowl can pose a problem in terms of routine feeding. This is the Stifftail family. As they hardly ever come ashore their diet ought to be carefully thought about. Pellets are very difficult to give under these circumstances, they become next to useless when immersed in water. Also, Stifftails in the wild eat mostly vegetation. A palatable and nutritious diet can be provided for them: as a vegetational part of their diet use chopped lettuce, water cress, bean sprouts, or if available, the tiny pond weed or duckweed, *Lemma minor*. One point to remember with duckweed is that it is normally found in semi-stagnant water. This water can be contaminated with agricultural pesticide sprays, and the weed can contain leeches, snails and water fleas or daphnia. It will have to be washed, and if possible the leeches, etc., should be removed. This is not because they are unpalatable to Stifftails, but rather, the water snails and daphnia carry harmful parasites and bacteria. Leeches can get into nasal passages and behind the eye.

An efficient method of washing and separating is to get a large, plastic container—such as a garbage can—and fill it halfway with duckweed. Fill the remaining space with water and drop in an aerator or small pump and switch on. The pump's action will spin around the weed, and whatever else may be in there, and after a few minutes you can switch it off. You should find the snails, water fleas, etc., at the bottom of the tub. After a short while the weed will float to the top and can be scooped up.

Grain can now be considered. Wheat, millet and canary seed all make a good mix, and a lot of the millet and canary seed will float among the vegetation providing a marvelous floating diet. Stifftails will happily dabble and dive among this floating feast as will other pen mates. Make sure that most if not all the grains are picked up or they can stagnate and spoil in the water over a period of time. Some people feed stifftails in a shallow pan next to the ponds' edge. The problem here is that competing species, often more agile than stifftails, climb in and get most of the food. Secondly, droppings from feeding birds fall into the pan, contaminating it. It is hard to provide stifftails with crumbles or pellets as these turn to mush very quickly. From my own experiences with several varieties of stifftails, I have found that they will if necessary come out on land and go to the food bowl for crumbles or pellets. Make sure your food bowls are accessible to these rather clumsy birds and don't locate it right at the water's edge. Feeding ducks love to take food in their wet beaks down to the ponds' edge and dunk it. Over time a nasty mess builds up both in the pond and in the food bowl. (I have bred stifftails in areas where they had no access to crumbles or pellets. Maybe this aspect of diet is not as important to them. From the point of view of good nutrition, it is probably better to keep them separate, in their own pens. Also, as some types can be timid or belligerent, this is probably the best idea for them from a breeding standpoint, and from that of nutrition.)

5

Nesting Requirements

Waterfowl nest in a variety of locations in the wild, but can easily be catered for in captivity. They can be divided into two types; cavity nesters (those that use a raised box or log), and those that nest on the ground. This second category can be further divided into natural nesting (i.e., constructing their own nest), box nesters and burrow or hole nesters (See diagram 2).

Cavity Nesters

Cavity nesting waterfowl display certain physical and behavioral traits. Most cavity nesters are well equipped with strong claws for climbing and the young are very agile, as anyone who has ever tried to keep young Wood Ducks in a small box will testify!

Adults produce light-colored down. This acts as a signal to other home seekers not to enter a cavity as the down is easily seen in the darkness and indicates tenancy. Also, departing females leave flecks of down around the entrance hole, a further "stay out" signal to roving nest seekers. This is why a box must be cleaned of every speck of down and old material, otherwise birds are reluctant to use it, thinking it already occupied.

When making nest boxes there are several important points to consider. Regardless of box shape, hole sizes need to be gauged according to the species of duck. In other words, don't put a 4½-inch diameter hole in a box for Ringed Teal. They may

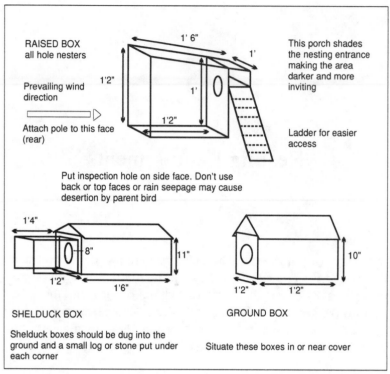

Diagram 2: Nesting boxes.

use it, but any bigger duck can get in and throw out the teal. Design boxes with the bird's general size in mind. It should be large enough for the bird to turn around and must have a small drop to the nest site. It needs a removable top that won't blow off in a gale and an access ladder if birds are pinioned, or a perch near the entrance if the birds are fully winged. It must also be waterproof.

There are variations on the basic design of nest boxes that incorporate separate porches from nesting cavities. My own preference is for a box with a nest area off to one side of the exit and entrance chamber. This way birds do not drop straight onto eggs with obvious results or scramble them getting out of the box. (For nest box design see diagram 2.)

Cavity Box Siting

Position boxes firmly to a post or tree trunk so they face the water. Remember that boxes facing inland are usually ignored. Shade the box, perhaps by placing near trees on the bank side: boxes can get hot inside. Don't face the box into the prevailing wind, and use a lid that will not blow off and that overhangs the front of the box, shading the hole and making it look more inviting. Many hole-nesters like a small drop to the floor inside, so make boxes deep enough, remembering to put coarse hessian cloth or weldmesh wire on the inside of the front face as a foothold for outgoing ducks. This avoids scrambled eggs! Cut a piece of sod to the size of the box interior, invert it (earth side up), and punch a depression into the earth. Then add two or three inches of peat or potting soil and a little dried grass or a large handful of wood shavings. Hole-nesters tend to produce a lot of down so large quantities of material are not needed. When buying peat or bark compost, make sure no additives such as steer manure have been mixed into the peat. This is a good way of bringing parasites and disease into a collection, or promoting fungal growth.

For pinioned birds, an access ladder to the box can be made from a suitable length of 4-inch wide wood with rungs nailed on. A 45° angle is not too severe as most hole-nesters are well adapted for climbing. Some examples of hole-nesters are: Hooded Mergansers, Goosanders, Goldeneye, Smew, Bufflehead, Ringed Teal, Mandarin and Wood Duck.

Ground Boxes

Ground boxes should be oblong in shape, with a removable lid for inspection. Angle the lid to allow drainage during rainy periods. Make sure boxes are big enough for the intended species, leaving enough room to turn around inside the box and a hole just large enough for the entrance. A snug fit makes the bird feel safe and content. Position ground boxes in cover if possible or, in the case of shelducks and Maned Geese, into a bank looking onto the water. Remember, if it rains quite hard, a puddle can build up under the floor of the box, so raise the corners on a piece of stone or log and position it with the back slightly higher than the front, to facilitate drainage. (For design, see diagram p. 60)

Some geese nest very early. From October and November through February, Cereopsis, Ne-Ne and some early Greylag may be nesting. It is worth noting that Cereopsis and Ne-Ne mate quite happily on land, as can some others, so deep water and large ponds are not necessary for these types.

Ground Nesters

Most geese will take advantage of artificial cover. Barrels, "kennels" and tea chests have all been used, as have old tires! Simply install these in and around cover and provide earth, peat and dried grass for materials within the site. Be careful when using metal drums because they get very hot if not well shaded and eggs of late-nesting birds may get overheated.

Most Arctic breeding geese (Ross', Brent, Red-breasted, Pinkfoot, Emperor, etc.) nest quite happily in long grass or in close proximity to a hedge, and tend to find their own nest sites. Open nests can be predated easily, so eggs should be picked up as soon as possible. Logs, laid in a triangular shape and about three high, can provide a good cover for nesting geese, as can wind-felled and split trees. Geese, being very alert, like to be able to squat down to hide and also peruse the area round their nest. Quite often with the log bunker-type of nest the gander will stand perched on the top log looking out for trouble while the female sits contentedly, incubating. Another attractive nest site for geese can be a wigwam of bamboo or willow branches. Cut straight willow branches in leaf, or best of all, bamboo, and arrange them in a circle encompassing a tree base, big stump or stone. Plant them closely together leaving an entrance. Bend the tops and gather them together, tie them with string, and secure to the tree base. Add peat and dried grass to make the job complete.

Swan Nests

Swans of all varieties like a good pile of vegetation for nest sites. Build these nests yourself, providing two or three within the pen, giving them a choice. Locate nests above any expected high water levels and backing onto some sort of cover. Arctic nesting swans (Trumpeter, Whistling, Bewick and Whooper) usually nest out in the open in the wild, but of course they have no choice of cover in the tundra and usually respond well to natural protection in captivity. Make two protected and one unprotected nest so they can choose. Utilize any available islands or consider building a floating structure surrounded by water. Both swans and geese feel more secure on an island nest. A good floating nest can be built using logs piled in log-cabin fashion secured with wire and chain-link fence stretched between the logs. Sticks and brush are piled on the chain link and the nest is anchored off shore. A nice feature of this nest is that it goes up and down with water level and never gets flooded as long as you allow for this variation in the length of the anchor line.

Make the base of the nest with sticks, then add lots of willow herb, rush, sedge, pampas grass and so on, capping it off with dried grass. Leave bits and pieces lying about so that the swans can finish it off as joint nest building helps to strengthen pair bonding. The nest when complete ought to be about 3-feet high, it will settle in time. Black, Black-necked and Coscoroba nests can be made slightly lower. Black and Black-necked Swans can lay very early in the season, so provide good cover as protection against inclement weather.

Stifftail Nests

Nest sites for stifftails need a little closer consideration. Stifftails (the Oxyura family) need a dark and protective rushy environment in which to breed. For these ducks build a raft having a wooden frame, square in section, and having a weldmesh or stiff wire floor. Diagonal wooden struts for strength are a good idea as a good raft will be quite large—about 5-feet square. If you decide your raft will be of the floating variety you will have one big advantage, but also one disadvantage over a permanently fixed one. The advantage is that during floods and summer low water they maintain their surface position, whereas fixed ones either drown or are left high and dry. The disadvantage is that they can be deposited during floods on the bank side or simply drift into the bank allowing predators access. Your raft type will therefore be dependent on the type of water you have. The following instructions can be applied to both; except, of course, your floating raft needs to be buoyant for at least four months of the year and well tethered to the bank so that you can haul it in (if in deep water), to inspect for eggs, etc.

When making a permanent fixture, drive four poles into the pond bed, one for each corner, plus one to support the middle where the diagonals meet. Attach the square section to the poles and insert the diagonals leaving the raft bed an inch or two out of the water. In large waterfowl collections, situate these nests well away from the bank to discourage rats or water voles from swimming over and onto them. Unfortunately, not much can be done to stop voles, rats or snakes from getting to nests, except a good trapping and/or poisoning regimen. Line the edges of the raft with Juncus Reed or rush, leaving on the roots. You will find that the weight of the reeds is just enough to enable immersion of their roots in the water so that they will stay growing for a month or two. In the middle of the raft, build up a good rushy nest like that of a coot or moorhen. Take some fully leafed willow or bamboo branches and push them into the pond bed as close to the side of the raft as possible, then using exactly the same wigwam technique as for the geese, gather all the tops together and tie them.

If your water level might fall an inch or two, attach a runged ladder, at a very gentle angle. Remember that stifftails are staggeringly inefficient movers on land and therefore will require easy access.

This type of nesting cover is what stifftails really adore—a dark, quiet rushy environment. Some stifftails will nest in a ground box on the land however, so it may be worth supplying a few extra boxes, dug into the ground and thickly surrounded by vegetation.

6

Eggs

Once nests have been created, the next thing we all hope for is large quantities of eggs.

First, a sound knowledge of the birds' nesting habits and clutch size is useful. Second, some knowledge of what time of year birds are likely to produce eggs is helpful, especially considering the geographical location of your collection. Generally birds lay slightly earlier in warmer areas where winters are mild, and later in more northerly latitudes. Arctic breeding geese, who generally lay later in the year, need to be kept very fit to breed properly. Ducks and geese of this type respond to lengthening daylight. The eye acknowledges this lengthening and signals the brain, which in turn signals the pituitary gland. The hormonal message travels through the blood to the sexual organs. If the sexual organs of your birds are encased in a layer of fat, fertility suffers. There is evidence to suggest that cold water helps with breeding of these Arctic species—possibly a connection with the melting ice water experienced in the Arctic just prior to breeding. Artificial lighting (extending daylight periods) can be used with these types of waterfowl. It artificially extended their breeding period which tends to make them lay earlier in the year and thereby made it possible for them to produce second clutches. If you decide to try this, make sure that other varieties of waterfowl that are naturally earlier layers than Arctic species, are not exposed to the light as you can wreck their breeding frequency. I would generally advise against using artificial lighting for this purpose.

Freak January temperatures can convince some species it is spring, and arctic species sometimes respond earlier in a season, especially if artificial light is provided for a few hours after dusk. I have seen Bewick's Swan clutches complete by April 14—giving the female ample time for a second clutch. Similarly, Red-breasted, Brent, Ross', Emperors, Eiders and others can be duped into believing "the time is right." However, I would only recommend this in areas where late spring is relatively warm and the weather stable. With the Bewick's mentioned earlier, she was in her fourth day of incubation (on dummy eggs) when it snowed very heavily overnight, engulfing her and her nest. (She sat calmly through it though, eventually hatching 3 of her 5 eggs.)

Waterfowl change in temperament during the breeding season. Females become secretive and eat more; building up reserves for the period spent incubating eggs. During this period they loose as much as a third of their body weight, so it is sensible not to allow birds to incubate too early in the season, when it may become cold and wet. Take the first clutch away and if she lays again, she will do so when the weather is warmer and more stable.

Finding waterfowl nests can be quite a lot of fun especially in large collections. Not all your birds will obligingly lay in their prescribed boxes so a sharp pair of eyes and a gentle step is needed to locate them. When I was younger and just learning my trade, we used to look for eggs early in the morning and I thought this should be standard procedure. I realized later that in large collections that are "unroofed" (this one was nearly 100 acres), early morning predators, especially Jays, Magpies, Carrion Crows, Jackdaws and Rooks can decimate the nests of laying birds. Also there was a lot of work to do every day and we were all involved in ongoing projects. Unfortunately, this part of the day saw a lot of birds nesting and we had to go out of our way to avoid disturbing them. Later on, when I was looking after birds in enclosed pens, I would leave the early mornings to the birds and wait until individuals had reappeared before I started to look for eggs. The last thing birds need when laying is disturbance or stress, so a rule of thumb should be, leave well enough alone! There are plenty of hours in the day. If you are lucky enough to be with your birds all day, have a quiet walk around first thing, maybe even with a morning cup of tea or coffee, and see if any of the birds are missing. Later on, when the bird shows up, you can go and check the nest boxes or nesting areas knowing you will not disturb her. As I mentioned in the chapter entitled Stockmanship, observation is vital in the successful propagation of waterfowl. Take the time to sit and observe your birds. Look for that characteristic bulging around the vent indicating that the bird is laying, or is "heavy." Make sure female birds are not in distress or egg bound. You may see a bird whose nest you can't locate, frantically bathing and feeding...trying to keep her ardent male away by quacking and gaping at him. Wait until she has finished and watch her disappear back into the undergrowth.... There, she's just led you to her nest!

Ducks normally lay every day until their clutch is complete. Geese and swans lay every other day, so you need not inspect and possibly disturb a parent goose or swan each day. Waterfowl eggs are not incubated as they are laid as is the case with some other types of birds. The eggs lie cold in the nest until the last one or two are laid, then the female plucks out her own down from the breast area, exposing a brood patch. Then she lines the nest with down and starts incubating or "sitting" the eggs. In this way all the eggs are started together and they will hatch together. As young waterfowl can swim and feed themselves immediately upon hatching, the mother bird can lead the whole family to water and safety.

Some birds, especially Smew and Buffleheads, can be very finicky about sitting on dummy eggs, and indeed sitting their own. Because of their value it would be wise to remember two points. First, use a dummy egg of similar size and weight. Usually, bantam eggs are a good bet, or, if you have some, those of a Ringed Teal. You can also, if you have a dependable and already-sitting Ringed Teal female, use her as a sitter for the Smew or

Bufflehead—she will take care of these more delicate eggs as they are very much like her own. If you want your Smew or Bufflehead to sit (always a good idea first time) let them sit the Teal eggs.

As each egg is laid, it should be picked up and a substitute egg placed in the nest. Even if you intend the female to sit her own eggs, you must collect each fresh laid egg; this way her eggs are fully protected by you while she spends seven to ten days laying. You need not use more than four or five dummy eggs even if the bird lays ten eggs or more; waterfowl are not very good at addition! Some propagators use infertile eggs from other species as dummies and this can be a good idea as you can use the correct type of egg as a substitute for the real one. However, never use infertile eggs that are more than two weeks old as they can decay quickly when warmed and spread disease to new laid eggs in a nest. Dummy eggs can be made in wood, plastic, china, fiberglass and many more materials. Some sizes are sold commercially like chicken, turkey and goose, but eggs for Teal, small duck and swans will need to be specially made. I like to pick up eggs as they are laid, because they can be given better protection this way. Birds sitting or laying for the first time should be allowed to hatch something expendable. You don't have to leave them sitting for their full incubation period. Say you are going to allow an Eider duck to hatch something. Mallard would be a good bet as the egg sizes are fairly similar. Find some Mallard that are within a week or 10 days of hatching, and put these under the Eider. This way she need only sit 10 days—enough so she thinks she has done her job, without losing too much weight and getting out of condition.

Keep a close eye on your stock during this part of the year. Eggs can be thrown out of nests by other birds, predated, flooded out and soaked. Laying birds may become egg bound and need veterinary treatment (see Disease and Control chapter). Above all, go about your egg collecting quietly and slowly at a sensible hour of the day.

Egg Storage

If you are going to rear your birds by hand and therefore are collecting their eggs, you will need somewhere to store them prior to incubation. Don't leave eggs in a nest box even if you are going to let the parent incubate. The weather could get very hot and spoil the eggs before they are ever incubated. Rats, snakes and other predators can get them. The parent bird herself might drop onto them heavily, breaking one or two, or puncturing the shell.

Eggs should be stored in a room with a steady, even temperature and humidity—about 55°F and 50 percent humidity being ideal. One of the best substances for storage before setting is sand. This must be sterilized: easily done by filling containers and baking the sand in an oven for an hour or so at a high temperature (400°F). When it has cooled, make a tray about 3-inches deep and having spread out the sand on the tray, place the eggs on the sand in individual clutches. This way you can see how many eggs are laid by individual birds and variations in shape or size of shell structure. Write on the shell the date each egg was laid. (When doing this, use a fine felt-tip pen that has nontoxic ink. Don't use a regular pen or pencil; you could puncture the egg shell.) This will help you keep an eye on the age of various eggs before they are put in the incubator or returned to the parent bird. Although waterfowl eggs can lie cold for a while, it is best that the egg is set within four days of being laid. This is not always possible to do when using a parent bird as an incubator, because she will need to finish her clutch and then it is best to watch her for a few days to make sure she is going to be a good sitter. By the time all this has happened, the oldest egg could be two weeks or more old! However there are ways around this situation. For example, you can use another bird that might just have started to sit, as the "mother." The bird doesn't have to be the same species either, just as long as she is about the same weight and size and has a similar-sized egg. This is where records come in.

Just as writing the date on an egg helps you keep track of its age, records will help you keep track of your eggs during incubation and at hatching. They will also show you, year after year, your success rates (or otherwise), with various species. Records are vital to a successfully run operation. I can't emphasize this enough.

An example of a suitable recording method might be as follows:

Ring No.	Species	Date of First Egg	Date Set	Incubator or Hen	Tray or Box No.
245	Eider	March 21st		Incubator	Tray 6

Candling Date	No. Fertile	No. Infertile		Comment Bad position in egg?	
April 3rd	4	1	1	Inadequate adult diet?	

Eggs should be turned every day during storage. This will help stop any portion of the fluid inside sticking to the membrane or shell and also keeps the yolk agitated. Turning an egg simply consists of rotating the egg through 180° along its longitude. In other words, you turn the egg over rather than twist it about its axis. To make it easier to remember if you have turned all your eggs, most people mark an O and an X on opposing sides. Having turned them, you can see if you have missed any as they should all register the same symbol.

To wash eggs before setting them, a gentle disinfectant in a weak solution is best. Blood or droppings on eggs will promote bacterial growth in the warm environment of an incubator, sometimes with disastrous, possibly explosive, results. Wipe eggs clean with cotton wool soaked in the weak disinfectant solution and dry the shell before setting. There are strongly held opinions on this subject among waterfowl breeders. Some say that it is of paramount importance to clean eggs, some just get the worst off, others don't bother. All, however, will tell you they have good results. I have noticed a slight increase in hatchability when eggs are cleaned, but a rise in chick mortality between hatching and

70

the following three or four days. This may be due to being hatched in an almost germ-free environment and then suddenly exposed to the outside world. Chicks in this situation don't seem to have the resistance to infection that youngsters from unwashed eggs have. As a general rule I would advise any blood or droppings or heavy earth deposits on the egg to be wiped away and the egg cleaned, but don't worry overly with slightly dirty eggs, especially if you have a fastidious incubator cleaning regimen. When handling eggs, at any stage, be gentle with them: don't jerk or jar them unnecessarily.

Broody Hens

If a broody hen is used instead of the parent bird (a good idea as most ducks are disastrous mothers) select one which is the right size for the eggs. It's no good using a Buff Orpington to sit Ringed Teal, or a game bantam to sit goose eggs. Make sure she is the right weight so she won't crush the eggs, and that she doesn't have long toenails that might puncture the eggs. Once the hen has become broody, sit it in a box in a cool spot on dummy eggs for a day or two to make sure she's not just kidding. This will get her used to you when you take her off to be fed and watered, once a day, about fifteen to twenty minutes being sufficient. When you know she is right, set the eggs under her.

Broody hen boxes can be laid out side by side, under shade if possible so that they can be fed and watered and eggs checked in one operation. Modern sitting boxes are much like the raised nest box in design, except the roof lifts off and the front face has a sliding door for access. Boxes can have a sort of wire cage into which the broody steps, having come off her eggs for food and water. It is best, as soon as she is out to shut her access door or she may spend valuable feeding and drinking time fluffed and complaining while she can see her eggs. Once the nest is out of sight they normally get on with feeding. Allow all broodies to walk out of boxes on their own if they will and only handle them if absolutely necessary. While she is out, inspect the nest for signs of lice, test the overall warmth of a couple of eggs (hold them and rotate them against your upper or lower lip) to make sure she is doing a proper job. Ensure the eggs are not cracked or damaged in any way, see that the nest isn't becoming too dry (damp the surrounds down with an atomizer spray containing warm water) and make sure she has defecated before she re-enters the nest box. The nest box interiors should be filled in exactly the same way as an ordinary duck nest box (see Nesting Requirements chapter).

If lice are found within the nest compartment dust the hen down with louse powder, transfer the eggs to another bird and reset some dummies for your freshly dusted hen to make sure she settles again. Next day, if no fresh lice activity is found, put the eggs back. When the broody is out feeding give her reasonable time. If it is very hot, half an hour is not too long to leave the eggs. Again, make sure she defecates before going back to the nest as droppings in and around the nest can send eggs bad. If you have to pick her up, do it gently, and put her back slightly to one side of the nest to avoid any possible damage to the eggs by her feet. Watch that she doesn't "pedal" with her feet as you are lowering her, or she may scatter and crack the eggs. Small cracks in eggs can be mended with a typewriter "cover up agent" or fingernail polish. "Mended" eggs should be put in an incubator where greater care can be taken of them. Don't set eggs with cracks that have torn the membrane that lines the shell or those with cracks of star-burst shape which exceed $\frac{1}{4}$ inch in diameter; they won't hatch. The very valuable egg or the egg that is only a few days from hatching is an exception.

Another problem associated with broody hens is that they can, at hatch and during the first few days, inadvertently crush youngsters. Also, some hens, seemingly on a whim, turn around and kill youngsters. Some species of duck, upon hatching, don't make the usual piping cheep, but make unusual sounds which disturb the hen, resulting in the hen killing them. During bad weather, the hen may not take them under cover to brood, or individual ducklings may not want to be brooded, leading to a soaking and eventual death through chilling. If you are on hand 24 hours a day you can take steps to ensure that all broodies and youngsters are shut away during rainy weather. However, not all breeders can be on hand all day and every day.

If you are keeping domestic waterfowl with your wild waterfowl, you can use some of these as broodies. You have to watch individual females to make sure they are good broodies. This does not mean sitting on the eggs continuously and never coming off. Never use a domestic bird that acts this way. People often think that this is the correct sort of devotion to incubation. I have seen many birds (normally geese) become thin, parasite infested and pneumonic quite apart from the total neglect of nest hygiene. Even when incubating, birds should come off the nest periodically for a wash and some food.

Using domestic geese as broodies for my goose eggs, I only recommend the China and Buff, and only then with a comparably sized waterfowl egg. Larger or smaller goose eggs tend to come to a sticky end. The problem is, or seems to be, that an oversize "foster egg" cannot displace the weight of a slightly smaller webbed foot bearing down on it, with the inevitable result. It seems nature has adapted egg size and foot size rather well, if not intentionally. A swan standing her own egg folds the foot right round her egg, evenly displacing her weight. But if that same egg, even under a big domestic, gets more pressure on a smaller area, a toenail bites in and breakage occurs.

It made interesting experimentation the first time I came across this; having used a few infertile swan eggs as experiments, I found this principle applying every time, even Embdens, weighing 20 pounds, cracked infertile Trumpeter swan eggs, whereas the swan herself some 10 pounds heavier, never did. I have tried broody domestic ducks with great success. Some were entrusted with very valuable eggs.

Call Ducks seem far and away the best. Kept in aviaries with some decently designed nest boxes, you can get four good results from these little birds.

Whatever reasons I have for setting the eggs of various different species under a broody, the bird itself is the main item. Call Ducks are nice, steady and can be downright belligerent to any intruders. They settle onto their eggs delicately and have a nice weight distribution over the egg, via the foot, should they ever stand directly on the eggs.

Calls can be fed once, in the morning, and, in aviaries, the females can be free to come and go as they please for both food and water. They keep beautifully clean and have a better chance than a hen to wash out any feather parasites. They also impart that lovely oily sheen to the egg shell which gives the impression of a good, healthy egg.

Candling

Now we have our broodies all sitting, we need to know, at some point during incubation, whether the egg is fertile or not. This is done by shining a light into the egg to look for embryonic development. There are many types of "candlers" available from poultry equipment outlets and from some incubator companies. Candlers range from relatively small output machines, to intense beams needed to penetrate the very thick shells of birds such as Ostriches.

Luckily for us, most waterfowl eggs are easy to inspect with a regular strength light. I have been using a small Mag Lite flashlight for some years now and it is quite capable of candling teal, Bufflehead, Smew, Hooded Merganser and many other small duck species' eggs. Stifftails, with their large and relatively thick-shelled eggs present a problem, but can easily be inspected with a normal candler. Goose and swan eggs may require a stronger light source. I have seen several good homemade devices which use an old slide projector. One word of caution when using high intensity lights for candling. These bulbs tend to be very hot, so don't take a long time looking at the egg, it will get very hot and could damage the embryo.

If you use a broody duck or hen and can easily inspect the eggs at feeding time, candle them at about 7 days to determine fertility. With a good egg you will find a little blackish red blob in the middle with red veins radiating out around it to the edge of the air sac. Often you can see the little blob (its heart) beating. If there is just a small black blob in the middle and nothing else, the egg is no good. Also, if the veins appear to be receding from the air sac edge and are black in color the egg is no good. Sometimes a red ring can be seen inside the egg. The egg has ceased developing when this occurs. If the egg is completely clear or devoid of any development, it is infertile and can either be disposed of or blown out and used in your own egg collection. Toward the end of incubation you may want to check on the development of some eggs. Occasionally you will see a sort of moving shadow in the center or slightly to one side of the air cell. This is the chick preparing to break its membrane and come into the air cell. Sometimes you will find that instead of a normal black mass and clearly defined air space there appears to be a yellowish area between the chick and the air sac with the last black remnants of veins. The chick is usually dead although on rotating the egg on the candler you may see movements. This is only the fluid. If you are in doubt leave the egg another 24 hours and if no further development is noticed throw away the egg. This condition is usually caused by too much humidity, especially when numerous eggs have the same problem. As the art of candling revolves around correct visual interpretation, it is extremely difficult to describe in writing.

I would advise all those who are dubious as to their prowess in candling eggs to go and see an experienced breeder and learn how it is done. If there is such a person relatively near by, pay his petrol or air fare (as long as it's reasonable) and you will inevitably win out. Half a dozen good eggs could be worth hundreds of dollars—spending 6 hours learning that the eggs are all right or taking remedial action under the supervision of a professional is not only worth it financially, but also you will learn a great deal.

7

Artificial Incubation

Modern technology has improved the incubator incredibly in the last fifteen years. However, artificial incubation is by no means modern in its conception.

The Chinese were hatching eggs using a compost heap method 1,000 years before the ancient Egyptians. Eggs were placed in a wicker-work tray which was shut within a clay box. A chimney with adjustable vents was fitted over the top and hollow bamboo pipes were laid out around the box. Semi-decomposed matter, usually vegetables, straw and animal dung, was piled around the box and the chimney vents opened or closed during the incubation process to let out excessive heat and humidity. The bamboo pipes provided oxygen and were plugged or unplugged according to the operator's fancy. This may sound like an incredibly chancy method of incubating eggs, but the operator's skill was undeniable as successful hatchings undoubtedly took place.

The Egyptians used the same basic method, but contributed to the development of incubation technology by using candle power! How this "modern" breakthrough worked I have no idea, but I presume the heat from the burning candles probably helped evaporate water and the whole thing was very much dependent on the skills of the operator. Oddly enough, this quality, skill or "feel," is one of the most important factors in incubation even now, 2,000 or 3,000 years later.

Incubator Rooms

Regardless of what type(s) of incubator you require, no machine can do its job effectively without a stable environment around it. Incubators should be situated in a room with a stable temperature (day and night) of around 60° to 70°F. Before you select a likely situation, check the room to see if it meets these criteria. Most houses with effective air conditioners and heaters can keep a stable temperature throughout the house. Outside buildings may not have heating or cooling systems. Make sure there are no drafts, but also, make sure the room is well ventilated. If there is some way of keeping the room in darkness, do so. This will help when you are candling eggs.

Incubator Design

There are two types of incubator design most used. One is known as a "still-air" design, the other as a "fan-assisted" or "forced-air" machine.

The still-air variety has temperature and humidity controls and uses naturally circulating air, whereas the forced air has all the same things but uses a fan to circulate the air within the machine. Which is best? Most modern operators will give you the same answer: forced-air machines. They are much easier to operate and are far more reliable. However, the old still-air machines had one quality I always liked; they were quiet and vibration free and more like the conditions found under the parent bird. However, there is no doubt that forced-air machines are easier to use and provide excellent results. In utilizing today's technology, there are machines available that keep the cabinet climate constant, within one degree or less. Computer technology has allowed for instantaneous detection of the smallest variation in temperature, which makes for a very stable machine. However, while the claims may be true at one location within the cabinet, I have yet to come across a machine that actually does not differ by more than one degree throughout the entire cabinet. Although this may sound contrary, this can work in the waterfowl operators' favor as different types of waterfowl can utilize these cooler more humid areas. Waterfowl that lay their eggs very close to or on top of the water (stifftails, swans) seem to deal with higher humidity levels easily and this is probably a reflection of their evolution in these environments and so can be set in these areas of the cabinet.

One of the unfortunate things about modern industrial incubators is that they were originally designed to take enormous settings of standard-sized eggs at once. The waterfowl keeper may find that he may only have 5 or 10 eggs at a certain time of year that he needs to incubate, or that he has a wide variety of shapes and sizes of eggs that do not fit in the egg trays properly. Luckily, there are many sizes of incubators available but we all end up inventing ways of keeping those odd-shaped eggs intact. The best way to deal with the number of eggs problem, is to use one small and one large machine. (I always use a separate machine in a different room for hatching. See Hatching.)

Thermometers

All machines will come with some type of thermometer. These vary in design (and greatly in usefulness!) from model to model. Some models use preset mercury-contact thermometers. Some use red alcohol thermometers and yet others use large dial thermometers. As one of the most important areas of incubation is temperature control, these types of thermometers must be checked to make sure that they are accurate to begin with. Don't just assume that because you have just paid hundreds of dollars for a state of the art machine that you are going to get a truly accurate thermometer. It is imperative that you check your thermometer when it arrives to ensure no separation has taken place within the mercury or alcohol. If it has, the manufacturer will usually have a set of instructions dealing with this predicament. It is usually put right by cooling the thermometer until all the mercury has been reunited.

There can be no doubt that electronic thermometers are currently the most accurate instruments available for temperature testing. Most of the operators that I know abandon the normally supplied thermometers in favor of an electronic one. There are literally thousands of models available now that will monitor temperatures as accurately as +/- .1°. While this is superb management of temperature, a thermometer need only (!) be accurate to +/- .5° to be effective. I urge you to use one. If you can't justify the additional cost, then you must be able to justify poorer results!

Prewarming of Eggs

Eight years ago, while I was absorbed in the studies of artificial incubation, I wondered if prewarming eggs before setting them was desirable. I found a marginal increase in hatchability using this technique. To this day I cannot say for certain whether it is something that will result in better hatches because of the many variables that exist. Genetics, diet, compatibility and weather conditions all play a role in successful incubation and hatching of eggs. There was no standard or placebo group to cross refer to. All I can say is that a parent bird will only bring her eggs to optimum incubation temperature gradually. An incubator can advance this process by a time factor of almost ten. My efforts were aimed at trying to simulate the conditions that waterfowl eggs experience under the parent bird. I hoped that this more natural approach would lead to better hatchings. While I feel I had slightly better results using this method, I can't say for certain. Here lies an enigma.

As I write, a house finch has built her nest in a strawberry plant that is in a hanging basket by my front door. Every time I go into the kitchen, she sees me and flies off the nest. This means that the eggs are being heated and cooled on a totally irregular basis due to my presence. She recently hatched all five of her eggs despite this interrupted incubation. If we were to try and mimic these sorts of conditions in an incubator, we would hatch nothing. Who knows what goes on in an egg under a female bird? Might it be that embryos are responsive to the heartbeat of the mother bird? Child psychologists tell us today, that the reason a baby may cease to cry when held closely to its mother's breast, is because it remembers the comforting sound of the mother's heartbeat, something it remembers from its days in the womb. Logically, we should be able to conclude that contact between the parent bird and its egg should be beneficial. Perhaps a machine designed to mimic all these exterior influences could become the ultimate incubator. All I know for sure is that by sticking to proven temperature and humidity settings in incubators, you will get a good hatch result overall. (More about egg communication in Hatching.)

Incubator Temperatures

A temperature of 99.3° to 99.5°F should be maintained for waterfowl eggs in a fan-assisted machine, and slightly higher (100.5°F) in a still-air machine. This temperature can fluctuate under conditions where the incubator room varies in temperature. Also, constant opening and closing of the incubator door will be detrimental. During hatching, the machine can operate at a lower temperature, 99°F. The most critical part of operation is that these temperatures are maintained and do not vary by more than half a degree during the incubation of eggs. Occasional fluctuations of 1° or more can be tolerated but not on a long-term basis. Remember that when you fire up the machine dry and stabilize the temperature, it will go down when you introduce water. Always test the machine for at least two days prior to setting eggs in it with water included. (Use only distilled water, otherwise the wet-bulb thermometer may get calcium deposits on the wick and give a false reading. Also, in some areas a slime can build up on the wick.) When eggs are set, the temperature may go down for a while as the eggs absorb heat. Always check the temperature one hour after setting eggs. Preheating the eggs to at least room temperature or more (80°F), may offset this a little, but a check is needed. Take notice of temperature fluctuations when eggs are turned. Some machines I have encountered varied 2° or more when the egg trays were turned. This was because of the design of air flow in the machine, over the trays and eggs when at a different angle. Make sure all these criteria are tested for.

Finally, make sure you have backup power in case of a power

outage. A \$300 generator is worth every penny when the power goes out during a storm and you have thousands of dollars worth of eggs in a machine. I did find a very good automatic alarm system once. There was a machine sold through Radio Shack outlets a few years ago that monitored temperature in a house room. It could be programmed to monitor high and low temperatures via a small thermometer at the back of the machine. Once programmed, and if the room temperature rose above or fell below the programmed temperature, it would automatically dial three preprogrammed telephone numbers with an alert message provided by the user, and would continue dialing until the message was picked up. I bought one of these systems, and set the thermometer probe into an incubator I was using at the time. The machine contacted me on several occasions when I was fast asleep and once when I was not available it went on and dialed my assistant. In all cases, I would never have known that the power had failed and would have slept blissfully through the outage, never knowing that my eggs were in danger. I supplied a similar system to a state agency that were incubating eggs of an endangered species on a remote island, notorious for power interruptions. As far as I know, it was a great success.

Humidity

Waterfowl eggs need warmth and humidity in order to hatch successfully. Keeping a stable humidity is almost as important as keeping a stable temperature. The old belief that waterfowl eggs needed lots of humidity, killed more embryos than it ever hatched. Too much humidity will result in fluid build up in the egg, eventually drowning the chick. Too little dehydrates the chick.

Humidity levels are measured in two ways; by a wet-bulb reading, and by a hygrometer. The wet bulb is a normal thermometer which has a wick attached to the bulb. The wick dangles in the water, drawing moisture up the wick to the bulb that then registers in degrees F or C. The hygrometer reads the percentage of water in the air and so records the humidity level by percent. Most hygrometers have a membrane of some sort (some of the best use a human hair!) that expands or contracts when exposed to differing levels of humidity. This membrane is attached to a spring and as the membrane expands and contracts, an indicator relays the information on the hygrometer's face giving the reading.

Different machines use different ways to get moisture into the air, but all work to the same principle. The larger area of water there is, the more evaporation can take place. I once owned a machine with one long narrow tray that provided humidity. Regardless of the depth of water in the tray, you could not raise the humidity level as there was no more area! I ended up redesigning water pans for it which worked much better. I sometimes wonder (and from the letters and phone calls I get, others are wondering too) if some of the designers of these machines ever used an incubator!

Differing geographical and climatical locations will have an effect on humidity levels within your machine. For instance, if you lived in the Bahamas where the humidity is naturally elevated, you would not use as much water as someone in Arizona. Simple testing of your machine will show you how much water to use. Manufacturers sometimes give guideline approximations to help start you in the right direction. As a guide, I have found that readings of 83.5° for 10 days, followed by 85° for the next 10 (give or take a degree), culminating in a reading of 86° to 87° for the last 6 to 8 days, produces good results. Some operators use more humidity, some use less according to location. Follow the guidelines set down by the manufacturer at first, as this would give you some good baseline readings from which to experiment with. The following conversion table from degrees to percentage may be useful to those who have hygrometers in their machines:

WET BULB (degrees)	HYGROMETER (percent)
91	70
90	68
89	65
87	62
86	59
85	56

WET BULB (degrees)	HYGROMETER (percent)
84	53
84	50
83	48
82	46

Turning Eggs

Just as cold eggs in storage need turning, so do incubating eggs. The motion of turning an egg during incubation helps the developing embryo from being stuck in one position and trapping blood vessels or nerves and it also facilitates the distribution of heat around the egg.

Most incubators have a method of turning eggs while they are incubating. Those that don't, rely on the operator to do it. The methods employed vary. Some machines are designed so that eggs are set upright and are rocked through 120° to 180°. In other machines, eggs are laid flat and rolled through 180° one way, and back 180°, the other. They are both ways of doing the same, vital thing. A developing embryo must not be allowed to sit in one position for too long. Simply rolling an egg about its axis the same direction every time does not turn the embryo, it helps to twist it up in its own umbilical cord, strangling it eventually.

Make sure that whatever method your machine uses to turn the eggs, that it is actually doing it. I have seen many machines that, because of different egg sizes and shapes, merely slid the egg to one side of the machine and back to the other, without ever turning the egg properly. Unless you had witnessed it, you would think that all was well. In machines where eggs are set upright, no egg is excluded from being turned, as all are rocked through 180° when the tray turns, regardless of shape or size. As a help, do the same thing I recommended in the section dealing with egg storage. Mark one side of the egg with an X and the other with an O. This way, when you pass by, you can tell at a glance any eggs which are not being turned properly as they will be showing the contrary symbol to the rest. Also make sure that any bars or grids used to roll the eggs, cannot ride up and over an egg at turning, or roll it against the side of the machine, trapping and crushing it.

Turning frequency is important to good hatches. Most automatic turners turn the eggs every hour or two depending on design. If you are hand turning eggs, you will have to do it at least 6 to 8 times a day at regular intervals...no 8 hours of sleep here!

Finally, some operators like to cool the eggs down in their machines, every third or fourth day. The female bird does this in the wild when she gets off the nest to wash and feed. Should you wish to try this, simply switch off the machine and open the door for about ten minutes if the room temperature is approximately 60°F. Allow less time if the room is cooler, and never allow the incubator room to get warmer than 70°F. Remember that the better control you have over temperature and humidity in the incubator room, the better your machine will run, and the better your success rate will be.

Hatching

Developing embryos can die before they hatch and the reasons for this are many. Too much heat or too little, fluctuations in temperature and humidity, poor egg storage practices, bad dietary regimen for adults and poor stock lines, all contribute to weaknesses in a chick. Overlarge chicks sometimes run out of air when they get into the air space at the top of the egg, prior to hatching. An egg shell is porous and each egg has evolved over time to accommodate the particular requirements of that species, be it oxygen exchange or humidity exchange or both. As mentioned earlier, too much fluid in an egg because of high humidity levels, can drown a chick. An over large chick may need more oxygen when chipping and struggling to get out, than would a normal-sized chick.

To run a hatcher successfully does not require quite the same sort of thoroughness as does the running of an incubator. Here you can get away with a temperature variation of a degree or so. Humidity needs to be kept higher (but not dripping off the machine), at around 86° to 89°F wet bulb. Hatchers must be well vented to allow fresh air to enter the machine and to expel the much higher levels of CO_2 experienced at hatching time. As I mentioned earlier, I always use a separate hatching machine and this is one of the reasons why. Secondly, as we are constantly setting eggs of varying quantities for as much as nine months of the year, our incubator will be catering for eggs at all different levels of incubation. The last thing we want are elevated and potentially lethal levels of CO_2 flying around, combined with the threat of infection spreading to all our eggs via all the loose down and hatching membranes lying around. Add to this the fact that we can't keep two different temperatures and humidities going in the same machine, and you start to realize why I like a separate hatcher.

Eggs should be placed in the hatcher as soon as the chick breaks into the air sack. This is normally two days or so before hatching. Candling an egg will show you the chick's progress. Do not turn the eggs any more at this point. Let them lie exactly as they are when you transfer the eggs to the hatcher. Do this gently...do not jar the eggs or handle them roughly. As the chick breaks into the air sack, it adapts its position in the shell to enable it to start chipping. From one point, the chick rotates in the shell chipping all the time, until it has loosened enough of the shell to enable it to break free. Turning or disturbing the egg constantly during this period can interfere with the chick's orientation.

Place clutches of eggs together in the hatcher touching each other. In the wild at this time, the chick and mother are in constant contact audibly. Being next to each other in the hatcher will allow the chicks to hear each other. Occasionally, a single chick comes up to hatching and, surprisingly, dies, while seeming perfectly vigorous while in the air space. Most of the time the chick expires because there are no audible signals to encourage him. I have found that recording peeping noises (either of actual chicks or an imitation) on a tiny microcassette tape recorder and leaving it playing next to the egg in the hatcher, stimulates the weaker or reluctant chick into action and in using this method, I have saved quite a few lives. (If you want to try this, find a recorder that will automatically rewind at the end of the tape and then replay.)

As the chicks start to hatch, it may be necessary to assist weaker or trapped youngsters.

On occasion, helping chicks out of an egg will save valuable birds, but with poor bloodlines, even if the bird survives to adulthood and eventually breeds, you will create more problems than you solve. I would only advise the use of this procedure in "last ditch" efforts or on a valuable bird.

First, you have to determine whether you actually have a problem egg or not. It appalls me to hear of, or see, people pulling out young chicks because they are 24 hours overdue. This sort of action can become addictive and is a poor excuse for bad incubation procedures.

If an egg is 24 hours late, and does not seem to be responding to the noises of its cousins around it, pencil a mark onto the shell at approximately the position of the beak. Check it four hours later to see if any progress has been made. If not, with extreme delicacy, make a small hole in the shell. A small nail is a good tool for this job, as the end has four sides around the sharp point, and can be used as a drill between the thumb and forefinger. Having made the hole, slide one mandible of a fine pair of tweezers under the shell and take out a very small chip. Using the candler, find the beak and determine at what stage the membranes covering the chick is at. If only the beak is through (and he has oxygen), some shrinkage of the membrane will take place. Give the egg another four hours, and you will probably find the membrane has dried to form a skin. Put the tiniest drop of water on a Q-tip swab and dampen the membrane. If all is going relatively well, you will be able to see the blood vessels receding. Membrane may now be removed *above the blood vein level only*. This is the most hazardous of procedures as if you happen to tear a vein you can kill the young chick by blood loss or poisoning. You really must have a very steady hand and good eyesight. Repeat this process at intervals. Do it slowly—don't rush—the chick has enough food in its yolk sack for another 48 hours. Usually, by the time the bird's head is free it will kick out on its own. You can help by gradually chipping shell away from it. Sometimes a chick will chip most of the way round only to halt suddenly. Having removed a portion of the shell, you may find it is in a bad position, or that premature drying has "stuck" its wing to the side of the head. Dampen the wing and gently, with thumb and forefinger under the neck of the bird, pull the head free. The bird will usually do the rest. Allow all newly hatched young to dry in the incubator for at least 15 hours.

A condition known as "straddle leg" can occur in some hatchers. This can be due to the type of surface the chicks are hatched on. Plastic or glass offers no toe hold to chicks, nor do certain varieties of fine mesh or plastic-coated mesh wire. During their first struggle to stand upright their legs slip away from them on either side and quickly a mental signal makes them believe that this is the correct position. Two things must be done under these circumstances. First, supply a floor on which the bird's legs cannot get away from it (fine mesh, soft rubber mat) and second, tape the legs together, allowing a correct distance between them and enough "give" to enable the bird to walk a little. Remove the tape after 48 hours and the bird should stand.

One final point. If you decide to use your old incubator solely as a hatcher, make certain that chicks cannot jump out of their trays after hatching. Also that standing up they cannot be decapitated by the fan. Most incubators have a fan guard—*one or two don't!* A tray full of headless young is not a pretty sight, especially after a good meal!

Incubator Hygiene

Incubators, and especially hatchers, need to be kept clean. Hatchers harbor all sorts of potentially lethal bacteria after a hatch from the chick's down, to the afterbirth debris. Try to choose a hatcher that is easy to clean. Some incubators/hatchers are a nightmare to clean. For most ducks, a small incubator such as the Marsh Roll X is an excellent hatcher. They are easy to clean and even the fan parts that collect a lot of down, can be blown clear with the use of a hair dryer, a compressed air source or an air can, the type used for cleaning camera lenses. I immerse the bottom part of the Marsh in a strong chlorine solution made up from pool chlorine. After it has sat for a while, it is hosed off under pressure to remove all traces of hatching debris and, of course, the chlorine itself. I have found this to be a very hygienic treatment and since using this method, have not had one infected yolk in my hatchlings.

Because I use a separate hatcher, my main incubators do not get dirty. I always wash eggs that have deposits of earth, blood or droppings on them in an egg disinfectant solution before they are set. I leave clean-looking eggs alone. I used to be a strong believer in incubator fumigation which was an acceptable practice when one incubator was being used to incubate and hatch young. As I now use at least two to four machines, I have found fumigation more work than is necessary. It is simpler and quicker to clean hatchers and incubators in the manner previously described.

8

Rearing

Successful rearing of young waterfowl can be very time consuming and on occasions, heart breaking. Total dedication is necessary to obtain satisfactory results. If your stock lines are good, your task will be much easier.

Nowadays, most breeders raise their waterfowl by hand—that is, they are reared without natural or foster parents. This reflects a breeder's reluctance to entrust the rearing of his charges to the true parents or a foster parent such as a broody hen. Generally, ducks are dreadful parents, especially in the presence of other species. Apart from the normal dangers on a quiet stretch of water in the wild, a captive bird has the threat of harassment from pen mates. The breeder's problems are magnified with this method of rearing—he must catch his ducklings before the parent takes them to water. He will want to pinion them or toe clip them. Once on the water, especially a large pond, young birds are very difficult to catch. Also, stress to other nesting birds due to this activity can cause desertion and great upset. The breeder will have no way of protecting the young birds from predators, and he will be unable to medicate or feed the ducklings properly, as the parent's natural instinct is to take the ducklings away from danger. Broody hens are little better, although they actually pay a little more attention to their broods than ducks. However they may inadvertently crush youngsters, turn on them and kill them, pick at blood spots on newly pinioned birds, transmit disease or fail to brood their charges during inclement weather.

You can understand why most experienced breeders rear by hand. The only drawback to hand rearing, besides time involved, is expense of outfitting the "duckery," or rearing room.

You will need brooders of various sizes to cater to birds as small as Teal, all the way up to Cygnets. Then there are more specialized species that need swimming water. All the youngsters will need heat of some sort and when they're large enough to go outside, they will need swimming, grazing and recreational areas. They may also need heat and protection from the elements.

Indoor Brooders

There are hundreds of designs of brooder units for waterfowl. I have seen everything from a cardboard box to a specially designed and cast fiberglass unit. I've seen them made of wood, metal, cement, plastic, plexiglass...you name it! Most probably worked to the breeder's satisfaction. There are a few criteria that affect the design of these units and these should be taken into consideration.

Firstly, ducklings make a mess! The unit that they are in is going to need cleaning out at least once a day so it must be lightweight and made of a durable material. Years ago, brooders were made with what was available, usually wood. This had to be sealed or waterproofed and the coop was heavy and needed maintenance. Nowadays, we have many strong, light varieties of plastics. There are hundreds of industrial uses for plastic containers, totes and boxes. I have used one particular design for the last seven years, called "Sky Kennel." I use the large-dog size and separate the two halves giving me two brooders that measure, 40 inches in length, 27 in. wide and 15 in. deep. A unit of this size is large enough to allow chicks to get away from the heat source should outside temperatures rise and also large enough to be able to place food and water containers with enough room around them so birds will not become trapped between the containers and the side wall, where they would get sodden and trampled. Because the unit is plastic, it is light, easy to carry and clean, and after making a few minor alterations needed for bird rearing rather than Great Dane transportation, it makes an excellent brooder.

The modifications are as follows should you like to use these units as well. When the kennel is split into two, the gap created by removing the door needs to be filled. It is a simple enough task to do this with wood, plastic or any other material that can stand a good soaking when cleaning. Don't use wire as some species will constantly try to climb out or become frightened or distracted by what is happening outside their brooder. Mount the new door on the inside of the gate aperture and secure it with some carriage bolts through the unit.

The next step is to make sure you provide a top to the unit so species such as Wood Ducks, Buffleheads, Smew and Hooded Mergansers can't get out. With the smallest toe hold (such as the head of the carriage bolt securing the blank) they can leap, pull themselves up and leap again. Also, they can get on top of a waterer and jump out from there. I use a piece of hardware cloth cut to fit the top of the unit and having a $\frac{1}{2}$-inch mesh. This is secured to the top lip of the unit with clips, the type artists use to secure their paper to the drawing board. A floor screen is cut to fit the interior of the unit. The material used is heavy-gauge hardware cloth or weld-mesh and this is covered by a piece of Neo-Tex matting so it is gentle on the feet of the ducklings. There are four round protrusions (probably casting lugs) that stand up from the floor of the unit, and these are ideal supports for the floor screen, keeping the birds off the floor and out of their own mess.

Finally, I use the gate aperture as the front of the brooder. Later on, when the birds are big enough to go swimming, I have a swimming unit that attaches to this aperture. For now though, the blank is in place. The area just inside the front of the unit is used for the food and water containers. Obviously, this is going to be the messiest part of the brooder. Luckily, the matting the birds are on, allows spilled food and water to drop through onto the brooder floor. However, we don't want wet food and droppings lying around, so I use a jigsaw to cut out a slot 20 inches long and 3 inches wide that runs across the front bottom part of the brooder. This is covered with hardware cloth and allows most of the spilled food and water to exit the brooder.

We also don't want old food and water on the floor of our rearing area. I have found the easiest solution is to mount all the brooders on a trestle or frame at about waist height. A waste gutter is now installed directly under the slot in the brooder floor. The frame is built to slope slightly from the back to the front and from one side to the other to facilitate drainage both in the brooders and in the waste channel. The waste channel is plumbed into the sewer or can drain into a receptacle such as a large trash can, from where it can be disposed of properly.

The only disadvantage to using Sky Kennel brooders is that individual groups of young still have to be caught and either isolated or moved into another brooder while the old one is being cleaned. I always try to avoid stressing the young, but it seems there is no practical way around a physical round up! Even this can be less stressful to the birds if done slowly and calmly. I have found a box that almost exactly fitted the width of the unit. Having taken out the food and water, I gently lower the box into the brooder and advance it up the unit until the young are all inside. Then I close the lid and either transport them to their new brooder, or leave them inside for a couple of minutes while I clean out their old one.

The best units I ever had were made of fiberglass. I designed them and had some made up when I was in Montana, working for William Hancock. These units had doors cast into the sides so groups of young could simply walk from one unit to the other without having to be manhandled. They had cast in food and water receptacles and a similar floor and food spillage operation. Their only drawback was the front was solid and didn't allow for a swimming unit. A "Mark 2" unit solved this problem. See photos page 152.

Indoor Swimming Units

All waterfowl need water to exist. They feed in it, bathe in it, mate in it, play in it and some even sleep in it. Some breeders still like to rear waterfowl "dry," that is only exposing the young birds to water when they are almost completely feathered. While some people have had successes using this method, I prefer getting the birds onto water as soon as is possible. After all, it is their natural element and there are benefits to giving them early access to water as there are disadvantages.

One of the main benefits is that the birds' preen glands start to work properly as nature intended. Dry rearing can lead to poor feathering later on when the birds first get wet. However, young birds need to be watched very carefully during their first swims, as they can get too wet and chilled, leading to eventual death. With a well-designed swimming unit, the birds should be both safe and happy.

Any swimming unit needs to be easily accessed by the youngsters. Getting in and out of the water can be difficult for some species. Stifftails, Cygnets and some geese are especially clumsy at first. I have always liked to get goslings and swans outside as quickly as possible for a number of reasons. Geese especially like to graze and exercise from the start. Swans likewise, but they like to be on the water more. Therefore, using an indoor swimming unit for these birds is unnecessary. They can be inside in a brooder large enough for them for a week or so and then go outside. This is not always possible in some areas as early breeders may encounter bad weather. Luckily, some of the earliest breeding birds, such as Ne-Ne's and Cereopsis don't need much water, but Black Swans and some others do, so swimming water for these types may need to be provided.

Some duck species may be a little more delicate at first and require a longer brooding period indoors and I like to have them swimming at about 4 or 5 days old. In California it is easy to get the birds outside quickly because of the beautiful weather, but in some areas, this is not always possible for 10 days or so and the birds need to be introduced to water inside. It is important to the birds' well being to get the preen gland working as soon as possible.

All waterfowl have a preen gland that supplies oil that the birds apply to their feathers when washing and preening. In the wild, they get an initial coating from contact with the parent bird's feathers during their first day or so of brooding. In this way, they are waterproofed and ready for their first swim. In captivity, most of the young birds come to the brooder straight from an incubator and so are not naturally waterproof. However, the preen gland functions immediately when they take their first dip, allowing them to coat their down properly and become waterproof. Initially they look like little drowned rats, but soon fluff out after they have preened and oiled their down. This first exposure to water can be a very stressful encounter. I have seen young ducks leap joyously into water, swim and dive straight away and on getting out, collapse into a shivering coma. I'm not sure what exactly happens to the bird's metabolism in order to bring on these sorts of attacks, but it does occasionally happen. Some subsequently die, others recover. It does seem to happen more in certain species than others and could even be genetically related as I have observed this happening to badly inbred birds most of all. Therefore, it is best to make the young birds' first encounters with water as brief and stress-free as possible.

In order to achieve this, the swimming unit should be easy to get in and out of. I have been using a plastic pan that was originally designed to catch waste oil during an automobile's oil change. This makeshift pond works well when slightly modified. This particular design is 26 x 19 x 7 inches and holds about 10 gallons of water. It has a rigid lip around the outside that is ideal for attaching a weld mesh wire screen to, so the birds can't jump out. The screen also has a hinged top on it so that more agile species such as Buffleheads, Hooded Mergansers, Wood Ducks, Mandarins, Smew, Ringed Teal and others, cannot climb out! Because of the pan's size, it fits snugly against the Sky Kennel-type brooder that I mentioned previously. The screen around the pond attaches to the front of the Sky Kennel and is secured with carriage bolts. As the water will need changing and the pan cleaning from time to time, I installed a drain pipe. There is a ready built unit for evaporative coolers that is very handy. It acts as an overflow pipe for these units and is easily installed into the pan. Once this is achieved, a threaded portion of the drain sticks out under the pan and can take a female garden hose attachment and a suitable length of ⅝-inch hose. I built another frame to hold a row of six ponds that butted up to the front of the Sky Kennels so each brooder now had its own swimming unit. All the ponds could now be drained independently and this was achieved by fitting the short length of hose into a 1½-inch PVC pipe that ran the length of the frame under the ponds. In order to separate the birds from the water for cleaning purposes or for enforced drying off periods, I used the blank that I originally made up to seal off the area of the kennel that housed the wire door. This could be dropped down like a shutter between the brooder lid and the swimming unit lid. The whole thing worked like a charm and was easily manageable.

After the birds had spent their first few days in the brooder and had started to feed and become strong, I let them have their first swim. I had made a little ramp of hardware cloth (weld-mesh), that fitted to the inside front of the brooder so it would allow the birds easy access to the pond and also easy access out of the pond back to the brooder. I would remove the blank from between the brooder and the pond and encourage them verbally. (Yes, I DO talk to my birds!) Little by little they would cautiously approach the water and eventually one would either jump in or topple in. Once someone had taken the plunge, everybody wanted in and enthusiastic diving and swimming would immediately ensue! After they had got slightly wet, I would shoo them back into the brooder (some not wanting to get out they were having so much fun), and drop down the blank to seal them off from the water. This is when they started to preen and waterproof themselves. After a few hours, when they had preened, fluffed up and rested, I would open up the pond to them again, and from that point on they usually had free access to come and go as they pleased. However, I would take the precaution of separating them from the water for the first two nights as things can go wrong with any young stock when left for long periods unattended in unfamiliar surroundings. This way, the birds got their first swim in a stress-free environment and I had the added benefit of being able to observe their behavior and look for possible problems that might arise.

Heat Lights

There are many types of heat source available and all have advantages and disadvantages in their usage.

The infrared or white bulb is probably the commonest type of heat source used in rearing facilities. While they work well, the breeder must remember to get shatterproof (or waterproof) bulbs so they will not break when water is accidentally splashed on them by the birds or by the breeder. Most of the time, these heat lights are suspended on a chain, and in order to raise or lower the available heat for the birds the breeder must reach up and lean over the brooder, panicking and scattering the young. If you wire all your lights to dimmer switches and have the whole panel remotely situated from the brooders, you can hang your heat lights at one level and you can adjust heat values by the turn of a switch and without the accompanying panic.

Infrawhite bulbs keep birds in the glaring light too much and I prefer the red, although these too emit light but not as intrusively. When I was in England, we could get a bulb made of porcelain called a dull emitter. This was the best bulb I ever used and it gave the birds the dark period they need to rest in as it emitted no light.

Remember that most lights can give off considerable heat. Birds must have room to move away from the heat. Also remember that temperatures outside can fluctuate affecting the temperature inside your rearing center. Heat will have to be increased and decreased accordingly.

From the Incubator to the Brooder

The first 24 hours that young birds spend in their brooders are a critical stage of life. This period will see them starting to explore their surroundings, drink and eat for the first time and do an awful lot of sleeping. During this stage, the breeder must pay close attention to the young and observe them as unobtrusively as possible and on a frequent basis.

When my birds were drying off in the hatcher, I would start to communicate with them whenever I was in the hatching room. Simply talking to them helps them start to recognize you or your presence and has a calming effect on them that will greatly assist you during their first few days of life. Once they are dry (normally 18 to 24 hours after hatching), it is time to transfer them to a brooder to get them to start eating and drinking.

Because I only had 20 or so species, I would never have a lot of birds hatching at once and so had the luxury of being able to keep the birds in a small brooder in the house. Other collections that I worked in had substantially more young and I always introduced them to their brooder first thing in the morning so I could spend the majority of the first day checking in on them. Even if this means leaving the birds in the hatcher for a little longer overnight, don't worry. Newly hatched young have a yolk sack that they internally digest for 30 hours or so and this will keep them sustained for that period.

To start with, I would set up their brooder with the wire floor screen and Neo-Tex mat as described previously. Over this I would put down newspaper and line the first half of the brooder (the area under the light to half of the way down the brooder) with paper towel. A heat light would be set up over one corner of the brooder and was adjusted on a vertical bar set outside the brooder to give a temperature of about 85° to 90°F an inch or so above the floor, this being the approximate height of the birds' backs when under it. This way the birds could brood directly under the heat source, or move away slightly when warm. A standard chick watering pot was filled with fresh water to which I added vitamin and electrolyte-soluble powder as an additive to get the birds fit and strong quickly. The normal waterer of this type has a lip of 1½ inches width and this is enough space for young birds to get into and get wet quickly. To offset this, I would put marbles in this space which still allowed the birds to dabble and drink but stopped them from getting completely soaked. The water pot MUST be positioned so that there is a good space around it. Never place a waterer right in a corner or exploring young may get stuck between it and the brooder wall and be

97

trampled by their brood mates. Also, make sure that the water container is a decent distance from the heat source so flying water will not shatter the light and so that birds don't tramp a wet mess back to the brooding area, soaking it. A wet, warm duck can die from chilling as easily as a wet, cold one.

Starting to Feed

Initially, your birds may not want to feed because they may still be digesting their yolk sacks. It is always a good thing to have them recognize the food though, so I usually put in a small food dish anyway. Birds won't necessarily go straight to the food and may need some encouragement to start feeding and so I would sprinkle a little bit over them when they first were under the light so they could pick at it. Sprinkle some around the waterer too and even in it, on top of the marbles. During their first explorations they will start to pick at it and will find the water. Usually, as soon as one bird finds the water and starts drinking, the rest will respond. If there is no evidence of drinking activity after the first two or three hours, gently pick up one bird and push its beak into the water. This often starts them off. If it seems that they are not feeding, there are a few methods to help.

First, you can take a bird from another brooder that has already started feeding and put it in with the newcomers. He will help the others identify the food and start them off. (Don't use too big a duckling for this. Use a bird a day or so older than the new ones. Ducklings, especially, grow extremely quickly and an oversize roommate can suffocate other smaller birds when brooding.) This is a well-tried and proven method.

Second, some birds require slightly more specialized food and so live food is an alternative. Small mealworms ($\frac{1}{4}$ inch) can be dropped onto the brooder floor or onto the food itself and their wriggling often attracts the young ducklings' attention. Similarly, small crickets can be used. I have seen breeders use brine shrimp in an open pan, and while this is a good food source, it does create an awful mess in the brooder! Birds of the sea duck family (Harlequins, Buffleheads, Mergansers, Smew, Goldeneyes, Eiders, Old Squaw, Scoters, etc.), do well with a little

98

live food additive to their diets. (When they are older, live fish can be given both as a food additive and as a recreational item.)

Some breeders report initial difficulties with stifftails. I always had one or two Laysan Teal or Mallards in with every brood of stifftails and they found and devoured the food very efficiently, showing the stifftails where it was. Again, make sure that when the more clumsy stifftails have started to feed, that you remove the Mallards or Laysans immediately otherwise they may squash the stifftails while sleeping. You will notice that all young waterfowl like to sleep in a heap, heads twisted this way and that. Just make sure no one is being suffocated. Day by day you will notice that the heaps move a little further away from the heat source and may fan out in smaller piles around the outer edge of the light. The heat source can now be adjusted down a little. Make sure that at night, the heat lamp is accessible as brooder-room temperatures can fluctuate greatly in some areas.

Feed

There are many and varied food supplies available to start young waterfowl on. Some are made specifically for waterfowl or game birds, but a good standard poultry crumble is always available. Don't use the powdery mashes if you can help it as they get reduced to mush very quickly under the web-footed stampede! They can also stick to the birds' down, caking it. Don't buy medicated foods. If your birds need medication it can be given via the waterer.

Young waterfowl are normally started on a crumble-sized food and progress to a small pellet and finally to a larger pellet with added grains, greens and dog chow. Crumble rations can vary in protein levels considerably. To start with, use a feed that is around 18 percent protein and this level can be reduced as the birds grow older and start to consume additional feed such as grains, greens, duckweed and live food which can be added to their diet. Make sure that the feed is fresh. Most manufacturers have a date stamped onto the sack. Don't use food that has been stored for more than a month. Vitamins added to the feed can break down quickly under less than perfect storage conditions and any bags that have holes in them or staining on them should be avoided as well. The stains can indicate water damage or the presence of rodent-urine contamination.

To stimulate initial feeding, a lot of breeders use finely grated hard-boiled eggs which are mixed into the initial diet. The softer feel of the egg along with its dietary functions help start young birds feeding well. Overeating of hard-boiled eggs can potentially cause a problem such as constipation. Birds suffering this way will often exhibit the symptoms of lethargy and listlessness; playing with food rather that ingesting it. These symptoms are often misdiagnosed, and antibiotics are fed to the bird on the assumption that it is suffering from infected yolk. There is an easy way to treat constipation in waterfowl, and it is discussed in the chapter Diseases and Ailments of Young Waterfowl.

The role of protein in diet has been greatly overestimated. It used to be thought that certain types of waterfowl needed high levels of protein in their feed at first. This belief probably killed more young than it raised by putting unnecessary pressure on the kidneys, leading to renal failure. Certain types of waterfowl are adapted for life in certain geographical locations and may need special attention paid not so much as to what is in their diet, but more to how much they should eat. Most young waterfowl are veritable pigs and need to be dieted in just the same ways as humans, to stop them from becoming overly obese.

In the wild, many of the Arctic breeding species of geese are hatched into a daylight cycle of almost, if not actually, 24 hours' duration. As they also have a weather-imposed deadline of 6 to 8 weeks in which to fledge before the onslaught of winter and their migration south, these goslings are programmed to eat. Even when they are raised in more southerly climes where nighttime lasts from 6 to 7 hours, the light of their heat lamp illuminates the feed in their brooders, so they will eat all night if given the chance. Naturally, these birds need more green stuff than crumble and should be exposed to clean grazing as soon as possible. They should be fed sparingly and be given greens at night rather than crumbles or pellets. These can be provided during the day.

Other slightly specialized waterfowl young need exercise to

offset unnecessary weight gains. Young of the sea duck family are notorious eaters and great sloths if let be. Live fish can be used to get them swimming, diving and chasing prey. The ducks benefit from not only an additional food source, but also from a good work out! Most breeders further supplement these birds' diets with a puppy or dog chow. Most of these foods are high in protein and should be fed sparingly. It can be broadcast onto the water or mixed into the solid feed ration. Try to use a chow that is easily digested by smaller sea ducks, such as the Buffleheads, Smew and Hooded Mergansers, and find one that does not contain a meat source formerly fed on steroids and subjected to all sorts of medications. These residues do not always break down in the manufacturing process and end up in your birds' systems. I have been using a chow made from grass-fed lamb and rice and have found it to be both palatable for the birds and healthful.

Basically, most waterfowl are started on a crumble and egg mixture until they reach the size when they can take a small pellet. The egg is phased out and pellets are added to the crumble. Later still, grains, such as wheat, can be added. Variations to this theme include the addition of crumbled dog chow for young sea ducks until they can eat normal-sized chunks, added greens such as lettuce, cabbage, spinach or bean sprouts for goslings and cygnets and duckweed, millet, canary seed and added vitamins for stifftails, Pink-eared Duck, Pygmy Geese, Black-headed Duck and a few other more specialized birds. Overall, most breeders use combinations of these diets.

Outdoor Brooding

After your birds have spent an initial time indoors, they need to be put outside where they have space to grow and recreate. The great outdoors can be a forbidding place for young waterfowl.

They are easy prey to a variety of predators. Sudden rainstorms can drench and chill them. An overnight power cut could rob them of their heat source leaving them shivering and dying. They may become infested with parasitic worms as a result of grazing on overused ground. Literally, there are hundreds of dangers to the growing young. Luckily, most of them can be catered for by vigilance and common sense on behalf of the breeder.

The outdoor brooding area must first be secure. Owls, hawks, crows, magpies and other aerial threats must be kept out and I would advise that the outdoor rearing area be completely netted over. Next, we must secure our stock from rats, weasels, stoats, raccoons, coyotes, dogs, cats, mink, otters, snakes and snapping turtles! This will entail making certain at construction time that these animals can't burrow into the area, or climb up or through the wire around the area. If you can use one, an electric fence is a great help. Correctly positioned wires will keep away the vast majority of ground-based predators and I have even seen breeders use electrified plates on top of poles to scare off owls and hawks. Snakes can be kept out by using a very small mesh wire, which can be overlaid the normal wire if necessary. When you build, think about all the types of predators you have in your area and design your outdoor area to suit.

We all know that sudden weather changes and power outages happen, and while nothing can be done about a power outage, a back-up generator may save some birds from a long, cold and, potentially, deadly night. Sudden storms of hail, rain or wind will make it necessary that your young birds have proper and sturdy protection against the elements. Never have boards or sheets of plywood that you may have been using as sun shelters, leaning against fences. They have a habit of falling or being blown over and crushing youngsters. Make sure that swimming ponds are easy to get into and out of for all your birds. Never walk away from a draining pond! Inquisitive birds will get sucked down the pipe or jump into an empty pond and hurt themselves. Make sure that the grazing is good and worm free. Over the years, the grazing of young birds and the accumulation of their droppings can make for ideal conditions that lead to parasitic worm build up. The ground may have to be limed and rested and a new grazing area will be needed. You may have decided not to have grass and provide greens yourself. You will have to keep whatever surface the birds are reared on (sand, gravel, dirt) clean and renewed. Brushes used in the cleaning of ponds can shed bristles which the birds can pick up and ingest. Make sure that the pond is hosed down well after cleaning, so that any bristles are washed away. Don't use wire partitions in ponds. These are death traps to young birds. This may sound like a litany of disasters and it is meant to. Believe me, if there is a new and unique way of dying, or being predated, young waterfowl will find it first! The waterfowl area should be checked for any of the potential killers ducks pick up and swallow such as wire, staples, glass, string, polythene bags, wire bristles, nails, tacks, *et cetera* (a metal detector is an advantage).

Check the ares that birds will be in. Make sure the wire has no holes or gaps where birds could get through into the next area and be beaten or killed by neighbors. Check that the area is vermin proof and that overnight brooders have wire floors to prevent rats from burrowing in. Also make sure the coops are big enough so that birds can get away from the heat source on warm nights.

Finally, fine hardware cloth screen should be fixed between the heat light and the birds. If the bulb should shatter, it prevents the birds from being showered with hot glass. Until they are fully feathered, your young waterfowl will still need protection from the elements and some additional heat at night. Remember that Arctic species are particularly prone to heat stroke, so make sure that sun shelters are provided in hot areas, during the day.

Outdoor brooding units vary in size and shape, according to their designers. I have seen simple A-frame structures, large wire-bottomed runs, plywood houses, most of which overhung the water of a large cement pond. For smaller ducks of all types, I have used the previously mentioned Sky Kennels. When one of these units is split in half and turned upside down they afford good shelter from the sun. And when outfitted with a heat lamp (suitably protected with a screen of fine mesh in case of breakage) that has been wired to a dimmer switch, these units work very well for nighttime brooding. Of course, they have no solid or wire floor, but my rearing area could not be accessed by burrowing or aerial predators.

In rearing areas where a top net is not used and a larger mesh perimeter fence is employed, youngsters will have to be shut in at night. To prevent predators (including snakes) from burrowing in, it will be necessary to outfit a unit with a sturdy wire floor to prevent just such an occurrence. Also, the shelter part of the unit will have to be designed to withstand the attention of raccoons. These units will need to be physically moved each day to new ground as the birds' dropping build up, fouling the grass underneath. I have seen units designed with a large removable "litter tray," like the type used in parrot cages, which preserved the grazing under them, and these worked quite well.

When birds are outside overnight, I like to use a heat bulb made of porcelain. These bulbs (dull emitters) give heat but no light. The dull emitter will give the necessary heat and the darkness encourages them to sleep more.

When sea ducks and stifftails are big enough to go outside they will have different requirements than dabblers and teals. Sea ducks are not grazers, so there is no need to provide grass. In fact, in wet climates grass can be a potential killer; birds will sit on wet or dew-soaked lawns and chill. Sea ducks need a diving and swimming pond with a gravel surround. Gravel can be washed or changed and drains surface moisture quickly. Shelter from the elements is required for both sea ducks and stifftails. Also, when you have mown the grass in rearing pens, make sure it is picked up. Decaying grass clippings are havens for infectious spores such as aspergillus.

There really is no science attached to outside brooding of birds. It is more labor intensive than looking after adults and requires watchfulness on behalf of the breeder. As soon as the birds are able to eat grower pellets or maintenance pellets, they should be switched onto them. This is also the time to start adding some wheat and/or millet to the diet. These grains can be fed in the water, but don't allow old millet or grain to sit in water and rot. Waterfowl of all types love additional greens, such as lettuce, cabbage, bean sprouts, cress, etc. Your local grocery stores often throw away old green stuff on a daily basis (greens that have gone past their sell-by date), and these greens are perfectly good for your birds. Give just enough and don't "baby" your waterfowl...they may become hooked on one particular thing and refuse to eat anything else. Just make sure that when they are first put outside, they have warmth, protection from the elements (including the hot sun), a safe place to swim, a good diet and clean, predator-proof surroundings. Keep a watchful eye on them as much as you can and try to identify problems or diagnose disease early. In this way, you should end up with good, fit, healthy stock ready to sell.

Diseases and Ailments of Young Waterfowl

Young ducks, geese and swans can fall foul to a small number of ailments. These ailments swiftly descend upon young stock and quickly take their toll. Young birds are particularly hard to diagnose and treat for a variety of reasons. Firstly, their physical size is so relatively small (when compared to a cow or sheep). Secondly, their metabolisms are very fast and medicines often can not be given in sufficiently large doses to offset the ailment, without harm to the bird. Thirdly, young birds tend to exhibit the same sort of distress reaction to most ailments, i.e., they lose weight and become listless. Our first and best line of defense is to keep young birds warm, clean, stress free and properly fed. This on its own, will almost totally eliminate the chances of birds becoming ill.

Infected yolks kill a lot of newly hatched waterfowl and can be treated with a broad-spectrum antibiotic. Soluble Terramycin products are good for this. Deaths occurring mysteriously from one to three days after hatch can normally be traced back to an infected yolk; the result of a dirty hatcher. Visual symptoms exhibited by birds with this infection include distended abdomens and general lethargy. Most often, the birds will show no interest in food and/or water. Medicating them is almost impossible, as the stress involved in trying to tube feed so young a bird will generally be enough to kill it. Physically sticking the young bird's beak into medicated water in the hope it will swallow some, is almost as futile, but I have seen birds saved using this very time-consuming process.

Occasionally a bird will get into respiratory distress as the result of chilling, air saculitis or gape-worm infestation. The first two conditions can be treated with soluble antibiotics, and gape-worms can be eliminated by treating the individual with Levamisole or Ivermectin.

One of the problems with the treatment of young birds is that they stress and pine immediately when they are removed from the rest of the brood and therefore, in order to treat one bird with medicated water, the whole brood gets a dose too! I don't like to medicate birds which don't need medication and some medications (especially antibiotics) can destroy much-needed antibodies in the bird's system, leaving it more vulnerable to infection. Unfortunately, there is often no choice and the entire brood may get medicated, like it or not.

Another condition that can occur in young waterfowl is constipation. This can be caused by the bird eating too much egg and/or not getting enough water. Also, birds that become dependant on live food occasionally experience this. You will generally notice that the bird becomes listless and uninterested in food. They may sit around more than usual poking at food tid bits but not ingesting anything. If you pick the bird up, you may feel that its weight seems good. Look at the vent to see if there is any caking of fecal matter around it. Often the feces can become rock hard and obstruct the vent completely. If this is in evidence, the matter will need removing. Sometimes you may have to crush it with your fingers and wipe the remainder away with a wet paper towel and warm water. Any still stuck to the down can be snipped off with a pair of scissors. Once all is clean turn the bird on its back and apply GENTLE pressure to the lower abdomen area just above the vent, just as if you were going about the initial movements of sexing. Make sure the vent is facing away from you, your loved ones, walls, furniture or anything else! The internally backed up fecal material can fly a long way and you may well end up with more than egg on your face! This condition is so simple to remedy but seems to account for many deaths in young waterfowl, probably because we are looking for more exotic causes and something this simple can easily be overlooked.

Impactions of the intestines can sometimes occur in birds that

are exposed to various sources of hardware. Goslings and cygnets love to pick at and tear at things, a natural conditioning for
feeding. If they are initially raised on paper they will chew this.
Artificial turf is particularly bad when it starts to fray. Birds just
love to chew on it and will accidentally ingest it. Similarly, they
can pick up paint chips from brooder walls or scrubbing brush
bristles shed from the brush while cleaning. Sometimes, when
the birds are still in the hatcher, it may be observed that they are
having difficulty standing up. You may notice them lying around
with their legs pushed out to both sides. This occurs most often
because the hatcher's tray surface is too slippery for them to get
up. Use a surface that gives a secure foothold and the problem
will disappear. Those birds that still can't stand up, can have a
small pair of "ankle cuffs" made from electrical tape or bandage
material. Leave some slack in the middle (just like a prisoner,
similarly manacled, needs in order to walk) and the bird will be
up and about quickly. Take off the cuffs after 24 hours or so.

Occasionally, a bird is hatched with a crooked neck. You will
immediately notice the bird's condition as it is so abnormal. While
it does not seem to cause any pain to the individual, the reason for
its occurrence can only be guessed at. If all other birds in the same
hatch are unaffected then something has to be amiss with the
individual bird. It may be a genetic problem or the result of a bad
position in the egg. Whatever the reason, this condition seems to
be irreversible. I have tried neck splints and other devices to try
to straighten out the neck in infancy, but so far, I have found
nothing that works. Obviously, these birds will be of no value
when fledged and ready to sell. The good news is that this occurrence seems to be very limited and is a relatively rare problem.

Skeletal-related problems are occasionally seen in growing
birds. Their growth rate and weight gains are both enormous and
fast when compared to other animals. Rickets is sometimes in
evidence in geese and this is the result of poor diet or specifically
one lacking in vitamin D. If any slight bowing of the legs or leg
joint irregularity is noticed, immediately cut down protein levels
and supplement the diet with vitamin D or multivitamin powder.
Also, give the birds more grazing (and therefore, exercise).

"Angel wing" or "flip wing" is another skeletal deformity. It most often occurs in young geese and cygnets and is evidenced by the wing(s) twisting over and sticking out from the body. As soon as any semblance of this condition is seen, the bird can be caught and the wing folded into its proper position and taped at the "elbow" and (if necessary) at the "shoulder" so that the wing is held in its natural position. The tape is normally left on for 4 to 5 days and then the same operation is needed again. As goslings grow so fast, the bird is in danger of having the tape cutting into its wing as it grows, so it will need replacing regularly. NEVER forget about a bird treated in this way and always check it on time. When removing the tape, make sure, especially around the end of the wing where the new pin feathers are growing in, that you don't pull any of these feathers out. To offset this occurrence, cut two lengths of tape, one slightly shorter than the other and lay the pieces face to face on each other (i.e., sticky side to sticky side). Now you have a piece of material that will not adhere to the wing feathers or the down around the birds elbow yet it will have two ends that will adhere to each other when wrapped around the wing. Alternatively, there is a new nonadhesive bandaging material called Vet-Rap^{TM} Bandaging Tape which is an excellent product available from 3M Animal Care Products, St. Paul, MN, 55144 or from your local vet.

Closely related to angel wing is another condition normally associated with goslings (although cygnets and ducklings are not immune), and commonly referred to as "droop wing." You will notice a bird constantly pulling its wing back to the fully folded position and then see the end of the wing start to droop back down. It is rather like watching someone trying to work in a pair of pants that are way too big and constantly need pulling up every few seconds! This generally occurs at the fledging stage, when a bird's new primary feathers are still in their blood feather stage, wrapped in their bluish sheaths. The wing is literally too heavy to hold up and this could be due to poor muscular development or too much protein in the diet causing the wing feathers to develop faster than normal. Give the birds more grazing and less protein when this occurs and to remedy the wing, use the same taping procedure as described for angel wing.

There are three conditions which are sometimes evidenced in the leg joints of young waterfowl. We have already covered the bowed appearance of the legs as a result of rickets and vitamin D deficiency. Secondly, birds are sometimes observed sitting on their hocks and on rising, the back of the joint appears to be flattened and elongated. This is usually the result of a medially luxated Achilles tendon and a small operation to realign the tendon can be done. Thirdly, there is a condition commonly referred to as bumblefoot. These cyst-like growths occur on the underside of the bird's foot and affect the toes and webs. They are thought to be associated with foot damage due to overly rough surfaces and are practically impossible to treat. Very large swellings may be surgically removed but small swellings can be left alone. Make sure the birds are reared on soft surfaces to offset this condition.

Other conditions, such as Salmonella, Pasteurella and coccidial poisoning, can be discovered by fecal exam. Fecal examinations are extremely useful in identifying a particular condition and a veterinarian should be consulted for this work. All these areas of potential danger to your birds can be offset by being observant and around them as much as possible. Just the same way as you would not leave a child unattended all day, you will benefit by being around your young waterfowl charges as much as possible, and they in turn will benefit from your diligence.

Finally, a sometimes common problem that afflicts goslings and cygnets (sometimes ducklings as well) is food that becomes lodged under the tongue. The afflicted bird will be seen to be developing what looks like a "pouch" underneath its beak. On catching the bird and opening its beak, you will find compressed food, in a wad, under the tongue. Simply slide your finger in and dislodge the food wad. Make sure this problem is not left unattended or the skin under the tongue will become stretched as more food is lodged in there, making this problem a reoccurring one.

9

Pinioning and Sexing

Unfortunately, some of your birds may need to be pinioned for later sale, and the time to do this is when the birds are quite young. I say unfortunately because I abhor any unnecessary mutilation of waterfowl. I know that we can not have our stock flying about and that not everyone can have enormous aviaries where their birds can fly around. Nevertheless, it is such a shame that it should be necessary to rob any bird of its powers of flight.

A tendonectomy is another form of flight restriction that requires a small operation but that leaves the bird with two complete wings rather than one and a half as pinioning does. The old style tendonectomy simply removed part of the wing tendon and was only partly successful at grounding a bird. The more modern method involves the removal of not only part of the tendon, but also part of the flight muscle (pectoralis) and it seems to be effective. Both these operations are normally carried out on mature birds by a veterinarian.

Pinioning involves the removal of the end part of the wing, from the "spur" or bastard wing (alula), through the primary feather section. It is best to pinion waterfowl at 2 to 5 days old. At this very young stage, there will be little or no blood loss and the whole stressful experience is soon forgotten. If you can sex the birds just before they need pinioning, you can establish a routine that will pay off later. Pinion one side for one sex and on one side for the other (i.e., males right wing, females left wing). Later on you can see easily, who is who and this is particularly useful in species where both male and female are similar. Do this operation on a cool day if possible and if there is a little blood, keep an eye on the bird for the rest of the day to make sure it heals properly and is not being picked on, or picked at, by other brood members. Bleeding can be stemmed with the use of a silver nitrate stick.

Hold the young bird in your hand, with its head pointing toward you. On extending the wing, you will notice the spur forming an offshoot of the wing, almost like our thumbs. Hold the wing briefly between thumb and forefinger to help cut off initial blood flow, and position a sharp, sterilized pair of scissors at the junction of the wing where the bastard wing leaves the wing proper. Snip across the wing at this point cutting toward the body of the bird. If you cut straight across or toward the end section of the wing you will leave a tiny section that, later on when the bird grows, will give it a few extra feathers...just enough for it to get airborne.

Sexing waterfowl can be difficult and requires a lot of practice. It involves the manipulation of the vent in order to expose either the penis or clitoris. Telling someone how to do this is almost impossible and I can only advise you to visit with a breeder experienced in this art and learn from him. Once you have had some practical experience at both pinioning and sexing, you can perform both operations together. It is important to learn to do both properly because you don't want to sell badly pinioned birds that can get airborne, or wrongly sexed birds to your customers.

It is important to pinion correctly. There will be more upsets later over poor pinioning than in any other area of waterfowl management. It is not good to sell long-pinioned birds to someone and have him telephoning irately next day saying they have all flown away. Likewise, birds that can clear the perimeter fence may fall foul of local predators. It is not good for your heart either, chasing birds miles with a net (although amusing to onlookers)! Nor is it good for breeding males to have badly pinioned female birds constantly a few yards in front of him, while he is flapping away like a demented paddle boat trying to rob her of her most treasured maidenly asset!

10

Waterfowl Ailments and Remedies

Since first writing this book ten years ago, avian veterinary science has progressed enormously. It used to be a very tricky business having the smallest of operations done on waterfowl and quite often the birds would not recover from the anesthetic. Nowadays, with the use of gasses such as isoflurane, halothane and methoxyflurane, anesthesia is both practical and safe. Far more is known about avian medicine today, and drugs used in the treatment and prevention of waterfowl ailments and diseases are legion.

Today's waterfowl keeper should work closely with his or her local veterinary surgeon. Most of your bird's ailments can be diagnosed accurately and quickly by using fecal exams, throat cultures or by blood samples. You will find that in time, you will be able to identify what ails a bird, not so much by its reactions, as by the probability of disease repetition. This in turn will allow you to treat the bird yourself, where possible. In the last resort, (a post mortem), you will still learn much about a bird or the course of its disease from the outcome of the procedure and may be able to take life-saving steps in the future.

The most difficult job in the avicultural spectrum is the identification of infection and its treatment. Sick birds tend to show no symptoms until it is too late. Symptoms themselves can be baffling. Commonly, sick birds go off food, weaken and lose weight. These symptoms are typical of at least fifteen or twenty common ailments of waterfowl. So how does one cope?

Daily observation of each bird, during routine chores, is by far the most effective disease control measure. This is where stockmanship will score. Look for signs of unusual behavior; diving ducks spending a lot of time on land, birds seeming listless or uninterested in what everyone else is doing, brightly colored eyes appearing off color, birds appearing "leggy," or in poor feather condition, etc. The minute you make one of these observations, catch the bird and look it over closely. How old is the bird? How is its weight? Does its stool look normal? Has it been moved to a new area lately? What has the weather been like lately? The answer to these and other observations will go a long way in determining the problem. Take a fecal sample at this point and run it through the lab. It might confirm your diagnosis point out a different problem, or tell you nothing, but you have little to lose and potentially a lot to gain. Act quickly and don't wait for something further to develop, it may then be too late. The most effective time to treat a bird is when it is starting to become ill, but don't be surprised if you are only able to spot a problem early enough in only 50 percent of the cases. Ducks, geese and swans tend to make up their minds once they are ill that they are going to die come hell or high water, and usually do so.

Most causes and solutions to illness are right around you, so be observant, know your local parasites and diseases. Look for common causes; don't invent exotic ones.

Few breeders have epidemics that wipe out a lot of birds. An epidemic, ironically, is the easiest way to treat stock. A post mortem can at least establish cause of death and other ill birds can then be suitably treated. The odd bird that becomes ill is always the most difficult. (I remember Frank Todd in one of his superb lectures caustically announcing that scientists have a cure for death in waterfowl. "Don't keep ducks" was the answer!)

So what are these killers and how can we deal with them?

Stress

One easily treated problem that indirectly accounts for 90 percent of bird mortalities is stress. This point must be rammed home. Throughout this book I have commented on stress. Stress can be induced by your own behavior around the birds, by other people's behavior, by the behavior of waterfowl to each other, or by conditions within the pen.

I remember touring one waterfowl collection with the owner. He brought his dog along, and throughout the dog ran wild panicking the birds. Subjecting waterfowl to this barbaric and totally unnecessary harassment or to any harassment is inexcusable. A little appreciated fact in the ownership of any animal is that you have a responsibility to it, just as you would to your child, and looking after it, or them, properly, requires dedication and feeling. If neither of these qualities are apparent, the owner simply should not be allowed to have them; I make absolutely no apology for that remark.

I have already pointed out in the chapter on stockmanship how one should behave around waterfowl, therefore I will not repeat myself. Mixing varieties of waterfowl sensibly will also reduce stress. Once stress has been minimized, the treatment of sick waterfowl is easier.

Prevention

One area susceptible to infection in any collection is the duckery. The old adage, "an ounce of prevention is worth a pound of cure," certainly applies. As mentioned previously, young birds are more susceptible to infection. In order to prevent disease, several factors concerning the construction of the brooder house need consideration.

First, air within the building should be kept moving and at a stable temperature. Second, all coops, drinking fountains, food bowls, etc., should be regularly cleaned and floors disinfected.

Food should be stored off the ground and used as quickly as possible as moldy food can harbor lethal spores and bacteria. Birds in their brooder units should be kept clean and dry. These simple procedures should almost negate the outbreak of infection. Young stock are almost impossible to treat anyway, so this is the best course.

Newborn chicks can have medicated water for two or three days to protect them from infection or until they start producing quantities of natural bacteria themselves. Avoid routine treatment of stock with antibiotics. Broad-based application of antibiotics will predispose birds to fungal infection by reducing populations of competing bacteria.

Medicated feeds are also quite useful for young stock. Feeds medicated with one of the coccidiostats such as Amprolium™ or Coban™ can be used right through the fledging period at the low levels found in feeds with no harmful effects. Coccidiosis causes the death of many young waterfowl. This protozoan parasite in the digestive tract is easily diagnosed by examination of a fecal sample and treatable with a variety of sulfa drugs. The medicated feed protects the young bird until natural immunity is established.

For years waterfowl breeders have insisted that medicated feeds kill young birds and shouldn't be used. You need to identify the type of medication in the grain and use the proper type. Possibly this position started years ago when breeders used medicated turkey grower for their waterfowl. The medication, Nitarsone (Histostat-50), was used for Blackhead in turkeys. It is toxic to ducks and they probably died from it. Incidentally, coccidiostat-treated grains are highly toxic to other livestock such as horses, so be careful.

Treatment

As I am not a veterinarian, I am not trained in the specific identification and treatment of the various maladies that beset our birds and therefore, I propose to give a broad overview of one or two of the most common ailments waterfowl suffer from. At the time of writing, there is a new book entitled, *Avian Medicine: Principles and Application* by Ritchie, Harrison and Harrison. It is an enormous book and, at the time of writing, fairly expensive. However, it is far and away the best work on avian medicine ever, covering a wide and diverse section of aviformes. Chapter 46 is dedicated to waterfowl and is most insightful. I would recommend all waterfowl keepers buy a copy and if you can't afford it, maybe a waterfowl club could buy a copy for all its members to read.

As mentioned earlier, birds are difficult to treat as one symptom suggests so many maladies, but there are things one can do. Let's start at the head and work down.

Ailments of the Head

Infections of the sinus and eye can be readily dealt with. Two more common infections are sinusitis and coryza. Birds with sinusitis develop a swelling just below the eye in the sinus sacs. When touched, the sacs feel watery as they are swollen with fluid. Tylan injected into the breast muscle of a bird will clear this up quite quickly. Use $\frac{1}{8}$ cc for teal, $\frac{1}{4}$ cc on Laysan or Hawaiian Duck, $\frac{1}{2}$ cc for larger duck (Mallard size) and for smaller geese. Large geese can be given $\frac{1}{2}$ to $\frac{3}{4}$ cc, as can swans.

Waterfowl can get infections of the eye. Sometimes this manifests itself as a small amount of frothy discharge around the eye, or a large amount, with the bird constantly scratching at its eye or rubbing its eye on its back feathers. It is best to get a culture from the eye before establishing a treatment, as a variety of bacteria can be responsible. If caught early, a wide range of ophthalmic antibiotics are available for treatment depending on the organism responsible.

Ailments of the Respiratory System

The trachea, air sacs and lungs are also areas prone to infection by parasites and bacteria. Gape worms, saculitis, aspergillosis and pneumonia are common ailments of the respiratory system.

Aspergillosis can cause heavy mortality, and the only effective treatment is a fairly time-consuming procedure researched and developed at the Gamebird Research and Preservation Center in Utah. This technique involves treating the infected bird by direct endotracheal injection with a mixture of Amphotericin B (1 mg/kg of body weight increased each day of treatment by 1 mg/kg until 3 mg/kg is reached), and Gentamicin (3 mg/kg for bacterial involvement) twice daily. In conjunction with this, the systematic antifungal agent 5-Fluorocytosine is administered.

Results at the Research and Preservation Center have been encouraging, particularly in cases where the disease has not reached the acute stage. However, if hygienic conditions are provided and air is kept moving inside buildings this disease may never be encountered.

Air saculitis can cause damage within the air sacs—although this is of no particular relevance, as this damage is found at post mortem which is too late anyway! Birds suffering from this complaint, wheeze and gasp. Since this is almost the exact symptom of aspergillosis and gape worm infection, you should try both remedies for air saculitis and gape worms. Tylosin can be administered to birds suffering from saculitis but it is advisable to consult a vet depending on the extent of infection. Tylocine is a water soluble drug that will combat this disease, but if the bird is in an advanced state of distress, injections of Tylosin may be quicker.

Gape worms infest the trachea. Infected birds gasp or produce a kind of sneezing cough accompanied by swallowing and shaking of the head. This parasite has the earthworm as its intermediate host and is found just about everywhere. It is easily diagnosed by fecal analysis and in many instances can be seen sticking out of the upper end of the trachea. The most efficient way I have found of dealing with these beastly little worms in cranes and waterfowl is tubing them with levamisole hydrochlorite, the active ingredient in many all-purpose wormers. Tubing is done using a long plastic catheter and hypodermic syringe in exactly the same way as you would force feed. Both are available from your local veterinarian. Just make sure that the tube goes down the throat and not the trachea. I use 20 mg of active ingredient per pound of bird but you should consult your vet on the proper quantity and mixture which is dependent on the brand name drug you use.

Another but less precise method of treatment is to blow Thiabendazole down the trachea with the aid of a rubber air bulb and slim plastic tube. Catch the bird and wait for it to gasp or forcibly open its beak and puff down the powder. A good dose is about ¼ of a teaspoon. You may have to repeat the procedure once or twice depending on the extent of infection.

The Organs

The body's major organs, the heart, liver and kidneys can prove the most difficult to treat, not because drugs aren't effective on these organs, but because of the difficulty involved in pinpointing which organ or organs are suffering.

The liver, for instance, can suffer from Salmonella, Pasteurella and hepatitis, apart from any one of the major vitamin deficiencies. With Salmonella or Pasteurella infections you may have time to get droppings analyzed and locate the specific organisms. This requires a specific type of fecal exam and should be requested if you suspect Salmonella or Pasteurella. Either one of these diseases can be caused by moldy grain or decaying organic material—a dead bird for example. Care should be taken to stop feeding bad grain and to remove any dead animal from your pens as soon as it is discovered. Once identified they can be treated; but because both Salmonella and Pasteurella organisms can be dealt with by the use of Furazolidone or Sulfa-based drugs, it pays to dose the bird while samples are being tested.

Leucocytozoonosis is a disease of waterfowl and poultry caused by a microscopic blood parasite, *Leucocytozoon simondi*. Related to the protozoan parasite that causes coccidiosis, Leucocytozoon boasts a more complex, two-host life cycle involving a definitive host (waterfowl) and an intermediate host, a black fly or midge. Outbreaks of Leucocytozoonosis coincide with peak hatches of these insects, late spring to midsummer, depending on climate. The disease is perpetuated by chronically infected older birds, who show no signs of disease.

Young birds are severely affected by Leucocytozoonosis. Symptoms include depression, anorexia, thirst, weakness, anemia, loss of equilibrium and labored breathing. Affected birds may die or improve and themselves become carriers. Mortality is often high. Internal lesions include enlargement of the liver and spleen and evidence of anemia.

The best treatment is prevention. Care should be taken in

119

choosing sites for aviaries. Black flies breed in fast-moving, cool water. In high-risk areas, the type of birds stocked should be carefully considered. While native and north-climate waterfowl may exhibit varying degrees of resistance to Leucocytozoon, many exotics are extremely susceptible. As a further safety measure, the coccidostat clopidol (coyden) has been used successfully to prevent Leucocytozoonosis in poultry and captive waterfowl. It is administered in feed at 1.6 ounces per 100 pounds (0.0125 to 0.025%) for 14–16 weeks, or throughout the risk period.

Nutritional Ailments

Kidneys can be rapidly broken down by bacterial action and also by the effects of too much protein. If diets are correctly formulated and vitamins and trace elements provided, kidneys should not suffer; however birds can get gout by overfeeding protein. Slipped tendons can be attributed to a manganese deficiency. Sometimes the instances of tendon slip are localized to one brood or just a few birds. Sometimes you can train the tendon back into position, but unless it affects a very valuable bird, it is hardly worth the effort. Find some latex tubing (the thin, stretchy type) cut a length, and roll it around the leg joint to create a sort of elastic bandage. Tape the ends of the bandage to keep it in location, and allow at least ten days before removing it. My success rate is probably only 50 percent with slipped tendons, however it's 50 percent better than none at all. If the problem is a medially luxated Achilles tendon, it can be operated on by a veterinary surgeon.

Other vitamin deficiencies can cause problems but are not too common. A lack of vitamin D can bring on rickets, or a lack of vitamin E can bring about a condition known as white muscle disease, which reflects a shortage of the element Selenium in the diet.

Infections of the Intestinal System

Intestinal tracts can suffer from bacterial or parasitic infections. Birds affected by internal parasites can be treated with Thiabendazole in drinking water, or if they remain in their breeding pens, the powder can be mixed into food.

Bacterial infections of the intestines or blood can be effectively treated with antibiotics. Several years ago I tried a penicillin-streptomycin mixture marketed as Pen-Strep. It was so effective at dealing with unidentified problems, that I now use it routinely as a first remedy, injected in the same quantities mentioned earlier for Tylan, according to the bird's size. Usually I inject into the breast muscle, but with leg or leg joint infections I inject into the leg muscle for quicker results. Antibiotics such as Pen-Strep can also help clear up preen gland infections. For all injections use a 23-gauge, 1-inch needle.

Ailments of the Extremities

The feet and legs of waterfowl can suffer from a range of ills. Tropical species can suffer frostbite damage in cold areas. Prevention is the best remedy as birds can be wintered indoors or provided with heat lights, straw, open water and perches outside. Perches can be insulated with polystyrene or a similar heat-keeping material. Cover any insulation with plastic mesh wire of a very fine gauge so birds cannot pick at it. Plastic will not freeze flesh to it as metal will. Further, heat tapes can be strapped to perches to give a warm base on which tropical ducks can perch. Should frostbite occur, there are ways of treating it. The victim should be brought inside once frostbite damage is evident. Normally a bird will display visible stiffness in the leg joint or hip. Affected parts can appear inflamed and sore, and should be swabbed with an antiseptic of some variety. The bird should be placed on a soft, dry surface to recover. Most frost damage is observed too late when it is obvious that a toe or part of the webbing has been damaged. As with most ailments, a bit of forethought will prevent many of these maladies from arising.

Broken bones, especially wings and legs, are common injuries in captive birds. Vets are a great source of help in these situations. Their skill, combined with the aviculturist's understanding of the needs of the bird can result in resourceful solutions to save valuable birds. One solution I devised to cure a broken leg on a Smew illustrates my point. The vet said the break was too high on the leg to repair, but an hour's thought came up with a tape splint. A double width of tape and some Q-tip sticks Cut to ⅜ inch were laid out along the tape with a gap between each of ⅛ inch. A V-cut, made midway along the bandage allowed the bandage splint to push up the leg as high as possible. The leg was braced in the normal sitting position and the splint wound on. A further large strip of tape was wrapped around the body, (under the wings) and the bird was hospitalized for 10 days. He was babied—fed goldfish and crickets as an attempt to relieve boredom and stress. Ten days later, the body tape still intact, he was allowed to swim for 20 minutes. After 15 days, off came the tape and splint. The leg hung lifeless. He was allowed to swim even more (half an hour), and two days later started to use the leg again while chasing goldfish in the pond.

Egg-bound Waterfowl

Another problem the waterfowl keeper comes across occasionally is a condition known as egg binding. This appears during the laying season and is the effect of an over large, or badly shaped egg being trapped in the oviduct just prior to laying. Sometimes the oviduct itself may be congested in some way, but the outcome is usually a dead bird with an egg still inside it or more usually an egg breaking in the oviduct and the bird contracting egg peritonitis. This condition can be the result of a number of factors including bad diet, too much calcium or bad stock lines, it can also be a factor during very cold weather when early nesters start to lay (Cereopsis, Ne-Ne, etc.).

Your best clues come from knowing how frequently a bird is laying and if it is 48 hours late, still heavy, and appears weak (sitting down a lot) or walking with difficulty, suitable action must be taken.

Needless to say, the bird must be handled gently when being caught and must be brought inside and isolated under a heat light at about 75°F. The effect of the heat on the bird will generally allow it to pass the egg without too much trouble. Sometimes some vaseline or jelly lubricant may be needed at the opening of the oviduct or vent to help.

If the egg bursts inside the bird there is only a one or two percent chance of it surviving. Stress, peritonitis or hemorrhaging of the oviduct will cause the death of the bird. Unless you are on hand and have a veterinarian very close by, little can be done. If the egg breaks without injuring the oviduct and you can get the bird to the vet, I believe it is possible to wash out the oviduct to prevent the onset of peritonitis, but I've never had the chance to find out as the birds I have dealt with have either died suddenly or recovered after being brought in.

If the bird should die with the egg intact, it is still possible to salvage the egg which can be incubated after being washed and suitably disinfected.

These then, are some of the more common ailments affecting waterfowl in captivity. Avian health and nutrition is a subject that, in itself, could fill a volume. Unfortunately, as with most specialized pursuits, the veterinary world has yet to supply detailed diagnostic facts and remedies concerning avian medicine. Still, the best remedies for any disease are observation and prevention, and a close association with your local veterinary surgeon.

11

Predator Control

There are many animals that predate waterfowl in the wild and these same animals will try to get at your birds even when you think you have them securely locked out. The constant patrolling and subsequent threat by predators will keep your birds nervous, stressed and less inclined to breed and nest properly. A good regime of predator control is vital to the success of any waterfowl enterprise.

Predators can be divided into three categories. Firstly, there are those animals who will kill your birds for sport or for food. Secondly, there are the egg thieves and thirdly there are scavengers and vegetation destroyers. Some predators will fit into more than one of these categories and some will be seen not so much as threats to your birds, but rather to the landscaping and plants within an aviary.

Aerial predators come in many guises and at all times of the day and night. Hawks and owls are a definite threat to waterfowl and virtually every member of the crow family likes to eat eggs and some of the larger varieties are not immune from having a try at your young birds, and very occasionally, at the adults too. Even herons constitute a threat to the safety of your stock and not just the large Blue Heron. Night Herons can take a toll on young birds in a hurry, so do not assume that because they are small, they are not a threat. Quite simply, the easiest way to deal with these predators is to have a top on your aviaries. However this still will not deter them from perching nearby and alarming your birds. I have found that this tends to happen for a while when you first construct a waterfowl facility but the hawks and owls learn pretty fast, and after a few tanglings in the top netting, they normally give up. For those that won't, hot-wired perching poles seem to work fairly well and, I am told, flashing lights deter owls, but I can't help wondering whether this would annoy your neighbors as well as your birds!

If you do not have a covered aviary, your only defenses against the aerial predator are a firearm, trapping and poisoning. In all three cases, there are different local, state and federal laws to comply with and these laws must be taken into consideration before you do anything. Consult the local Fish and Game Division first. Never go ahead until you know the law and its consequences. You may accidentally kill someone's pet cat or dog and then the feathers will definitely fly! Five minutes worth of consultation is better than five years of incarceration.

Land-based predators exist in alarming numbers. To name a few, there are: raccoons, foxes, coyotes, mountain lions, bobcats, domestic cats, dogs, stoats, weasels, ferrets, mink, otters, rats, snakes both venomous and egg eating, badgers, possums, skunks, fishers, wolverines, martens...need I continue? I haven't even mentioned the dreaded *Homo sapiens* who likes to break in and steal your valuable birds from time to time or who will shoot at them from a distance to annoy you. Luckily, most of the aforementioned group can be trapped relatively easily. In most states, some of these creatures, if not all (excepting *Homo sapiens!*), are considered pests. And state trappers will happily oblige you in getting rid of them. Good strong aviary wire dug well into the ground will help deter burrowers and strategically placed hot wires will zap those who attempt to climb. Here again, make sure it is legal to use a hot wire/electric fence in your area...in some places it is not. Some predators are small enough that they are able to access your aviaries via the underground runs of ground squirrels, rats, moles and even gophers. Weasels, stoats, mink, snakes and others use these corridors as ports of entry. Any underground runs originating outside of your aviary fence should be closed off and where permissible, a spoonful of cyanide powder placed in the run to discourage reopening. Constant vigilance is necessary on behalf of the keeper as predators will challenge you constantly and when you least expect it. Make it a part of your daily routine to walk around your fence line looking for tracks or signs of predator movement. I like to have a two to three foot strip of sand around the entire fence line and the tracks left show me immediately who has been visiting and therefore what I should be trapping or looking out for. If you have trees around the exterior of the fence, check around the base for signs of hawk or owl pellets...you may have a nighttime nuisance you never knew about.

Snakes can be a serious threat to your birds and even to you. Rattlesnakes and Cotton Mouths are perhaps two of the nastiest varieties and will kill birds on occasions. Sometimes they will get in through the wire mesh when they are smaller and hunt for a long time in your aviary before you ever see them. They tend to hunt in the cover that you planted for the birds to nest in. This is where the mice and voles live. I have found snakes stuck in the aviary netting...thin enough to enter, but when well fed, too fat to exit! Gopher snakes should be encouraged as they will hunt and kill voles, mice, rats, gophers, ground squirrels, and I have been told, small rattlesnakes. Similarly, King Snakes and Bull Snakes will provide the same service. The only drawback to their presence, is that they will disturb nesting birds and eat the occasional egg. One way of keeping snakes out of an aviary is to install plastic or fiberglass sheeting all around the fence line, from the ground up to about two or three feet in height. While this will deter snakes if installed properly, it creates an eyesore!

Threats from under the water can come in the shape of snapping turtles, bullfrogs (yes, really!) and various fish such as bass and pike. All will eat young waterfowl and large pike and snapping turtles will take teal-sized birds on occasion. Mink thrive in water and use this element to ambush waterfowl. Otters will also attack waterfowl from the water. Mink are especially nasty little customers not only because they prey on waterfowl, but also because they will clear other water-using creatures out of their territories by their sheer aggression. In England, where the mink is not a native but an escapee from mink farms, it has become a real threat to the dwindling otter population not to mention anything that lives on or near water. They are quick, agile and ferocious creatures often getting into waterfowl aviaries via an underground run or by scaling the fence. You will know in a hurry when you have a mink around, but you can fight back by trapping, shooting and, on occasion, by poisoning.

The last group of animals are not so much a threat to your birds as they are to the landscaping in your aviary and to the area's cleanliness. As mentioned previously, ground squirrel, gopher and mole runs can allow predators to enter your aviary, not to mention the damage one small gopher or mole can do to your plants! These smaller pests can be trapped, gassed and poisoned. In all cases where poisons are used, make absolutely certain that web-footed busy bodies can not get into it and can not pick up dead carcasses! Also make sure that the poison used is permissible in your area...just because the hardware store carries it, it doesn't mean it can be legally used, always check first. Other small pests include mice, voles and sparrows. Even the little field voles will dig up your plants or nibble out the roots from underground or eat the waterfowl food, contaminating it with their droppings and urine. They also attract the attention of hawks, owls and snakes.

Sparrows pop in and out of an aviary via the netting. They easily squeeze through 1-inch mesh and while they themselves are not a threat to your birds, their droppings can carry disease and parasites. I have found it next to impossible to keep hungry sparrows out. I suppose that when you take a piece of naked and uninteresting land and turn it into a luxurious green oasis, you're bound to attract the attention of all scroungers. I just make sure that the feed areas and bowls are cleaned at least once a day. I have seen exotic and ingenious feeders that are supposed to be sparrow proof, some that feed ducks in the water, but sometimes I feel this creates just as much mess as a sparrow makes, so I've learned to live with them and just make sure things are kept clean.

Overall, get to know which predators to expect in your area and the times of the year to expect them. Make sure you know all local, state and federal laws that govern the permissible methods for destroying predators. Know what you are after and always keep a watchful eye open for signs that predators are about. Never underestimate the abilities of these hunters. One of the reasons that they are so appallingly successful is because of their ability to do what we think they cannot!

Opposite page: Whistling Swan.

Pair of nesting Trumpeter Swans. While the female guards the eggs, the male is actually using his posture to tell the camera man to keep his distance!

Of all the swans, the Coscoroba Swan is visibly the oddest. Not only does it resemble an enormous mutant duck hybrid, but is the only swan to have patterned young. Here, a pair protects their young from an intruding adult (foreground).

Jankowski's Swan. Some naturalists are ready to reclassify this race as it is almost indistinguishable from the Bewick's Swan. Having worked with both, I found the Jankowski's to have a larger, thicker beak, with a more extensive area of color than its close cousin, the Bewick's.

Spotted Whistling Ducks engaging in mutual preening.

Cuban, or West Indian Whistling Duck. These are the largest of the Whistling Duck family, and to some aviculturists, the most aggressive.

Opposite page: Eyton's or Plumed Tree Duck.

Javan Tree Duck.   *Photo: Author*

Fulvous Whistling Duck. Probably one of the most numerous representatives of the family in captivity, Fulvous are the most widespread in the wild, spanning four continents.

Australian Shelduck (male).

European or Common Shelduck. Apart from the Radjah's, this family member is the smallest of the shelducks, and has several distinctive characteristics, among which is the very unshelduck-like beak. Here, the male (standing erect) clearly displays the large red knob at the top of his beak, reminiscent of a Rosybill.

Sheldgeese live in jungles, among the mountain tops and along the shorelines of the world. Here a pair of Kelp Geese (in the Falkland Islands) and their young forage among the Bull Kelp at the shoreline. Kelp Geese remain among the least captively studied or managed of the waterfowl family.

A sheldgoose representative from jungle regions would be the Orinoco Goose. These are the most arboreal of the family, even nesting in hollow trees.

Sheldgeese of higher altitudes, the Andean Goose (above), and the Abyssinian Blue-winged Goose (below) live at altitudes in excess of 10,000 feet.

Probably the most attractive of all geese, the pretty little Red-breasted Goose is under considerable pressure in the wild. Its population has been severely impacted by hunting, oil exploration and the decline in numbers of the Peregrine falcon, due to the insidious effects of agricultural pesticides such as DDT. (See page 245.)

Among the Brent or Brant Goose family, the Russian Brent, is less well-represented in America than in Europe, and is seldom bred.

Another rarity, both in collections and in the wild, the Aleutian Canada Goose.

Two oddities in the goose family, the Magpie Goose (above) may represent the oldest link between waterfowl and other bird groups and has many individual characteristics no other waterfowl possess (see page 248), while the White Spurwinged Goose (following page), an enormous bird of up to 20 pounds in weight, is currently classified as a perching duck! This whole family however, may be about to be reclassified.

African White-backed Duck.

White-headed Duck. The male is in a partial display posture, the drabber female is in the background.

Black-headed Duck, male. These curious birds are not only the least "stifftail" looking of the family, they are also the only truly parasitic nesters in the waterfowl family. Their eggs have been found in the nests of many different bird species, including Snail Kites and Caracaras!

The unusual Musk Duck of Australia. Here, a male is in mid-display. Note the distended throat sack.

Freckled Duck. These birds are almost completely unknown to aviculturists outside of their native Australia. A recent successful breeding program has led to the importation of the first 5 pairs of these birds into the U.S., and they will no doubt be bred soon.

Pink-eared Ducks feeding in the "star" formation.

Blue or Blue Mountain Duck. Opposite page: Green Pygmy Goose at rest among the lily pads.

Not particularly rare in collections, the Maned Goose possesses physical qualities of the duck, goose and shelduck families.

Abyssinian Black Duck. This race has more pink coloring on the beak than its African counterpart.

While superficially resembling a common Mallard, the Mottled Duck is more similar in appearance to the Florida Duck. Many field researchers feel that the Florida Duck represents a race of the Mallard, while others are of the opinion that the Mottled Duck represents a subspecies of the Florida. Confusing enough?

The rare and little known Bernier's or Madagascan Teal.

Andaman Teal.

147

Campbell Island Flightless Teal. Considered extinct, these birds were rediscovered on Dent Island, a tiny volcanic plug of 0.4 miles (57 acres), west of Campbell Island in 1975. Introduced rats killed off the main population on Campbell Island around 1810 and it appears that the only survivors were on the rat-free Dent Island.

White-winged Wood Duck, an endangered species.

Chilean Torrent Duck pair, the male (with tail erect) courting his female.

The very uneiderlike, Steller's Eider (male).

Pacific White-winged Scoter.

Male and female Harlequin Duck.

Male Red-breasted Merganser displaying to female (in foreground).

Falkland Island Steamer Ducks.

Fiberglass rearing units designed by the author. Note the wooden frame they are on, and the fixed heat lights. They were wired to dimmer switches on a remote panel.

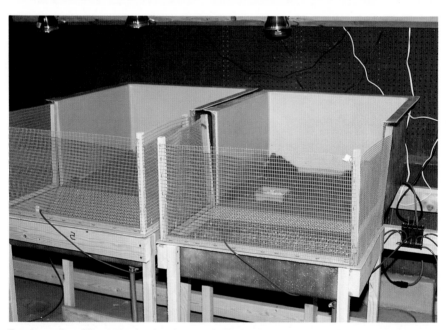

Rearing units with attached swimming ponds designed by the author. These units gave the young birds access to swimming water for a few days before they went outside. Each unit had its own water supply and drain. The wire screens on top of the units have been removed for photographic purposes.

Photos: Author

Aviaries and Enclosures

Whether or not your birds are kept in aviaries or on open ponds, these places are often the only homes your birds will ever know. As none of us would tolerate a high stress environment, neither will your waterfowl. Their environment needs to provide swimming water, shade and nesting cover, protection from predators and from other birds. I have always felt that a person's aviaries tend to reflect the personality of the aviculturist, and clean, neatly planted and visually appealing pens often promote better production from the birds.

The following photographs show different techniques and ideas in aviary design. Most use the idea of moving water, combining waterfalls and channels and a variety of plants that are either visually appealing, and/or provide nesting cover. Some show how to take advantage of naturally sloping terrain in order to show off the birds at different levels to the eye. Just because waterfowl live on water, it doesn't necessarily follow that they be displayed to visitors always at ground level, on a rather flat, two dimensional plane. Use as much imagination as possible, and a much natural material as possible in aviary design. Make your bird area a delight for your waterfowl to live in, and a showcase for you and your friends to enjoy. The following photos are all by Simon Tarsnane.

160

12

Dabbling Ducks

This chapter covers Mallards and closely related species. Included with Pintail and Shovelers and one or two near relatives, it makes up the largest waterfowl group. Teal, while classified as dabbling ducks, have not been included for propagational reasons and are described in a section dealing exclusively with them. You will notice some teal in this section. These birds display more characteristics in common with Mallards and related species than with teal. They include Falcated Teal, Cinnamon Teal, Garganey, Blue-winged Teal and Laysan Teal.

Mallards

The Mallard (*Anas platyrhynchos*) and its almost identical but slightly larger brother, the Greenland Mallard (*A. p. conboschas*), are probably to most people the definitive duck. Excepting the Greenland variety which seems almost isolated to Greenland and displays distinct sea-going qualities and physically is a larger bird, the common Mallard is found throughout almost every major continent in the world. It can live in virtually any type of water, climate, vegetation or terrain. Its food consists of anything edible at sea or on shore, including both meat and fish carrion. It has been introduced as a game bird in many areas. Unfortunately, its close affinity to Black Ducks in America and Grey Ducks in Australia has produced many fertile hybrids in these countries.

Their vigor does not limit them to wild hybrids either. Many collections have suffered—indeed it may well be said that Mallards may mate with any type of duck that tolerates it (and with some that don't). On occasions even geese are not immune to their amorous advances. One is forced to admire the tenacity with which these ducks have populated much of our planet.

For very logical reasons, it is rarely intentionally kept in collections: the Greenland subspecies may only be represented in one collection that I know of. One very interesting and slightly appalling observation is that because of the Mallard's sexual appetite, Laysan Teal populations in captivity may be hybridized to such an extent with Mallard and Hawaiian Ducks (and others) as to only resemble the real wild duck. True, unmolested specimens of Laysan Teal at San Diego's Sea World exhibit marked visual differences from nearly every single bird sold as a Laysan Teal. Might it be possible that people ought to be thinking of culling their Laysan Teal and getting new, pure blood? Certainly a thought that needs closer attention.

Mallards thrive and breed in almost any sort of conditions as long as food and water are available. Nesting cover of any vegetational variety is used, as is any sort of container, box, log, tin, tire, tree or gutter. They are wonderfully effective as broodies for sitting eggs and many aviculturists use them for this purpose, encouraging a few females within the collection every year. However, while the female is sitting the males must be kept away from anything with feathers and webbed feet!

As with most birds that lay large clutches, two-thirds of a brood may be lost before the survivors feather up and need no further protection. I have seen as many as 35 eggs in a nest, at least 26 of these laid by the same bird. Egg color ranges from white through cream, bluish white, blue green, green, light green to buff, and incubation is between 26–28 days. No special techniques for rearing, feeding or keeping need be discussed for this species.

North American Black Duck

Very closely related to the Mallard is the North American Black

Duck (*Anas rubripes*). In some ways, "just another Mallard," but they are marginally better mannered. A native of the North American continent, they are shot as a game species. Shier and more easily alarmed than Mallard, they nevertheless display almost the same breeding qualities and adaptiveness as their close cousins. Clutches tend to be smaller (10 on average) and the range of nesting locations more moderate. A ground nest or box are preferred sites. Again a great hybridizer, they should be kept away from close relatives. Food and care is much the same as for the Mallard, as is their incubation period.

Mexican Duck and Florida Duck

Again, closely related to the Mallard is the Mexican Duck (*Anas platyrhynchos diazi*) and the Florida Duck (*A. p. fulvigula*). True specimens of these birds are hard to find in collections as, again, hybridization frequently takes place. It is possible that since ranges overlap in Texas that these two species may hybridize in the wild. Both species are similar, the Florida being noticeably lighter in color. Neither are common in collections worldwide. Nevertheless, a pair or group of these birds, once established will breed fairly freely. Again a ground site or ground box in thick cover is favored. Incubation is 28 days in both cases and average clutch size is 8. Winter shelter helps these two types considerably, unless kept in mild winter areas.

Spotbills

The 3 races of Spotbills, the Indian (*Anas poecilorhyncha p.*), Chinese (*A. p. zonorhyncha*) and Burmese (*A. p. haringtoni*) all resemble each other superficially. The Chinese is darker and only occasionally displays the red patch at the upper part of the bill. The Chinese and Indian varieties are now becoming fairly well established in captivity but the Burmese is little known. As a member of a collection, they present little difficulty to aviculturists. They can become shy birds taken to skulking and hiding, especially in large collections open to the public. In smaller, private collections they display no particular spooky traits. Occasionally they can be bullied, especially on a large, well-stocked pond, usually by birds at least as large as themselves. A ground nester, they prefer dense cover or boxes located in cover. Average clutch size is 8 and incubation 28 days.

Meller's Duck

The Meller's Duck (*Anas melleri*) is practically unknown to most waterfowl enthusiasts. A native of Madagascar (also introduced into Mauritius) this is a rather drab, nondescript duck. At the Wildfowl Trust, in England, we had some imported from the Mauritius Islands. Prior to arrival they had been fed on grains (mainly rice) and, interestingly, guppies! Todd describes these birds as similar to a female Mallard, which they are, although slightly larger in the head, darker in overall color and with a larger bill (greenish in color) in both sexes, which suggests an adaptation for specialized feeding of some sort. The birds settled and bred within nine months. The young seemed no more difficult to rear than other ducks, but retained an element of shyness like their parents. The adults displayed some measure of nocturnal activity, often hiding during the day and feeding at evening and night. Also they were aggressive to other birds.

Along with other fauna of Madagascar such as Bernier's Teal, the Meller's Ducks' wild status is not secure. Although afforded legislative protection, it is one thing to sign a piece of paper, another to enforce its intent. If, as Frank Todd suggests, they breed readily in captivity maybe there could be some hope of reintroduction into the wild. The only nests I saw were on the ground in a typical scrape among cover. Average clutch size is 8 and the incubation period 28 days. Ducklings closely resembled Florida or Mexican Ducklings in color. Hopefully more aviculturists will become familiar with this duck; it certainly merits more study. Delacour was the first to breed these birds in 1929. Subsequently, they were bred in Holland and England in 1933.

Grey Ducks

Grey Ducks come in 3 types. The New Zealand (*Anas superciliosa*), the Australian (*A. s. rogersi*) and the Pelew Island (*A. s. pelewensis*). The New Zealand is marginally larger and darker than the Australian variety. Both types suffer from hybridization in the wild with introduced Mallards. Todd observed that the Australian variety selects tree cavities and elevated positions inland on the continent. The birds I have observed in captivity occasionally utilized a raised box, but mainly they were ground nesters and ground box nesters. The New Zealand variety and the Pelew Island nested almost exclusively on the ground or in a ground box in some sort of cover. Normal clutch size averages 7 and incubation is 28 days.

Wintering in captive conditions in England poses no problems as long as food, shelter and ice-free water is present—but in colder climates it may be more beneficial to winter these birds indoors. They need to be kept in their own pens otherwise, as with Mallards, hybridization may occur. (Interestingly enough, a hybrid produced by the Australian mating with an Indian Spotbill produced a bird looking exactly like a Pelew Island Gray Duck— so much so that several well known aviculturists were fooled by it.)

Philippine Duck

The Philippine Duck (*Anas luzonica*) although fairly common in captivity, appears to be very little studied in the wild. Here is another Mallard type which hybridizes easily. Many offspring that look like the real thing actually are not, breeders should ensure that these birds cannot mix with close relatives. Occasionally these birds use elevated boxes, but mainly nest on the ground in cover, in a ground box or tunnel box. Average clutch size is 10 and incubation is 26 days. They can have quite a long breeding season in fair climates, but need cover or protection during cold weather in cooler climates. Nothing more than standard waterfowl fare need be provided and youngsters respond well to normal rearing techniques and diet.

African Black Ducks

Of the 3 races of African Black Ducks, only the African (*Anas sparsa*) is fairly well known, and probably more so in Europe than America. The Abyssinian (*Anas sparsa leucostigma*) apparently was known prior to World War II and kept in several European collections. The Gabon (*Anas sparsa maclatchyi*) has only very rarely been kept.

The African race seems to be partly nocturnal in habit, and is only rarely observed during daytime, preferring to skulk in cover. They are cautious birds and fairly aggressive—although I know at least one pair who were perfectly tolerable to smaller ducks. They are quite large in size, as big as a very large Mallard, and only a little smaller than a Bronze-winged Duck. They have been known to use a ground box or a more typical scrape in good cover where they lay their clutch of 6 eggs. Incubation is approximately 28 days and the young retain their parents' alertness, often squatting flat and unmoving in a rearing coop when someone passes by.

The young eat quantities of pond weed (*Lemma minor*) but this may not be necessary as most young ducks if provided with it, will eat it too. I have noticed the young do not tolerate sustained high-protein feed—often suffering kidney failure. Pellets of the grower variety (14 percent) should be given with wheat as soon as the young can take it. Winter protection in cold climates should be provided.

Laysan Teal

The Laysan Teal (*Anas laysanensis*) is an astonishingly tame little duck with a remarkable story behind it. Down to 7 in number in 1912, on their only habitation, a tiny island about $3\frac{1}{2}$ miles in length, they were lucky enough to escape total extermination at the hands of Japanese plumage hunters in 1909 (Delacour). In 1918, 35 individuals were reported, and in 1950–53, some adults with young were reported by H. Smith, a visiting naturalist.

Introduced rabbits did a great deal of damage to vegetation on this tiny island and were thought to be competing with the Teal for food. However, stomach contents of one bird examined by W. K. Fisher in 1903 revealed that the birds apparently ate a great deal of insect life. The population in the early 1960s was almost 700 (Scott) but population crashes still take place in the wake of severe storms contaminating fresh water sources with salt water, presumably killing off various vegetational and insectivorous life. Interestingly enough, in Delacour's *Waterfowl of the World*, he related that as of 1951, Laysan Teal had never been kept in captivity.

Now the story is very different. Laysan Teal breed in captivity with the fecundity of rabbits, laying their small clutches (5) of large eggs in boxes and in ground cover. Incubation is 26 days and hatched young are very easy to rear. It may be safe to assume that there are more in captivity than in the wild, but captive stock is in jeopardy from hybridization from Mallard and Hawaiian Ducks kept initially either very close to or in the same pens. As mentioned in the Mallard section, pure individuals at Sea World in San Diego are visibly different from virtually all other stock I have seen. Todd, in *Waterfowl of the World*, states that Laysan Teal were first bred in captivity in 1959. In an effort to ensure the survival of the Laysan wild population, the U.S. Fish & Wildlife Service in 1983 established the National Zoo and the Game Bird Research and Preservation Center in Salt Lake City as official breeding centers and depositories for the species, and transferred the stock maintained at the Pulaukoloa Breeding Station in Hawaii to these collections. Progeny from this stock raised at the Game Bird Center is being distributed free of charge to those interested in helping to preserve the species and who will pledge to protect the genetic integrity and viability of birds under their control.

Hawaiian Duck

The Hawaiian Duck (*Anas wyvilliana*) also shelters under the endangered species umbrella. Estimated at around 3,000 in the late sixties, this is another type of waterfowl that needs watching to prevent hybridization. Many Hawaiian Ducks (or Koloas as they are known locally) are little more than a Mallard or Laysan hybrid. Often they display a markedly green head and double tail curl; these birds are not true specimens.

Hawaiian Ducks in captivity are often friendly as are Laysan Teal and present no difficulty in their keeping, breeding or rearing. Oddly enough, there are hardly any Hawaiian Ducks left in American collections, most being kept in Europe. Like the Laysan, they benefit from protection against the cold. A clutch of 7 eggs is laid on the ground in long grass or under leafy cover and the female incubates for 26–28 days.

Yellow-billed Ducks

The 2 races of Yellow-billed Ducks, the African (*Anas undulata*) and the Abyssinian variety (*A. u. ruppeli*) at first sight seem almost identical, but the Abyssinian is darker with a pinker bill.

Again, notorious hybridizers in captivity, these birds are always active during their breeding season, which may be quite long in warm climates. The African race is far better known to propagators, the Abyssinian having only rarely been kept. The clutch of 7 eggs is normally laid on the ground in cover or in a ground box. Incubation is 28 days and youngsters require no special care outside of routine maintenance.

Falcated Teal

The beautiful Falcated Teal (*Anas falcata*) is among the more showy waterfowl. Recent writers credit its ancestry with that of the Gadwall (*Anas strepera*) which itself is more closely related to the Wigeon.

Primarily an aquatic feeder, unlike its grazing counterparts, it is easy to see how its beak is adapted to water sieving and feeding, unlike the rather short, tough beak that Wigeon utilize for cropping grass.

Falcated are hardy birds in captivity, and breed fairly readily. Around 7 eggs are laid on the ground in a very tidy nest, and the slightly shorter 25 days of incubation only reflects its northerly breeding tendencies in the wild. No special rearing techniques need be employed for this beautiful duck.

Gadwall

The Gadwall (*Anas strepera*), as mentioned earlier, is possibly a relative of the Wigeon family. Although not such a grazer as Wigeons, it can and does graze occasionally, although it usually dabbles and up-ends in shallow water. It is a hardy duck and is easily bred in captivity. It lays an average of 8 eggs on the ground in cover and incubates for 26 days.

Wigeons

Of the Wigeons in existence, all 3 varieties are kept widely and without difficulty. The two northern hemisphere varieties, the European (*Anas penelope*) and the American (*Anas americana*) breed easily in captivity but propagators need to keep them apart, otherwise hybridization may occur. Eggs are laid on the ground, usually around 8 in number and incubation takes 24 days.

The Chiloe Wigeon (*Anas sibilatrix*) is a South American Wigeon. Widely kept and easily bred, it requires no special maintenance techniques. They are especially active during the prelaying season, and can on occasion bully other birds. The males often take on larger birds and beat them viciously. Eggs are laid either in a box on the ground, or in cover. Clutch size is 6 and incubation is 26 days.

Pintail

While Pintail are dabbling ducks, they exhibit specialized physical adaptations. A long neck helps them take advantage of deeper water than their short-necked cousins, so competition for food is reduced.

These birds are well known to many aviculturists. The Common Pintail (*Anas acuta*) is very common in captivity, and is also a well-known and much-respected game species. These beautiful ducks probably have the longest neck of all pintails when viewed proportionately. Their tail length seems longer too, but this appears necessary as a counter-balance when up-ending. A feeding Pintail flattens its tail along the water surface. Remove these long feathers and balance is completely upset. The common Pintail nests readily in captivity, laying 6 eggs in a ground location and incubates for 24 days.

Another familiar Pintail is the Lesser Bahama (*Anas bahamensis b.*). With its domesticated and artificially developed Silver Bahama cousin they represent another well-represented and much-loved captive waterfowl. They are easily bred, hardy and generally have no vices.

There are two very closely related varieties of Bahama or White-cheeked Pintail, which along with the Lesser, make up the three races.

The Greater Bahama Pintail (*A. b. rubrirostris*) is almost identical in color to the Lesser but is markedly bigger. I have only seen one, a male, and while they were formerly the best-represented variety of these Pintail in wildfowl collections (unfortunately being allowed to hybridize with the Lesser), the Lesser now is by far the most common. Lesser Bahamas nest on the ground or in boxes and average 8 eggs which have a 25-day incubation period.

The third member of this sub-complex is the Galapagos Pintail (*A. b. galapagensis*). There are no representatives in captivity at this time. Few have been maintained and there are no breeding records.

Yellow-billed Pintails

There are 3 Yellow-billed Pintails that represent South American varieties.

One, the Chilean Pintail (*Anas flavirostris*) is extremely well known to aviculturists and breeds easily. The other 2 have probably never been seen in waterfowl collections. Certainly the Niceforo's Pintail (*Anas niceforoi*) which is probably extinct, has never been kept in waterfowl collections. They have hardly ever been seen in the wild. The South Georgian Pintail (*A. g. georgica*) has occasionally been kept—I have only had experience with one old female at the Wildfowl Trust when I started work there in 1971. It was smaller and slightly darker than the Chilean, and was thought to be 11 or 12 years old. (Since, the Trust has hatched and reared young from eggs collected on South Georgia Island.)

Chilean Pintail lay about 7 eggs which have a 26-day incubation period. They utilize a ground box or the more usual ground nest in cover. I have known these birds to use an elevated box, but only rarely.

The last two varieties of Pintail represent insular populations. The Crozet Island race (*Anas acute drygalskii*) are considered by some authorities to be invalid as a race and have never been kept in captivity.

The other race, the Kerguelen (*A. s. eatoni*) has been and indeed is represented in captivity currently, although it is extremely rare. At least two pairs at the Wildfowl Trust have bred and I remember they looked very much like a Common Pintail female, slightly smaller and darker, the male still having that bluish gray color pattern each side of a dark stripe along the length of the beak. They bred infrequently, but the young seemed no more difficult than any other Pintail; although presumed delicate this probably was because the adults were closely related. They nested on the ground and 5 eggs were normally laid, the incubation period was 25 days.

Garganey, Blue-winged and Cinnamon

An interesting group of ducks of teal size, but bearing a closer affinity to the Shovelers are the Garganey, Blue-winged and supposed five races of Cinnamon Teal. A sort of pseudoShoveler, they have visibly specialized, elongated and relatively wide beaks, like true Shovelers. Also they display Shoveler feeding habits, sieving the surface layer for microscopic vegetable and insect matter. The Garganey (*Anas querquedula*) is relatively common in captivity but some propagators find them difficult to breed. Bloodlines play a big part in all captive waterfowl.

Genetically diverse strains of these birds often prove easy to breed while inbred stock remain stubbornly unproductive. Garganey seem to do best in small groups (6–10 birds). They are easily bullied, so pen mates should be picked with care.

Some breeders keep them fully winged in aviaries where they do well, but no better than pinioned birds overall. I believe the main criteria for these birds (and with most teal) is to have well settled, tame birds. Full-winged birds do actually seem tamer, but this is hardly surprising since the confidence of a bird is easily built when it knows it can fly from danger. However, good breeders should be able to achieve the same results with pinioned stock.

Their substantial clutch of 9 eggs is laid on the ground in cover and undergoes a short (22-day) incubation period.

Young Garganey sometimes suffer from being fed too much protein during their first few weeks. This may be dependent on blood lines, but I have seen birds achieve a feathered state while walking with distinct difficulty as if considerably aged. Birds that died had enlarged, overworked kidneys when examined post-mortem. This particular strain of birds, when fed differently with lower protein levels and grains, did much better. Some protection in cold winter areas is beneficial. Interestingly, the Garganey is the only summer waterfowl visitor to England, and is known as the Summer Duck.

The Blue-winged Teal (*Anas discors*) is divided into 2 races according to some, the other race being the Atlantic Blue-winged Teal (*Anas discors orphana*). Orphana is shown in Scott's *Colored Key* but Todd describes it as "suspect." Regardless of classification it is widely kept in collections where it breeds freely. As with all smaller ducks it is vital they get proper winter nourishment, and if kept among large groups of bigger duck, make certain they get their fair share and are not bullied. They nest on the ground, sometimes causing egg-collecting breeders concern as the nest is small and well hidden. Up to 10 eggs are laid and incubated for 23 days.

Of the 5 races of Cinnamon Teal, I have only experienced two, the Northern (*Anas cyanoptera septentrionalium*) and the Argentinean (*Anas cyanoptera c.*). Many breeders keep the Northern variety, and from what I saw of the Argentinean race, the general care and activity of these two types were more or less similar. Not a brave bird, they can be bullied by larger waterfowl but generally do not attract much attention from others, especially when pen mates are of the same size and disposition. Nine eggs are laid in an extremely well-hidden nest in cover. Incubation is 24 days. Young Cinnamon, like young Shovelers, occasionally get caked up with a wet mash of chick crumbs when in the close confinement of a rearing coop. They tend to take food in beakfuls and dump it in their water and then happily dabble away splattering food around in the process. This rarely happens but it is as well to be alert to the possibility. The other three races are the Andean Cinnamon Teal (*A. c. orinomus*), Borrero's Cinnamon Teal (*A. c. borreroi*) and the tropical race, (*A. c. tropica*).

Shoveler

Of the 5 races of true Shoveler, 3 are commonly kept and reared. These are the European (*Anas clypeata*), the Cape (*Anas smithi*) and the Argentine Red (*Anas platalea*). Although the Argentine variety is less well represented in American collections, they are endearing birds. One is tempted to almost feel sorry when watching these birds with their incredibly unwieldy and ugly beaks. However, their specialized feeding equipment enables them to earn a living. Groups of feeding Shoveler are truly comical. A group will form a circle in single file and swim round and round, gradually sieving away at the surface layer. You wonder just exactly what the one at the back gets to eat, but the paddling of those in front, at least in shallow water, stirs up the muddy lake bed enabling everybody to get something. I often wondered whether as in formation flying during migration, the one at the front drops back and someone else moves to the front. So far though, I've not seen it happen enough to conclude that this may be common behavior.

Shovelers, Teal and Dabbling Ducks, of course, cause havoc around small ponds when a puddle builds up behind the pond edge. They dabble away merrily until a large sloppy mess is produced. (See facilities chapter for suggested methods of curbing this activity.) These birds are ground nesters although the Cape and Argentine often choose a box located in cover. Clutch sizes vary slightly, the European averaging 8 eggs, the Cape 9 eggs and the Argentine 6 eggs. Incubation periods are 25, 26 and 25 days respectively.

Australian and New Zealand Shovelers act in much the same way as the other three. The Australian (*Anas rhynchotis*) is unfortunately losing ground in the wild as its preferred shallow-feeding ponds are drained for agricultural use.

The New Zealand variety (*Anas rhynchotis variegata*) seems to be stable in the wild at present. In captivity they suffer during

173

cold weather so some measure of protection ought to be available. Both races are not hard to keep, although ducklings are not particularly hardy. They are not widely represented in captivity and prove difficult to breed. They nest on the ground in cover or sometimes in a box where 10 eggs are laid and incubated in 26 days.

Aberrant Dabbling Ducks

The Bronze-winged Duck (*Anas specularis*) is a rather large and beautiful duck from South America which is relatively well known to aviculturists world wide, but has recently been declared an endangered species with maybe no more than 1,000 birds left in the wild. Usually kept in their own pens, they can be savage to other birds, though of course there are exceptions. They also can be very tame, the male charging about uttering his lovely little trilling whistle, the female close by his side uttering a vaguely doglike noise with frequent head stabbing to the side (as in female Mallard). Indeed, this noise the female produces has apparently earned it the name locally of *pato perro* or dog duck. Bronze-wings thrive on standard waterfowl fare and benefit from winter protection. Sometimes laying on the ground, they usually choose a box or kennel, if available. Five eggs are laid and incubation is 30 days.

Young pairs of Bronze-wings can be helped to better pair bonding by being placed in a pen adjacent to that of a breeding pair. The mock charging and general hooray of the adults that goes on next door may incite a young pair to breed early. There is controversy as to whether this species is a dabbling duck or an aberrant Shelduck.

To complete the aberrant dabbling ducks I will briefly mention some strange, rare and hardly ever kept birds.

A little observed and very rarely kept duck (certainly none at present in collections outside of New Zealand), is the Blue Mountain Duck (*Hymenolaimus malacorhynchos*). These birds were once kept at the Wildfowl Trust in England. All I know about them is what I have read in Delacour and Scott's volumes and Todd's *Waterfowl of the World* and McKinley's work studies.

Apparently they are rather tame and very bad parents, especially as both parents are credited with brood care.

It lives in the rushing mountain streams of New Zealand and is insectivorous. The beak is reminiscent of the Pink-eared Duck at first sight. Apparently they lay 5 eggs and incubate for 31 days. Virtually no captive records exist.

Equally perplexing to the Avian student is the Salvadori's duck (*Anas waigiuensis*), a species I have never seen except in photographs. It was formerly kept at the Wildfowl Trust and bred by Sir Edward Halstrom in 1956 (Delacour and Scott). They were reported as aggressive, and females with young often swam with their young on their back. However, Todd relates that they are shy, nocturnal and feed almost entirely on invertebrates. They lay 3 or 4 eggs, which are incubated for at least 28 days.

The Freckled Duck (*Stictonetta naevosa*) is also a little-known duck which only a handful of European and American aviculturists have ever seen. It feeds filter style, on algae, tiny fish and invertebrates. Todd reports its young have no patterning color and suggests it may be a sole survivor of a very ancient genus of waterfowl.

They lay about 7 ivory-colored eggs and the incubation period is about 27 days. After a successful breeding program in England, the Wildfowl and Wetlands Trust recently sent the first 5 pairs of Freckled Ducks to the U.S. They are currently housed with M. Lubbock in North Carolina.

13

Diving Ducks

The 18 varieties of the *Aythyinii* family are better known to most people as Pochards, White-eyes, Scaup and Tufted. Typically, these birds are short and round bodied, with powerful legs set toward the rear of the body. They are well equipped for diving (sometimes to considerable depths) and have a distinct, sharp-winged silhouette when flying.

Pochards

Three of the family display distinct physical adaptations. Two are the Red-crested Pochard (*Aletta rufina*) and the Rosybill (*Netta peposaca*). These are more elongated, almost dabbling duck-like in appearance. This reflects an adaptation to natural terrain. They are quite capable of diving, but spend 50 percent of their time upending or dabbling on the surface. Neither type is difficult to keep or breed and both are birds many people start with. The Rosybill does not have a distinct eclipse plumage and is attractive to some breeders since it is "in color" all year. Both species can be aggressive in close confinement, so select pen mates sensibly. Few birds are as feisty as a broody Rosybill. I remember one case when this behavior came in very handy. They were deliberately selected by Mike Lubbock as broodies for the little-studied Black-headed Duck, a native of South America. These birds are parasitic egg layers and prey upon all sorts of nests, ranging from indigenous *gallinules*, through waterfowl varieties nesting close to water, and eggs were even found in a Snail Kite's nest. It was incredible to watch such a protective mother as the Rosybill, decoyed and physically thrown off a nest by a teal-sized Black-headed Duck, so the female could dash in and lay an egg. However, due to the Rosybill's tenacious mothering instinct it always returned soon to brood its precious eggs.

Rosybills lay 8 eggs in close cover or occasionally in a box on the ground and incubate 26 days. The Red-crested Pochard lays 8 eggs and incubates for 28 days, choosing virtually the same nesting site as the Rosybill.

The 2 races of Southern Pochards, the African (*Netta erythropthalma brunnea*) and the South American (*Netta erythropthalma e.*) also display adaptations peculiar to their environment. Like Rosybills, they are well equipped for diving but spend a fair proportion of their time dabbling or upending at the surface. I find it difficult to write a great deal about these (to me) rather characterless ducks. The ones I have worked with were neither bullies nor weaklings, and were exceptionally nondescript. Both lay an average clutch of 9 eggs and incubate for 26 days. They nest in cover on the ground or in ground-located boxes.

The European Pochard (*Aythya ferina*) and its close relative the Redhead (*Aythya americana*) are widely kept and known to most breeders.

The 2 races when kept in close association readily hybridize and produce youngsters only very faintly distinguishable from each other—even to the exceptionally well-trained eye. The females are very alike, and when genes of the opposite race get mixed in, resulting males can be almost indistinguishable.

The European variety is physically a "true" Pochard. Short broad-based, and a strong, direct flyer once airborne, it is considered quite a hard target by sportsmen. They dive to enormous depths to locate food. While fishing on Loch Maree in Scotland, I saw one dive and come up with a rack of weed. Having just passed over the spot with the boatman (or "ghille" as they are known in Scotland), I noticed as he plumbed the water with his weighted line just how deep it was. We were on a bank seventy-five-feet deep and the water was clear (not the normal "tea" color that Scottish peat Lochs usually are) as a fresh-water spring flowed in nearby. Even if the weed grew 10 or 12 feet from the bed of the lake, it still was locating food at 63 feet. Both varieties nest in close cover on the ground, or occasionally in a ground box. Seven eggs are laid and incubation is 27 days.

The Canvasback (*Aythya valisineria*) is well known to breeders. It is not as frequently bred in Europe as in America, but among breeders on both sides of the Atlantic it has a "cult" following. The term "Canvasback nut" seems widely applicable to a lot of European, British and Americans. To a lot of American sportsmen it is considered the "Grand Prix" of ducks. Whatever mystique this bird has, I have not been taken over by it yet. (But there is still time!)

Many Canvasbacks I have seen never "fade out" but stay in their breeding finery year round. Captive diet may be responsible. Paired females can be very belligerent to their mates. At least one American propagator recommends placement of paired birds in sectioned aviaries with substantial land space for the unfortunate male to escape to, if he so needs. Maybe the female's actions are the results of being closely confined year round, coupled with a strong territorial urge. In England, waterfowl tend to compliment large houses or formal gardens, so water space is usually large and this trait is not noticed as much. In America, collections tend to be smaller and more intensive. Odd isn't it, when you consider the space available in either country?

"Cans" (as they are affectionately known) nest in either natural vegetation or in a ground box. Eight eggs are normally laid and incubated for 25 days. In the wild they build very substantial nests, sometimes far from water among overhanging shrubs or trees. This liking for "top cover" may explain why they like boxes.

The Ring Neck or Ring-billed Duck (*Aythya collaris*), although quite pretty, is to me a rather nondescript duck having no particular personality. It is often allowed to hybridize with other Pochards, Tufted or Scaup. Well known to most aviculturists, the

Ring-bill breeds well in captivity. They nest in cover or in a ground box and lay 9 eggs which are incubated for 26 days. No special techniques are necessary for the well-being of these birds.

The Tufted Duck (*Aythya fuligula*) is distinguished from other Pochards, by the male's distinctive tuft. A rather dapper bird, they are always active and breed easily and widely in most collections. They lay 8 eggs on the ground or in reeds close by water and incubate for 24 days.

Scaup

The 4 races of Scaup are essentially the same to keep, feed and breed.

The largest of the 4, the Pacific or Blue Bill (*Aythya marila mariloides*) is somewhat of a mariner, especially in winter. The Lesser Scaup (*Aythya affinis*) slightly resembles the Tufted or Ring Neck in appearance. It has a bluish hue to its head feathers, whereas all other Scaup have greenish heads. The female displays a smaller white patch at the top of the beak, like a Tufted. The European Greater Scaup (*A. m. marila*) is essentially a European version of the Pacific Scaup. In fact, its extreme eastern European range into Siberia and further, may bring it into contact with *A. m. mariloides*. This scaup is far more common in captivity in Europe than it is in America. (Indeed, the same may be said for Tufted and New Zealand scaup, and most of the White-eye family.) European Scaup lay 8 to 10 eggs in a ground nest close to water where they are incubated for 25 to 28 days. These three should not be kept together as they will interbreed.

The New Zealand Scaup (*Aythya novaeseelandiae*) is the only Southern hemisphere representative of the Scaup family. Easily reared by aviculturists these rather dumpy little Scaup have been known to utilize raised nesting boxes intended for Mandarin and Wood Ducks. These boxes had wide, gently sloping, ladders, so no prodigious climbing ability should be assumed. It might have been interesting to see if youngsters could get themselves out of these boxes upon hatching. I have a feeling

179

they might have been able to; ducks don't usually do things without reason.

Normally all Scaup are ground nesters and average 7 eggs, but sometimes use ground boxes in cover. Eggs are incubated for 26 days, except the Lesser, which has a shorter, 24-day period.

White-eyes

The White-eye group consists of 5 races, the best known to Americans is the Baer's Pochard (*Aythya baeri*) while European breeders, who keep Baer's extensively, also keep the Common, or Ferruginous Duck (*Aythya nyroca*) and Australian White-eye (*Aythya australis a.*). The Madagascan (*Aythya innotata*) and Banks Island (*Aythya australis extima*) are virtually unknown in captivity. Delacour kept Madagascans and first bred them in 1930, subsequently establishing this race in France and England. However, none survived World War II.

Of the 3 best-known races, the Baer's, Common and Australian breed well under captive conditions. Hybrids will occur, especially with the Common variety, but no special techniques or diets are needed. Large areas of open water are a must for Pochards during winter as their extensive diving activity often leads to their being trapped under ice and drowning. Also make sure that they can get out of the water, especially in near vertical-sided ponds. The use of a ramp will facilitate this problem.

While I was learning my trade in England, I asked a co-worker why the Australian White-eye was also called the "hard head." I was told that a noted English breeder who couldn't stop them breeding was culling his flock one day near Christmas. His method of dispatch was a swift blow to the head with a stick—however, for one reason or another it seemed that one blow was not doing the job and at least three were administered in quick succession along with the curse "God, these things have hard heads." I got the feeling someone was making fun of me!

All White-eyes are ground nesters or ground-box nesters, average 8 eggs and have a 26-day incubation period.

14

Mergansers

This family of waterfowl (making up a group known as Mergini, the mergansers) are poorly represented in captivity. There are 8 members, 2 of which are fairly common in collections in America and in Europe.

One is the lovely little Hooded Merganser (*Mergus cucullatus*). About the same size as the Smew, the "Hoodie" as it is affectionately known, is not a bird of fast water. It prefers quiet, woodland ponds and swamps.

They are agile fliers, and full-winged birds in collections can lift off the water with the ease of any Dabbling Duck. They nest in tree cavities, where they lay 9 eggs and incubate 31 days. Full-winged birds in captivity display remarkable perching ability. They can drop onto a 1-inch-wide wooden perch with ease. They were first bred in America by that remarkable aviculturist Chuck Pilling of Seattle, Washington.

Mergansers are physically adapted for catching fish. The Hooded Merganser eats quantities of fish and will also take crayfish and frogs. Some vegetation and seed matter is consumed during the breeding season. In captivity they normally are fed a poultry pellet supplemented with dog chow or trout pellets. They are hardy birds but still need open water during winter. When out of their eclipse period, the males will begin displaying almost immediately as if trying on their new breeding dress. The hysterical antics of a pack of displaying males are a sight to behold. A group of males, with crests erect and making a peculiar gargling sound, single out a female as the object of their amorous intent. She will often drive them away, occasionally responding but usually she just sits, looking bored. Copulation can take place in the autumn but is unusual. The fairly high incidence of infertile eggs in captivity could be a result of this early activity; it is not uncommon in spring to see males less active, and even being bullied into displaying by the then amorous duck. It could also be a blood-line problem—too many closely related birds in collections.

With good stock it is not uncommon to raise many young from two or three adult pairs. Indeed, for example, in 1982 we produced some 42 young from three pairs of adults.

Another beautiful merganser is the Smew (*Mergus albellus*). It is prized by aviculturists specializing in sea ducks and fish eaters. It is more specialized than the others in the family as its beak is shorter and stubbier. Indeed their diet, while similar to the Hooded Merganser, comprises more of invertebrates. Like the Hooded, they perch easily and are active, likable birds. They have sometimes proved difficult to breed under captive conditions, and the ducklings can be difficult to raise. In the account of the first captive breeding of these ducks (Delacour and Scott) in 1935, the writer observes that ducklings were easy to rear and very hardy. Most breeders of this bird that I know have lots of horror stories about ducklings or eggs dying, but I feel this is probably a genetic problem. It seems to me that with sea ducks, the mergansers genetic health is especially susceptible to breakdown due to sibling mating.

Smew are cavity nesters, and elevated boxes or old logs with natural holes are a favorite. When making these boxes, don't make them too shallow from the hole to the nest bottom. Cavity nesters (even pinioned ones) can climb remarkably well and are adapted with strong claws for this purpose. They like a drop down to the nest chamber, and a foot or so is about the right depth. Add hardware cloth in a strip on the inside front face to facilitate exit.

They normally lay 7 eggs and incubate for 28 days.

The Red-breasted Merganser (*Mergus serrator s.*) is poorly represented in captivity but very numerous in the wild. They are rarely bred in captivity, but in my experience, they are easy to maintain.

Unlike other mergansers, they are ground nesters. They are particular favorites of mine, always active, inquisitive and playful; traits which can cause their premature demise. Care must be taken that lethal bits and pieces of metal, glass, etc,. are not left lying around.

These are fairly hardy birds. Adults and young alike will eat pellets, dog chow, trout pellet, biscuit, bread, hamburger and fish. As with most of the fish eaters and sea ducks, diet plays an important propagational role.

As food for young birds, I find live fish excellent. Apart from their nutritional and fiber values, live fish are an excellent play item with great educational value. The exercise of young birds is very important. As you would not encourage your child to sit about the house eating all day, these birds should not be over fed or allowed to become lethargic.

One bunch of Red-breasted Mergansers I raised illustrates my point, which is, feed just enough. Fish time (afternoon feeding) was eagerly awaited. At my arrival the birds would frantically search their pond for fish, their heads half submerged looking to and fro. Once inside the pen I was mobbed—shoelaces and trouser cuffs were tugged and fingers investigated. Once fish were released, a tornado of activity broke out, birds diving and even pursuing fish out of the water onto the pond perimeter. It became difficult to make sure everybody got their share. Lazier birds would hop out of the water and stand waiting to be hand fed—something I never gave in to. After going hungry once or twice they learned to compete.

Adult mergansers quickly become the clowns of a collection and their neck-breaking curtsies to the females during breeding season are fun to watch. Most adults I have seen were kept with numerous other ducks which was detrimental to their breeding success.

Females construct a nest on the ground in which 9 eggs are laid. The incubation period is 30 days.

The other mergansers, the Brazilian (*Mergus octosetaceus*) and the Chinese Merganser (*Mergus squamatus*) have never been kept in captivity, so there are no breeding records available. Observations in Delacour and Scott's *The Waterfowl of the World* and Todd's *Waterfowl* need not be repeated here, but are well worth reading.

Three varieties of Goosander complete the Merganser family. These are the European Goosander (*M. mergus m.*) and its almost indistinguishable Asian cousin (*M. m. orientalis*). The only difference between the European and the third member of this group, the American Merganser (*M. m. americanus*), is said to be the presence of the strongly curved nail at the end of the bill in the European—a feature that while still present in the American, is less obvious. Birds of the *americanus* variety seen on the Yellowstone and Boulder Rivers exhibit a nail to a greater or lesser degree—some seemingly identical to the European.

Comparisons to birds in captivity may not be valid as, with Eiders, the bill can overgrow. Both varieties I have experienced in captivity appeared identical.

In captivity (as in the wild), their characteristics as far as nesting, etc., are almost identical.

Few of the varieties are kept in European or American collections. Considering their relative abundance in the wild this is surprising. The Goosanders I have cared for seemed hardy, and like other members of the family, were greedy eaters. They can be fed on dog chow, poultry pellets, bread (brown, if possible) or soaked biscuit. A fish additive is useful but unless live fish are used, vitamins must be supplemented as described in the Red-breasted Merganser section.

Apart from the family's general habit of picking up and swallowing lethal objects, Goosanders share other characteristics of concern to the aviculturist. Being a large and playful bird, they can upset and injure (though probably not intentionally) other pen mates, and are therefore best kept in their own pens in groups. Another malady they occasionally suffer from is known as "frothy eye," where the eye becomes sensitive and is covered by frothy mucous. Affected birds rub the eye on their feathers and scratch it with their claws. In fact, one American Merganser I observed actually scratched out its own eye in its efforts to ease the itching.

The organism creating this discomfort seems to occur in large, muddy-bottomed ponds with slow-flowing water. In clean, well-aerated water this problem seems rare.

Being cavity nesters, mergansers will take advantage of a raised box with a suitably-sized hole. They lay 9 eggs and incubate 32 days. They are difficult to breed and more research needs to these birds before we can propagate them successfully.

(The Mazuri Company, mentioned earlier in this book, make diets appropriate for a large variety of waterfowl, including fish eaters.)

15

Perching Ducks

This group of waterfowl exhibits great diversity in size and shape. From the lovely little Ringed Teal at ten ounces to the seven-pound White-winged Wood Duck, they all share the ability to perch. One particular anatomical similarity is the position of their legs in relation to their bodies in all the members. Unlike divers—perching ducks have legs placed more toward the front of the body. Virtually all are cavity nesters. Some waterfowl not included in this family should be on the basis of the previously described characteristics.

White-winged Wood Duck and Muscovy

Two related members of the *Cairina* representatives are the White-winged Wood Duck (*Cairina scutulata*) and the Muscovy Duck (*Cairina moschata*). The White-winged Woodie is one of the rarest ducks, whereas its cousin the Muscovy is the ancestor of one of the most numerous types of domesticated duck.

Apart from this difference in survivability, both species display a strong perching ability and are equipped with strong claws for climbing. (To which any breeder who has handled Muscovies can testify!)

Oddly, the true Muscovy is not well established in captivity, probably because it resembles its scruffy and often ill-bred domestic cousins. However, the wild Muscovy is beautiful and rather endearing. Its wine-bottle green iridescence is eye-catching. (Some domestic forms are kept and bred in standard show colors such as lavender, black and white, chocolate and blue.)

However, most breeders find them rather unappealing even considering their tameness and curiosity.

The White-winged Wood Duck is rare in captivity, but recent breeding successes suggest that this may soon become a better represented captive species. Their rare status and the difficulty of trapping them in jungle terrain meant that few were ever collected, but once established in captivity they were not too difficult to breed. They do suffer from inbreeding. Because the original young produced could not be outcrossed (as no other birds were available), brother-sister matings occurred. Odd wild birds occasionally become available, and certainly the outlook for this species seems better as the World Wildlife Fund and the Wildfowl Trust attempt a reintroduction program. Hopefully in the future more aviculturists will have the opportunity to study this rather pleasant duck.

The White-winged Wood Duck normally lays 8 eggs in a ground box or slightly elevated box and incubates for 33 days.

Muscovies will choose an elevated box, but are also content to lay their large clutch of 10 eggs in a ground box. Left full winged they will take advantage of old tree cavities of suitable size. Incubation is normally 34 days.

Hartlaub's

The third member of *Cairina* is the Hartlaub's Duck (*Cairina hartlaubi*), which some aviculturists have split into 2 varieties; eastern and western. These ducks are better represented in Europe than in America, although both continents can boast captive breedings. They are shy birds, often skulking in cover, and seem to prefer to feed in the evening. Not generally a threat to other ducks, males will fight viciously so pairs or trios should be separated.

Hartlaub's prefer an elevated barrel or box where their 9 eggs are laid and incubated for 32 days. All members of this family require warmth and shelter in cold climates.

They thrive on normal waterfowl fare of wheat and protein pellets, dog chow and biscuits. The addition of a multivitamin and mineral supplement is a great plus, especially in winter. Some of these supplements come in a coarse, powdered form which floats well on the water surface. With the addition of millet and dog chow this makes a fine food and an excellent dabbling medium which can be fed in a large pan near the pond edge.

Pink-eared Duck

Another fascinating perching duck is the Pink-eared Duck (*Malacorhynchos membranaceous*) from Australia. At first sight it appears to be an archetypal shoveler; it is not. A filter feeder, it has strange leathery flaps at the end of the beak and it differs from Shovelers in one very fundamental aspect. Young Pink-eared, unlike Shovelers, are born with an exact, scaled-down replica of the beak of the adult, something the true Shovelers only fully gain when they mature. They are also cavity nesters and display skillful perching ability.

Very few of these birds are represented in captivity; very few people outside of Australia keep these little ducks. My only experience with these birds was at the Wildfowl Trust in England. Michael Lubbock brought eggs back from an Australian trip. The young that were reared eventually laid and a first generation was produced in captivity. Subsequently, more American and European propagators keep these birds, and European breeders especially, seem to have had good success with breeding them.

The birds I saw ate a great deal of pond weed and, besides wheat and pellets, were provided with a nice soup to dabble in containing finely milled coarse biscuit, wheat, pellets and a multivitamin supplement. They required warmth and shelter at the first sign of winter and were quiet, unassuming birds, only occasionally uttering a very shrill whistle. Interestingly, unlike most ducks, the female's whistle was higher pitched than the males.

They are cavity nesters and average 7 eggs which are incubated for 27 days.

Ringed Teal

Another endearing member of this group is the Ringed Teal (*Calonetta leucophrys*). Well represented under captive conditions, it is extremely popular because it has no eclipse plumage, staying attractively "dressed" all year.

These little ducks are quite hardy. Although native to tropical climates, full-winged Teal will winter outside except in extremely cold areas. Like so many other warm climate waterfowl, the problem of wintering is not so much the cold weather itself, but the crippling effects of frostbite. Full-winged birds rarely display frost-related pedal damage. Of course, winter protection is always beneficial. The provision of good food, heat lights and shelters will bring all birds through cold weather better prepared for the breeding season.

Ringed Teal display an enormous perching ability and are often seen in collections on gates, fence posts, walls and nest boxes. They like an elevated nesting box, and a large clutch of 10 eggs is laid and incubated for 26 days. If eggs are collected on a regular basis birds will lay from May well into September with good fertility and a large number of offspring will result.

Mandarin and Wood Duck

Two other well-known members of this group are the Mandarin (*Aix galericulata*) and the Carolina or Wood Duck (*Aix sponsa*). Most waterfowl enthusiasts start with these birds, and more easily kept or finely attired birds would be hard to come by. These species breed easily and young are not difficult to rear (unless you happen across wild Wood Ducklings which are so highly strung it is unbelievable). Both are cavity nesters and are quite hardy. They are noted for hybridizing with other birds, but strangely I don't think there is a record of a Mandarin x Carolina.

The Mandarin normally lays a smaller clutch of large eggs, averaging 8, whereas the Carolina tends toward a larger clutch (9 or 10 average) of small eggs. As both species utilize elevated nest boxes, it is common to get large dump clutches of mixed Mandarins and Carolinas. Also birds will try and pull each other out of nest boxes, and cracked eggs result. It is best to keep both types apart and provide plenty of boxes.

The incubation period for the Mandarin is 29 days while the Carolina is usually about 30 days.

Some years ago, both European and American breeders possessed many Mandarin Ducks. Sadly today, this is not the case. These fluctuations in the populations of certain species in captivity, are symptomatic of a dangerous cyclical problem that seems to plague waterfowl propagation. What usually happens is that a particular species will become abundant in captivity, and soon, propagators find that particular species boring, and of no value. The species starts to die out in captivity, and suddenly one day, someone asks, "Where have all the 'so and so's' gone?" Many species have suffered this way in captivity, and the Mandarin is a prime example in America...and just as the bird is trying to make a precarious come back in the wild!

Maned Goose

Another member of this group which is occasionally referred to as a perching duck, is the Maned Goose (*Chenonetta jubata*) or Australian Wood Duck.

This quiet, unassuming bird is kept widely in collections and where blood lines are good, they breed regularly. Grazing birds by nature, they also feed extensively in the water, especially where corn is scattered along the margins. Full-winged birds show a peculiar grace in the air, and perch freely. Most breeders never see this aspect of their birds for most stock is pinioned. Interestingly, full-winged birds revert to normal nesting habits, favoring elevated boxes or tree cavities where 7 eggs are laid and incubated for 28 days.

When pinioned, Maned Geese favor a burrow or ground box. A modified shelduck box, with a pipe entrance seems to be a favorite. These birds benefit from winter protection, and can't take many subzero days or nights.

They represent a unique niche in the waterfowl family possibly as a link between shelducks, sheldgeese and ducks. Unlike sheldgeese, they have a colored speculum but share more traits of geese than ducks.

Pygmy Goose

Of the 4 varieties of pygmy geese, 3 are now represented in captivity outside of Australia. The 3 varieties kept at the time of writing are, the African (*Nettapus auritus*), the Green (*Nettapus pulchellus*) and the Indian (*Nettapus coromandelianus. c*), or Cotton Teal. First breeding of the African variety took place at Winston Guest's former waterfowl collection on Long Island in 1975. The adult pair were full-winged birds and had chosen a natural log cavity in which to nest. It seemed to me that the male was quite attentive to the young, which reminded me of Wood Duck young and the female did not seem too upset by his presence. This may just have been a reaction to me being in the aviary, although since, I have heard other aviculturists who have bred the African type, say the male will attend the young.

When I was working with Bill Hancock in Montana, we had 5 pairs which we housed in a large, old greenhouse that had been converted for waterfowl. Initially, the birds had some intestinal worm problems which were quickly treated, and they settled down well. I had a great opportunity to closely observe their behavior and with the addition of video surveillance, I finally obtained film of one pair mating. Males were very aggressive, flying up and down the aviary chasing each other; the females hotly in pursuit. Once a male had driven off other males, the whole bunch would pump and bob their heads up and down furiously all the time squeaking and trilling. Although they are classified as Perching Ducks, I never once saw an individual perch on any of the overwater branches provided for them in their pond. Later, when I kept them in California in an 8,500-square-foot aviary, I would see them perching on large rocks and perches and even fighting off Ringed Teal who wanted to land! It seems that a fairly large group of birds are needed to stimulate breeding activity and Mike Lubbock has had great success with his "flock," although as Frank Todd observed, "If you keep enough of one species together, it will only be a matter of time before they breed." Our Montana flock never laid despite the mating going on and the evidence of scrapes in nest boxes. After I left, Bill informed me that he did get some infertile eggs.

Currently Mike Lubbock is the reigning king of pygmy breeding in America, keeping and breeding the three varieties previously mentioned, and a few European and British breeders have had successes with the African. Many of America's larger zoos keep pygmy geese as well, almost exclusively the African variety, but the New York Zoological Society were the first to breed the Indian variety.

I once saw an old black and white photograph taken at Alfred Ezra's collection in England in the early 1920s. Amazingly, one large, open pond contained not only African pygmies, but also Cotton Teal. (And would you believe the now extinct Pink-headed Duck!) The fact that they were maintained on an open pond in England suggests that they may be hardier birds than they seem, although the birds maintained at the Wildfowl Trust were kept in the tropical house most of the time and seemed not to like cooler weather.

Pygmy geese will eat small pellets and grains. I used to feed millet (white prosso) in a large pan of water to which vitamins and electrolytes had been added. The birds loved this. Mike Lubbock told me that in the wild, they will take small fish (guppies) and they undoubtedly eat insect matter. The birds I had in California, would fight off others to get the small minnows I fed to the Smew, Buffleheads and Hoodies. (Interestingly enough, the Orinoco Geese loved minnows too!) I have also heard of trout chow being given to Pygmy Geese. The incubation periods of Pygmy Geese seem to range from 22 to 26 days, averaging 24, and preferred nesting sites seem to be natural log-type cavities.

Comb Ducks

Two races of Comb Duck, the African (*Sarkidiornis melanotos melanotos*) and the South American (*S. m. sylvatica*) are known and occasionally reproduced in American and European collections. Unfortunately, birds are often allowed to hybridize. Differing flank color in males tells the races apart, the African having a light flank, the American, a very dark gray. Females are identical in each race. One wild-caught specimen from Botswana displayed a mottled side with alternating white and dark feathers, so possibly a light-flanked bird is not necessarily positive proof of a pure African.

Comb Ducks, like Maned Geese, are probably survivors from extinct families of waterfowl. They are hardy birds but suffer from frostbite in colder climates. They rarely bother other ducks. Males fight quite savagely but usually the prefight "psych out" precludes injury: two males, standing on tip-toe with wings slightly open and heads bowed, circle each other puffing or grunting for several minutes before contact is made. Comb Ducks average 6 eggs. They favor an elevated box and eggs are incubated for 29 days.

Wheat and breeder pellets make up the standard diet, and they seem to like dog chow as a supplement.

Brazilian Teal

The final perching ducks are two races of Brazilian Teal, the Lesser (*Amazonetta brasiliensis b.*) and the Greater (*A. b. ipecutiri*). The Greater is more common in captivity now than the Lesser, which used to be kept. There are probably many hybrids between the two.

They are tropical birds, and definitely benefit from winter shelter. Included with perching ducks because of their arboreal tendencies, they choose elevated nesting boxes into which they climb with great dexterity to lay their average of 7 eggs.

They are aggressive birds and should not be kept with other teal or small ducks as the beatings handed out during the mating season can be very savage. Incubation is 25 days.

16

Sea Ducks

To most propagators the term "sea duck" refers to a variety of waterfowl that includes Eiders, Harlequin, Long Tails, Steamers, Goldeneye and Bufflehead. Scoters are also sea ducks, but for propagational reasons I have given them their own section.

Among my favorite waterfowl, most sea ducks have great personalities. While sea ducks have been represented in collections for many years, mediocre breeding success is achieved. Much mystique surrounds these birds which only until very recently have been studied in detail. Only a few breeders have achieved consistent success with some species.

Eiders

Of the Eiders, the 2 most common captive varieties are the American (*Somateria mollissima dresseri*) and the European (*S. m. mollissima*). The main difference between males is that the skin flap above the beak reaches right up to and slightly above the eye level in the American, while the European's ends below the eye. Females are also different in color, the American being a lovely chestnut-brown color, the European being grayer.

Both races are hardy and can live for many years in captivity. They fare best in drier, cool areas of the world as they are highly susceptible to sinusitis, aspergillosis and other respiratory infections. They also tend to pick up inedible items and die from impaction or puncturing of the intestinal lining. These items include feathers, sticks, tab pulls from cans, discarded Polaroid papers, nails, glass, wire, string (especially the modern synthetic variety), staples, nylon and wire bristles from brushes. These occurrences can be fairly regular and the breeder should take great pains to ensure none of these items are available for ingestion. The breeder ought to be aware that the bird is probably trying to find grinding materials and fiber. Eiders have very strong gizzards and in the wild swallow crustaceans whole. Shells and stones (which may be quite large) are used in the gizzard as grinding materials for digesting shellfish.

Two important organs in the Eider's body are the gizzard and the salt-extraction glands. Located on the inside of the beak at the top, salt glands extract and excrete salt through the nostrils of the birds while in sea water.

These 2 organs should not be allowed to become flaccid and unused while in captivity. I am sure that this is partly why leech invasions of the nostril, sinusitis and certain impactions of the gizzard occur in birds maintained in fresh water. Of course, metallic articles, chemically treated photograph paper and synthetic materials will kill birds, but a healthy bird should be able to overcome minor impactions. In captive birds the muscle surrounding the gizzard is usually not as large or as strong as in wild birds simply because it is not used as much due to a softer diet.

One has only to look at an Eider to see how beautifully it has adapted to oceanic life. Wide and powerful in stature, it is almost impossible to upset in the sea. Indeed a popular story in Scandinavian countries is that the Eider's shape helped determine the shape of the wide, flat-bottomed war boats of the Vikings. Not only did these vessels sail the Vikings around some of the wildest seas in the world, but also gave them access to shallow river estuaries from which to launch raiding parties.

Eiders have powerful legs set well back on the body. A large web spread, coupled with their powerful wings, help them forage beneath the water. Beaks are broad, nail tipped and very strong and are used for prying mollusks and crustaceans from rocks and out of holes. Their dumpy tails act as rudders for control. They can fly with surprising speed close to the surface, rising and falling with the swells.

Both varieties breed sporadically in collections. Several breeders produce young every year, but many more produce young only occasionally. Usually they are fed on pellets of 14 to 18 percent protein, supplemented with dog chow, trout chow, fish, hamburger, biscuit or bread. A mixture of ⅓ Hi Pro dog food, ⅓ trout chow and ⅓ pellets works well as a staple diet.

They sometimes choose a nest box, but prefer to nest on the ground usually in cover or just under a bush. Some lay quite a distance from the water's edge. They average 5 eggs, and incubation times vary from 25 to 30 days. Twenty-six is average.

The Pacific Eider (*S. m. nigra*) is the largest Northern Hemisphere duck, often exceeding 6 pounds in weight. The male has a striking orange beak and the female's plumage is a dappled grayish brown. Only a few American, Canadian and European propagators keep the Pacific variety as of 1995, but some have done extremely well with them.

At the Game Bird Center, George Allen has found them to be polygamous, or at least promiscuous in that males have been found to breed with more than one hen, something that has also occurred in Spectacled Eiders at the center. The birds at the center assume pair bonds early in the year, usually by January or February, and after the female has laid her complete clutch in May or June and has incubated for several days, its mate will often search out one or more other unmated females with which to breed.

At the center, clutch sizes range between 4 and 6 eggs, a somewhat larger clutch than is found in other common Eider races, and the eggs are somewhat smaller than most eggs of the American race which is surprising considering the larger size of the Pacific form, except that in an evolutionary sense the survivability of the young of a high Arctic species is somewhat lower because of higher predation rates and the shorter season than the lower latitude races, and a larger clutch size is advantageous in this regard. At the center the incubation period has been documented at 26–27 days. Pacific Eiders were first bred in captivity at the Gamebird Research & Preservation Center, Utah, in 1980.

The King Eider (*S. spectabilis*) is a beautiful and most striking bird. It is rare in captivity but has been bred at the Wildfowl Trust in England and in one or two other European collections. It has also been bred by three or four American propagators, and by at least one Canadian. They have beautiful "sails" (curled scapular feathers on their backs). These also occur on Pacific Eiders and some American Eiders I have seen. They are among the most northerly nesting waterfowl in the world. Their beautiful haunting call is a wonderfully wild experience. They favor starfish and sea urchins over shellfish and have been credited with very deep dives (up to 180 feet!). They lay 5 eggs and incubate 23 days. They pose some difficulty in their captive maintenance, as they can be rather delicate. Also a flock of birds is needed to create competition and sexual activity.

The Spectacled Eider (*S. m. fischeri*) is also poorly represented in captivity. In Europe it was bred for the first time in 1976 at the Wildfowl Trust and in America at the Game Bird Center in 1980. The pond on which they were kept at the trust was large, about (120 yards x 40 yards) and deep. Small islands had been provided all along one bank, planted with reeds and grass and scattered with rock. The female chose one of these to nest on. The ducklings could not have been mistaken for anything else as they had their spectacle outline around the eye, giving them a very sad appearance. At least six American collections currently have one or more birds. (One female collected in Alaska by Warren Hancock laid eggs every year but tragically had no male Spectacled with her, and was amorously courted by American Eider males.) Spectacled Eiders nest on the ground in low cover and lay an average 5 eggs which are incubated for 24 days.

Many Eiders have been brought into collections from Alaska. Almost all have died, usually because rearing facilities were poorly planned and maintained. Now breeders are coming up with better methods to keep these birds, but lack of money hinders many of them.

The last member of this family hardly resembles a true Eider. Because most people would expect to find it under the Eider section, I have included it here.

Steller's Eiders (*Polysticta stelleri*) possess some physical qualities of the Eider family, but are obviously adapted to a different lifestyle. Their beaks are developed to eat soft-bodied invertebrates and they spend more time foraging and dabbling than diving.

Steller's Eiders are incredibly beautiful in breeding dress and photographs cannot possibly do justice to their color.

They are rare in collections; a few are maintained in England, and probably no more than two or three collections in America. My experience with these birds is limited but I did have the opportunity to work with some that Mike Lubbock brought back to the Wildfowl Trust from Alaska as eggs. About 40 percent of the hatched young were raised and most encountered diet and health-related problems.

One of the only places that Steller's have been raised in America is in Utah, and George Allen writes: "There is probably less known about the breeding biology of Steller's Eider in the wild than any other North American waterfowl species, except perhaps the Surf Scoter, with no major study ever having been made of its breeding ecology. I have been fortunate in observing its breeding and nesting behavior in two areas of its breeding range in Alaska, near Kotzebue in western Alaska in the early 1970s, and southwest of Wainwright on the Arctic coast on several expeditions between 1977–1981.

"I found that its favored nesting habitat in the Arctic portion of its Alaskan breeding range is quite different and more specialized than that of other Eider species in that they prefer dryer terrain, located not more than 1 to 5 miles inland from the ocean. Nests were located not far from shallow (usually not more than 6 inches in depth), low-centered polygon marshes, and tiny ponds. Elevated nest sites are preferred, being placed along the polygonal ridges or atop mounds. The female makes a shallow scrape in the mossy, mostly brownish black-colored tundra, and deposits 6 to 7 eggs which are laid every other day (at least this was the laying schedule I observed in two nests that were fresh when first found and checked each day). In addition to the mosslike plants into which the nest scrape is made, other dominant plant species around the nests that we identified included *Carex, Epiophorum* and *Dupontia spp*. The vegetation around the nests located was very short, leaving the females with little cover protection, and predation from Parasitic Jaegers, Glaucus Gulls and Arctic Foxes was found to be extensive. Since their nests are not at all concealed by vegetation, the birds must rely on their cryptic coloration for protection against predators, and the birds blend in well with the brownish black soil on which the nests are often found.

"In captivity at the Game Bird Center, the few hens that have so far nested have selected sites that were in thick grass, in open-faced nest boxes in secluded areas, or against a tree or tree stump. The eggs, which average 61 x 44 mm, are laid at 48-hour intervals, and the drake often accompanies its mate to the nest site and remains nearby while the egg is deposited. The incubation period is 23–24 days.

"During the breeding season groups of males at the center often perform rather synchronized courtship displays, where several drakes rise upwards and backwards from the water, and this activity is apparently important to pair formation."

Harlequin

The Harlequin (*Histrionicus histrionicus*) is also poorly represented in captive conditions. A delicate and shy duck, it has not been studied enough in captivity to provide good breeding results. However, one or two of the European breeders, and Americans such as Mr. C. Pilling of Seattle, The Gamebird Research Center in Utah, and one or two others have experienced some success. Harlequins are beautiful and can have lively personalities under the right conditions. Often though, a single bird or pair is kept with other sea ducks, resulting in a shy, retiring bird. I feel unless the breeder is a born natural with birds (and a good stockman) these ducks should be kept in their own enclosure in groups, with sufficient space for each pair during the breeding season. Being a natural with birds is, however, a very rare gift.

Most people can keep and propagate 90 percent of waterfowl, but species that are shy, delicate and very specialized need a great deal of attention and good conditions. For example, Mr. Pilling successfully breeds Harlequins on his half-acre pond under city conditions. They seem to get along with his other birds but I feel this is because of his exceptional expertise. Visiting his collection, one can see how settled the birds are on their beautiful spring-fed pond. The same is true of an aviculturist in England who keeps her Harlequins among other ducks. They are not crowded and when I last visited in 1979, I observed two males vigorously pursuing and wooing a female.

In the wild, Harlequins breed from Alaska through coastal regions of British Columbia, and feed inland in the fast-moving streams that abound in this area. Vancouver Island has a breeding population, as does Washington State. Harlequins breed in Montana in Glacier National Park, and Yellowstone National Park, Wyoming. Pairs are found in northern Wyoming and eastern Montana in "wilderness" areas along mountain streams.

Bob Elgas and I found pairs nesting along the Boulder River near Big Timber, Montana. If it were possible to gather eggs from these southerly nesters, the young might turn out to be hardier. It would be interesting to find out.

They are highly susceptible to stress during molt; most birds are lost at this time. Like many delicate species, they stress easily and have a low tolerance to most drugs. Penicillin injections for ailing birds seems to be the best known remedy. Stress induced in trying to catch the ill bird may have dire results, hence captive Harlequins should be allowed to become as tame as possible.

The molt period is long and varies depending on latitude. Mr. Pilling's birds in Seattle, Washington, were in color in September, while ours in Montana were only just coming into color in November. Wild birds observed in the Boulder River area were, interestingly, still in color in late August and early September.

In captivity, Harlequins nest in cover and I have also seen scrapes in caves and raised boxes provided for them. Diets in captivity usually consist of a protein pellet and dog chow or trout pellets. Clutch size averages 7 eggs and incubation is 28 days.

(Rearing methods and breeding pens for sea ducks are discussed in their respective chapters.)

There are two possible races of Harlequin, the Pacific and Atlantic. European birds tended to come from Iceland while American birds come mostly out of Alaska. Side by side I find the two races indistinguishable and tend to side with other skeptics such as Todd, who question the existence of two separate races.

Longtail or Old Squaw

The Longtail or Old Squaw (*Clangula hyemalis*) is the only duck having two distinct plumage phases in addition to an eclipse plumage. I find these birds beautiful in either dress, but in captivity can rank among the most stupid (or unlucky) of waterfowl. One American breeder told me of an incident when a Great Horned Owl swooped low over a pond containing numerous birds, including his only Old Squaw drake. Everything else dived, and birds on land took to the water for safety. After the owl's third pass, all the other ducks had taken refuge in the water, heads up and alert. The Longtail just sat in the middle of the pond, and then decided to take to the bank for safety, where it was struck and killed by the owl.

There are similar stories of Longtail stupidity in England. One bird that was killed by a mink was on land when the mink found a way into the collection, and into this particular pond. The other birds (seeing the mink take to the water) leapt out of the pond. The Longtail leapt into the pond and was promptly seized from below the water and killed. A Canadian friend told me of one that managed to hang itself in the fork of a low shrub growing near its pond.

The Longtail is among the most numerous of Northern Hemisphere waterfowl, so it is surprising that more are not kept. It is poorly represented in collections in Europe and has little better status in America. In captivity they are either completely wild and hysterical, or embarrassingly tame, mostly the latter.

They have been bred in England, Europe and in Canadian collections.

Adults tended to be unassuming and easily bullied. Like the Harlequin, they prefer their own type and really only start "to come out of their shells" when kept accordingly. Youngsters I reared from eggs were started on chick crumbs and minced egg with a little hamburger meat and a vitamin-mineral supplement. Occasionally I gave them a dish of salt water and brine shrimp, which they loved.

The hamburger added to the food was probably unnecessary—the birds ate ravenously from day one. I fed them in the same fashion as one would feed baby cranes, three times a day for twenty minutes. Shrimp feeding was phased out after three weeks, and I am convinced that the sea water in the shrimp pan had beneficial effects on them. The adults spend time on fresh water before breeding and after the young are hatched they are led to the sea about the time they are half-grown.

The display of the drake Longtail is reminiscent of a Goldeneye, with a head throw accompanied by a call. The call is particularly haunting and, like the call of migrating geese, can be quite an emotional experience. Todd reveals that Eskimos know the bird (after its call) as "hohoalic," and Delacour eloquently and accurately describes the call as "ow ow owal-ow." Northeasterners in England supposedly call the bird "coal and candlelight" although those people that I have spoken to either have never heard this name, or didn't know what a Longtailed Duck even looked like.

Longtails construct a well-hidden nest and are tight sitters. Their 6 eggs have a short (22–23 day) incubation period.

Longtails have proved to be delicate under captive conditions, and are prone to respiratory troubles. Paradoxically some keepers who have had them for a considerable time will testify that they are one of the hardier sea ducks.

It seems that if they become established they tend to survive; birds that die are usually under stress. This duck stresses very easily, so it is beneficial to have them as tame as possible and kept under the least stressful conditions possible. The pen should be large, with good, clean, cold water.

Buffleheads

The petite and endearing Bufflehead (*Bucephala albeola*) is a much sought-after duck in waterfowl collections. Their color, personalities and size make them very attractive avicultural possessions.

Best kept on a diet of pellets, some breeders include a grain of some sort, usually wheat. Diet is supplemented with dog chow or trout pellets small enough to be easily taken by these tiny birds.

Buffleheads are lovely, busy little ducks, preening, diving and courting their equally petite females with a vigorous head pumping motion and viciously fighting off interfering males.

Currently well represented in collections worldwide they are being bred more and more each year. Like all sea duck families, the Bufflehead does best on cool, clean water. Losses among young birds tend to be at two or three days old or at fledging. Like others in this family (and most Mergansers) they are often put outside too quickly to "harden them off." A gradual acclimatization program is needed unless the stock is directly descended from the wild or within one or two generations. It is possible that hardiness regresses dramatically generation to generation. It happens with other species where brother-sister matings have occurred and the genetic mix gets weaker and weaker. Like all species, the breeder must ensure that his stock is outcrossed as much as possible. It makes the rearing of young much easier.

Wild Buffleheads nest in cavities excavated by flickers. These holes can be fairly small (3¼-inch diameter) and the Bufflehead often must squeeze to get in. Like most hole nesters, the slight effort required to get into a hole often seems to make the female more content within the nest—seemingly in the knowledge that she is secure. Old logs with such holes make excellent boxes for captive Buffleheads to nest in. Here they will lay their 8 eggs and incubate for 30 days.

They can be exceptionally finicky about dummy eggs; a bantam egg of the same weight and size should be used. Ringed Teal eggs are often acceptable dummy eggs.

Goldeneyes

Of the 3 races of Goldeneye, 2 are common in captivity in their native ranges. The American (*Bucephala clangula americana*) tends to be well represented in the United States whereas the European (*Bucephala clangula c.*) is rarely seen. In England and Europe, the European is more frequently kept, and a few *americana* are represented also.

The primary difference between the two is size, the American being larger. Both types are hardy, only being wintered inside in northern states. Winter protection and open water are beneficial—care should be taken not to alarm birds on water in winter as panicking birds may dive and become trapped below the ice.

These species prefer a raised box, but will also nest on the ground in cover. They lay 9 eggs and incubate 30 days. These two races easily hybridize and many supposed American types in England are hybrids. The results of American x Barrow's are quite interesting! I once saw two pairs of young birds that were sold as Barrow's Goldeneye, and that looked almost like Barrow's, with a bluish iridescence to the head, but the round American spot near the beak. The other had an atypical green head with a Barrow's-type profile, and perfect crescent-shaped, white facial marking. One female was almost indistinguishable from a pure Barrow's, but lacked beak color and the greenish tinge to the eye, that all pure Barrows hens have. The other female was short headed, short beaked, and short bodied, altogether a nasty-looking bird.

The Barrow's Goldeneye (*B. c. islandica*) is widely distributed in the Northern Hemisphere. Breeding areas range from Alaska to Iceland, and it also occurs in Greenland. A distinct Rocky Mountain population breeds through Montana, Wyoming and into Colorado.

These birds were displayed at Sea World in San Diego. One had to look closely at the "Rocky" birds and the Alaskan representatives in the adjacent pen to discern differences. Coloration was similar, but Rocky birds have narrower bodies and sharper tails. Alaskan birds are chunkier, stubbier-tailed and marginally larger.

Fairly well represented in collections world wide, most European breeders have Goldeneyes of Icelandic origin. Care should be taken when choosing pen mates. Eiders make good pen mates but should be allowed into pens first or they may be challenged for territorial rights by the smaller Goldeneyes. I always made sure that Eiders were settled in a pen before introducing Goldeneyes. Todd states that wild female Goldeneyes are protective of their broods, even setting up "brood territories" where visiting ducks are chased or savagely beaten. I remember a female Barrow's in captivity which was presumed to have started sitting some ten days after she actually had. She hatched out a brood, took them onto the pond and promptly cleared an area 60 feet in each direction, almost killing a Cinnamon Teal in the process. She even attacked the keeper when he came to collect the young.

They lay 8 eggs in raised boxes in captivity and incubate for 32 days. Fairly hardy birds, they will benefit from protection in severe weather. They are less inclined to breed in captivity than their European or American cousins, but a group of three pairs or more may start earlier, usually because one bird becomes quite active, encouraging the others. One breeder I know deliberately placed a five-year-old pair that showed no interest in each other next to a flock of active *americana*, and, as if the frenzied mating of the American was contagious, the Barrow's mated and produced fertile eggs for the first time. I have used this technique for swans, geese and some ducks, but never for Goldeneye. Initially, a larger ratio of males to females starts sexual activity. After a while it will become obvious which males are dominant and which females are preferred. This is probably the easiest way to start up a flock. Keep a close eye on the genetics of your birds. Icelandic Barrow's have a reputation for great activity and aggression in the males, but oddly these males tend to make bad breeders as they have a habit of not knowing what to do in response to the females copulatory display. Hence many infertile eggs are produced.

Scoters

There are 3 species making up the 7 races of Scoters. Very little has been done in the way of captive propagation with these birds for many reasons. Scoters are difficult to acquire, most are too specialized for the majority of breeders (but then so were many waterfowl which are currently widely kept), some appear to be delicate, others hardy.

Few aviculturists maintain Scoters and, like some of the rarer sea ducks, they tend to be representatives rather than a breeding viability in most collections.

Scoters appear to most enthusiasts as large, ugly sea ducks. They strike me as being rather pretty in the same way as are Steamers, Spurwings and Muscovies. Like most sea ducks they are very well adapted to ocean life. To see Scoters feeding in the aftermath of an Atlantic storm, with huge breakers pounding the beaches emphasizes this point.

They are highly specialized (like most sea ducks), eating a variety of shellfish, crabs and sea invertebrates.

Few have every been kept in captivity and my own experience is limited to three; this was only on a maintenance basis—as they never bred. (Glen Howe in Canada is one of the few people to breed Scoters in captivity. He has also bred Longtailed Duck, Harlequins, Spectacled and King Eiders. In England, Bill Makins, and in Scotland, Jane Dawson, have achieved notable successes with many types of sea ducks.)

Why are they so difficult? First, if they were easily obtained I'm sure more aviculturists would have tried them. Their own characters and preferences are the big stumbling blocks to their successful propagation.

Conditions needed for maintenance of Scoters include an abundance of clear, deep water. They seem to resent other birds and feel uneasy around them.

Todd kept his Scoters on salt water. Although they were alongside other ducks they seemed quite steady and in very good health. This tameness factor plays a big part in their successful maintenance. Why they are virtually impossible to breed no one knows. Having raised Scoters from Icelandic eggs I found them to be simple to care for.

Diet is probably enormously important combined with these other points. I would like to try feeding shellfish and crustaceans in salt water and see how this works. The recent availability of specialized waterfowl diets, such as Mazuri's Sea Duck Ration, have been of great help to aviculturists keeping these more specialized birds, and I highly recommend this ration as part of a well-balanced sea duck diet.

As demonstrated by the few people who have maintained Scoters, they can be fed normal waterfowl fare. They are especially fond of dog chow, trout pellets and bread. Delacour relates that a European White-winged Scoter that he kept for a time never touched meat—but ate dog biscuit greedily. The group of Pacific White-winged maintained at the Wildfowl Trust had a similar dislike of fish, except for one male. However, now and again the bags of sand eels which we fed to the Mergansers contained a crab or two. When feeding, I would always save these small green crabs for the Scoters—and they loved them. In the wild they are known to have a preference for small blue mussels which they swallow and digest whole in the same manner as Eiders.

Until recently, most Scoters came into captivity through oil spills or were cripples from shooting. These birds were extremely delicate and very difficult to acclimatize—but once this was achieved, they lived long lives. Perhaps if they can become established on their own in pens with cold, clean water and an appropriate diet (fresh water mussels, crayfish, etc.) they may be more successfully propagated.

Considering the enormous varieties of animals which have been bred in captivity, even when they are specialized, delicate and shy, I feel it will not be long before aviculturists succeed with these birds.

Scoters can be aggressive and often are seen gaping at intruders and chasing them away. Otherwise they seem rather lazy and shy.

I remember Scoters I cared for (especially Common Black's)

were so nervous and were bullied so much at feeding time by other birds (mergansers, dabblers and divers) that often they would only get a few mouthfuls before retreating from the horde. I would throw fish or bread well out into the pond so the mergansers and other ducks would leave the poor confused Scoters alone. This is why I feel they are better kept alone than in a group. Scoters present an enormous challenge to the serious aviculturist. More work must be done on these birds, especially in captivity. In the wild, they nest around fresh water—sometimes a long way away, which makes nest detection very hard. Little is known about brood care, clutch size or incubation periods. What is known is laid out in the following table:

BLACK SCOTERS

	Average Clutch Size	Incubation Period (days)
American Black (*Melanitta nigra americana*)	8	28
Common Black (*M. n. nigra*)	8	28

WHITE-WINGED SCOTERS

Surf (*M. Perspicillata*)	8	26
Pacific (*M. fusca dixoni*)	9	26
American (*M. f. deglandi*)	9	26
Velvet (*M. f. fusca*)	9	26
Asiatic (*M. f. stejnegeri*)	9	26

Steamer Ducks

The 4 members of this family of ducks make up one of the most perplexing, interesting and unbelievably savage group of waterfowl in existence.

The Steamers' niche is like that of the Northern Hemisphere Eiders, but they are not related. These birds are massive—12 to 14 pounds not being uncommon, and if Shelducks as a group are considered aggressive then the Steamer duck can only be described as lethal. All but one of the Steamer duck family is flightless, their short stubby wings being useless except as a paddle. Steamers have enormous, powerful beaks, and their

wings possess a bony knob at the elbow. Using these two append-
ages they seize and fight each other—and often kill lesser adversaries.

Few breeders have ever seen Steamer ducks. My experience
encompasses only two varieties, the Falkland Island (*Tachyeres
brachypterus*) and the Magellanic (*Tachyeres pteneres*). Once
seen, they are never forgotten. I remember one visiting American
aviculturist who, after scaling the low fence of the Magellanic's
pen to get a good photograph, was viciously attacked. Mopping
his brow and regaining his breath, he declared, "Boy—is that *all*
duck!?" "A cross between a battleship and a pair of pliers" was
how another breeder summed them up.

An escaped Falkland Island Steamer at the Wildfowl Trust
killed eight birds (including a brood of three-quarter-grown greylags) within the 20 minutes needed to recapture it. Undoubtedly
these birds are the "hit men" of the duck world.

I find them splendid creatures. When the female Falkland
Island Steamer laid at the Wildfowl Trust she constructed a nest
under a large Lonissera hedge and displayed the tight-sitting
qualities of a female Eider. When she was disturbed at the nest,
the male, ever loyal, thundered across the pond and shot out of
the water. With wings spread and beak agape, he stomped men-
acingly, waiting for the opportunity to attack the intruder.

Steamers at the Wildfowl Trust were maintained on wheat
and pellets, dog chow and brown bread. Their pond was deep and
clean, and had a moderate flow of water. Occasionally, a greedy
Mallard dropped in—a mistake they never made again unless
they had a chance to get airborne. The Steamers swam noncha-
lantly up and then attacked or seized the unfortunate duck from
underwater.

Steamers also have a peculiar way of submerging their bodies (as will alarmed Stifftails), leaving only their huge heads
above the surface, and steaming threateningly through the water
with beaks agape. In this posture they resemble a crocodile closing in for a kill. One particular Mallard seemed hypnotized by the
serpentlike gaze of an approaching Steamer and was seized and
beaten. I managed to separate the pair but received a short thrash-

ing for my pains! It really is sad that more is not known in captivity about these beasts.

Back in 1978 or 1979, both Frank Todd and Mike Lubbock speculated as to the existence of a fourth race of Steamer duck, the White-headed. They were correct, as in the early 1980s Dr. Phillip Humphrey documented the White-headed as a separate race. As their name suggests, these birds have a prominent white head, but this seems to be the only difference between this and other Steamers since their behavior (including breeding behavior) is presumably the same. White-headed Steamers have never been kept in captivity.

The final member of the Steamer family is the Flying Steamer duck (*Tachyeres patachonicus*), a much smaller bird that displays distinct freshwater tendencies. Steamers lay an average of 6 eggs which are incubated for about 34 days.

As mentioned, few breeders have kept these curious ducks. The Magellanic and Falkland Island varieties are most commonly represented in collections and so far, propagational success has been limited.

(Ten years ago when I first compiled this waterfowl book, Steamers were very rare in captivity and only two or three breeders had had any success breeding them. While they are still rare in collections, both the Magellanic and the Falkland varieties have been kept and bred by American, British and European breeders, and captive representatives are now more numerous.)

17

Stifftails

The tribe *Oxyurini* contains 12 members distributed through Eurasia, Africa, North America, South America and Australia. Of these 12, 10 exhibit most of the physical characteristics that people associate with stifftails, or Ruddy Ducks.

A typical stifftail is blue-billed, squat and dumpy. Universally shared is their ability to reduce human beings to apoplectic fits of laughter through their hysterical mating antics, their belligerence, and attempts at walking.

The Ruddy Duck is built for an almost totally aquatic life. Wide and flat keeled, they are unaffected by the enormous waves of the vast inland seas they inhabit. A broad, powerful bill enables them to grip and tear aquatic vegetation, as well as sieve edible bits and pieces. The Stifftail's enormous feet serve as stabilizers and provide powerful engine-room thrust to take them to the lake bottom or across the water surface in pursuit of females or rival males. In some species the feet are used as sails. The White-headed Duck has mastered the technique of catnapping with one leg drawn into the belly feathers and the other extended and spread to catch the wind. This behavior is not completely understood. Some believe that it prevents them from drifting into the bank while asleep, where they would be predated. In most species male and female are of dissimilar color (sexual dimorphism), the basic color patterns in the male being a rusty red body combined with a black head (with white cheek patches in some) and a distinctly outrageous porcelain-blue bill.

The females are generally the same size as the males. Some species have a distinct line above, through or below the eye giving the impression that they are always smiling.

The males have short, thick necks with inflatable sacs used during courtship display in combination with the blue bill. These displays are guaranteed to reduce the onlooker to a weak-kneed, rib-crackling wreck. I have seen males driving off Muscovy Ducks and geese, and in one instance a female, guarding a nest site, attack a fully grown Mute Swan; sitting in the middle of the swan's back, ripping out great beakfuls of feathers while the swan steamed around the pond in terror.

The "bubbling" display performed by the North American Ruddy has similarities to those performed by other stifftails. The air sacs contained in the crop area are inflated. After a series of vigorous head throws, the display ends when the bright blue bill is drummed on the inflated breast, forcing out a ring of air bubbles trapped in the breast feathers. Accompanying noises include grunts (rather like a bullfrog) and a whistle at the end during "deflation," apart from the noise emitted by the drumming of the beak, a rapid "thrumming" sound.

Maccoas and Argentine Ruddies follow a similar routine but do not seem to use the beak to drum and emit bubbles. They exhibit a variation which begins with inflation; after the slight head throw the movement is one more akin to a hen frantically tucking a nonexistent egg under her breast with her beak while emitting a range of tonal grunts, whistles and nasal snores.

The sound created by the approach of the males to the females is often alarming. The Ruddy Duck takes one pace back in the water before launching himself, using his large spread feet and wings to skitter across the water with a loud "bop-bop-bop" as the feet hit the surface. He then stops dead a few feet away from his bored spouse.

I have never seen the Argentine Ruddy use any sort of approach other than swimming quickly up to the female, sometimes with a brief wave of the beak. I have only seen the Maccoa make the "North American approach" once, but I have seen an approach rather more like the aggressive head-down drive of the Steamer Ducks (which sometimes alarms the female enough to dive).

The White-headed Duck usually drifts sideways toward the female, the body held perfectly still and head lowered, while the feet go like crazy. This culminates in a thin but quite audible "tic-tic-tic-tic" noise, again stopping just short of the female.

Black-headed Ducks inflate the neck and rapidly pump their heads, uttering a grunting "hop" noise sometimes finishing in a thin whistle. This noise and the inflation of the neck to near twice-normal size has earned it the nickname in South America of *Pato Sapo* or Toad Duck. It is also called the Cuckoo Duck because of its parasitic laying habits.

The Musk Duck has the most spectacular (although like art, it is in the eye of the beholder) and noisy display of the family. The fleshy lobe in the male which is situated under the bill, is enlarged and a neck inflation occurs with the body gradually flattened out across the water. The tail is spread and raised up over the back and the feet suddenly kick backward, sending a shower of water several feet into the air while simultaneously the birds emit a loud "plonk," and an ear-piercing whistle of such power that I have seen people leap into the air in surprise.

Copulation in most species resembles brutal rape and indeed several cases of females being drowned are on record. The Musk Duck female (being only one-third the size of the male) has a particularly tough time in the wild, being chased over and under water before being caught and mated.

This occurred to a small extent with captive birds housed in an aviary at Slimbridge, England. An escape grid, consisting of holes in a wooden shutter, dividing the male's pond from the female's was inserted to allow the female to escape. The female did eventually lay but the eggs were infertile. However, the Wildfowl Trust obtained some Musk Duck eggs from the wild and some of these hatched and were reared. I would like to try an adult pair on a large pond of their own, incorporating some escape mechanism for the female. I feel the chasing might be a necessary action, possibly arousing the males ardor to a necessary fertile pitch prior to copulation.

Stifftails engage in frequent inter-male squabbling, though it looks more savage than it really is. The Maccoa is exceptionally belligerent and is usually kept only with females. In the Maccoa's case single male/female pairings are better whereas with Argentine Ruddies I like to keep two males and one female; this stimulates sexual activity and speeds the egg-laying process.

Ruddy Duck eggs are among the largest eggs laid by any bird relative to the size of the adult bird. Except for the Musk Duck which averages 2 normal-sized eggs, clutches consist of 5 to 8 eggs, the total clutch weight often exceeding the female's own body weight. Most are round, white and have a chalky texture (rather like a large Whistling Duck egg) except the White-backed Duck who produces a beautiful rusty brown polished egg.

To my mind, the most bizarre of the Stifftail family is the decidedly untifftail-like Black-headed Duck (*Heteronetta atricapilla*). This bird does not resemble a typical Stifftail whatsoever, being about the size of a large Hottentot Teal, with a body shape more like a Cinnamon Teal and a large beak (relative to head size) reminiscent of a Mallard. The male has a black head and grayish black beak with a pinkish red crescent on each side at the top of the beak when in breeding condition. The back is an oily black and the side feathers range from a brownish gray at the top to a mottled gray-white at the water line. The female is a drab gray-black. The male has no eclipse plumage.

These birds have the oddest breeding behavior as they lay their eggs in other birds' nests, making no nest of their own. The youngster may spend a little time with the host bird on hatching, but quickly goes off and rears itself! Black-headed Duck eggs have been recorded in at least 18 different host nests, including that of a Snail Kite! The female either finds a nest in which to lay a single egg or sometimes the male will wrestle the occupant of a likely nest off her eggs long enough for the female to dart in and lay an egg. It is thought that the chipping noises of the hosts' young at hatching time, stimulate the Black-headed chick to chip out and hatch with the others. This would indicate a unique and speedy way of embryonic development on behalf of the Black Headed, as host incubation times vary and some eggs deposited in already incubating hosts nests have to play "embryonic catchup" in order to hatch at the same time as the hosts' young.

The young have considerably thicker down than most ducklings and this is probably needed as they leave their hosts very quickly upon hatching and are therefore not brooded. The egg is not at all like the typical stifftail egg, being much more akin to a regular duck egg and Mike Lubbock tells me that a female will lay 3 to 5 eggs, possibly more during her first cycle. Incubation ranges from 20 to 26 days. Once settled into a pen with suitable hosts (Red Shovelers or Rosybills), Black-headed Ducks can propagate themselves swiftly. At the time of writing, the race is being reclassified.

Stifftails do not produce down to line the nest, the exception being the Musk Duck.

Stifftails are among the longest lived and easiest to maintain of all waterfowl. Most large ponds with muddy bottoms with vegetational matter and invertebrates are ideal for stifftails. In these conditions Stifftails flourish, and through late spring to autumn rarely show an interest in conventional waterfowl fare. They also (as adults) seem practically disease immune although their young are susceptible to enteritis, aquaria, aspergillosis, tuberculosis, impacted gizzards, chilling (this, if they are being reared by hand, being normally the aviculturist's fault) and other assorted maladies.

Getting adults to breed is another matter. While the North American Ruddy is relatively easy, it is, in terms of laying, more equatable with a farmyard hen when compared to White-backed Ducks or Musk Ducks. To be fair to the keepers and breeders of these birds it has to be said that little work was done with these species until recently. Coupled with the scarcity and value of many species, this seemed enough to discourage most breeders from keeping them. African White-backed Ducks were first bred in England in 1978 and Mike Lubbock is the only breeder of this race in America to date (1995).

Now more breeders are keeping a variety of Stifftails and are steadily breaking down the barriers of nonproduction and making hand-reared young available. For example, in Britain you can buy North American and Argentinean Ruddy Ducks, White-headed Ducks, Maccoas, Black-headed Ducks, and maybe even White-backed Ducks. That represents one-half of the world's Stifftails. The ones which present the breeder with the most difficulty in terms of availability are the Australian Blue Bill, the Musk Duck, the Columbian and the Peruvian Ruddy, and the Masked Duck.

The family members consist of the following:

STIFFTAILS

	Average Clutch Size	Incubation Period (days)
North American Ruddy Duck (*Oxyura jamaicensis*)	7	24
Columbian (*O. j. andina*)	Probably as above	
Peruvian (*O. j. ferruginea*)	Probably as above	
Argentinean (*O. vittata*)	4	26
White-headed (*O. leucocephala*)	6	23
Maccoa (*O. maccoa*)	6	25
Australian Blue Bill (*O. australis*)	5	26
Masked Duck (*O. dominica*)	4–6	25–28
African White-backed (*Thalassornis leuconetus*)	6	27
Madagascan White-backed (*T. l. insularis*)	Probably as above	
Musk Duck (*Biziura lobata*)	2	Unverified
Black-headed (*Heteronetta atricapilla*)	Approx. 2 per host nest	20–26

18

Teal

There are some two dozen varieties of teal. While most are part of the Dabbling Duck tribe, they are numerous enough, and important enough to merit their own chapter. Many aviculturists are teal specialists, and to a breeder with limited space, teal make an attractive proposition in many respects.

As a group, teal possess similar traits. Most are shy, retiring and nonaggressive. One obvious characteristic of successful teal breeding establishment is the fact that the birds are usually very tame. This one factor is extremely important for the propagation of teal.

Teal are highly specialized and some are closely related to shovelers, perching ducks and the larger dabbling ducks. This is why Cinnamon Teal are placed alongside shovelers, and Ringed Teal are grouped with perching ducks. The Laysan Teal is really a degenerate Mallard, while the Falcated Teal is not really a teal at all.

Probably best known of all are the 3 races of Green-winged Teal.

The American Green-wing (*Anas crecca carolinensis*) and the European Green-wing (*Anas crecca crecca*) are very similar. One distinguishing factor is the white shoulder bar in the American variety.

Both races are kept fairly extensively, each in its own country. The American Green-winged Teal can become quite a producer of young under good conditions and while their longevity is not legendary, Bill Hancock had a documented eighteen-year-old female when I worked for him in Montana from 1982–1987. We would routinely turn out 40 young from 4 breeding females. The single pair that I had in California would routinely nest twice a year and provide me with 12 to 15 young. American breeders hardly know of the European Green-winged Teal and the Europeans don't seem to breed quite as many of this race as the Americans do of theirs.

The two previously mentioned races of Green-winged Teal lay about 8 egg which have a short 22-day incubation period.

The third variety of Green-winged Teal, The Aleutian Green-winged Teal (*A. c. nimia*) has adapted to the harsher environment of the Aleutian Island chain in Alaska. Said to be nonmigratory and common in the Aleutians, this teal has never been kept in captivity, but its nesting habits are probably similar to the other two varieties.

One of the most beautiful but stubbornly unproductive teal in captivity is the Baikal Teal (*Anas formosa*). *Formosa* is Latin for beautiful, a fitting description of the male in his breeding finery.

Baikal are exceptionally neurotic, and pen mates have to be very steady if the Baikal are ever to settle.

Collections in northern latitudes have successfully bred the Baikal, one of the most northern nesting ducks (70°N plus).

Some breeders have experimented with extending normal daylight with night lighting to mimic the longer cycles experienced in the Arctic. It is hard to know for certain whether the results (and there were some good ones) could be directly applicable to the extra periods of lighting. One breeder told me that he had produced Baikal Teal under "normal" conditions until I pointed to the light outside the barn next to the pen containing the teal. He admitted it was on a timer and he had forgotten completely about it! Having tried both ways myself, I can say that the vast majority of Arctic species that I have bred, have done so under normal light cycles. If you wish to try lighting your birds' pens for extra periods make sure that no other birds can see the light...it can induce early molting.

Baikal Teal are being bred in greater numbers nowadays, although before World War II they were one of the most numerous and cheapest of waterfowl. They are one of the hardier varieties of teal and only need shelter or heat during subzero weather.

Baikal will nest in cover or use a ground box. They lay about 7 eggs and these are incubated for 25 days.

Marbled Teal (*Marmaronetta angustirostris*) are perplexing little teal in many ways. As mentioned in the Crested Duck section, they have many similarities to Crested Ducks. Superficially they have the same shape, with a definite crest, a similar display and, even more intriguing, the young of both have similar markings and coloration.

However, Marbled Teal are fairly well represented under captive conditions, but are somewhat difficult to breed. Some propagators do well, most others only achieving sporadic breeding. The reasons for their lack of success are unclear. I have always found Marbled Teal rather personable, not particularly flighty or nervous. Perhaps the too common problem of inbreeding is responsible for their reluctance to breed. American aviculturists do slightly better with them than their European counterparts.

They normally utilize a raised box, and occasionally a ground-situated box. The nests I have seen in captivity were situated in cover on the ground, and wild nesting birds seem to breed under the same conditions. In their Mediterranean breeding range, they sometimes nest under the straw thatch of fishermen's huts, several feet from the ground. As ducklings, they display the same jumping tendencies as most cavity nesters. They lay 10 eggs which are incubated for 26 days. It would be interesting to know whether any brood rearing is done by males; with many waterfowl where sexes are similar, this is a fairly regular occurrence.

The 2 Versicolor Teal, the Northern (*Anas versicolor versicolor*) and the Southern races (*Anas versicolor fretensis*), are very similar. However, the Southern variety is larger and darker overall. The Northern variety is better known to aviculturists, the Southern only represented in a few European and American collections. Both are particularly beautiful, and like other species that do not have an eclipse plumage, are much sought after. They have no particular bad habits—but are easily bullied by larger ducks. Like most teal they like vegetation to dabble in (*Lemma minor*), and millet or a canary seed mixed with wheat and pellets is an acceptable, well-rounded diet. They lay an average of 8 eggs, and incubate 25 days.

A third, closely related, yet physically different adapted member of this group is the Puna Teal (*Anas v. puna*).

These are high altitude ducks (14,000 feet plus) and are very hardy. They tend toward a smaller clutch of 6 eggs but incubation is roughly the same, about 25 days. These birds are well known in collections worldwide and present no particular problems, but ought to be kept apart from their two other cousins or interbreeding will take place (as with Northern and Southern Versicolor if kept together). Normally a ground nester, they will use elevated boxes on occasions.

Sharp-winged Teal

There is a group of teal of which 4 races exist called Speckled Teal. This group consists of the Sharp-winged Teal (*Anas flavirostris oxyptera*) the darker Chilean Teal (*Anas flavirostris*) the relatively unknown Merida Teal (*Anas f. altipetans*) and the Andean Teal (*A. f. andium*).

The Chilean and Sharp-winged are well known and hardy. Similar in many ways, many examples of hybrids occur—these two should be kept separately. Both display a great perching ability if left fully winged, and even when pinioned can climb well. They like to nest off the ground. I have found nests of both varieties in raised boxes, half way up large Pampas Grass clumps, and occasionally on the ground. Brooding duties are shared by both parents. Clutch sizes are normally 5 to 6 and incubation is about 25 days.

The Merida and Andean Teal have never been kept under captive conditions.

Hottentot Teal (*Anas punctata*) are among the smallest ducks. They have been kept in captivity on and off for 50 years. An African species, they are remarkably hardy in colder climates, but shelter should be provided for them if possible as it brings a better bird out of winter, fit and ready for breeding.

Some people have found these little ducks difficult to propagate, but established pairs present no real difficulty in egg or young production. They do better in a full-winged state (as most teal do) and, like Silver Teal, they readily take to pond weeds and seed as a dietary supplement. Incubation records vary from 18 to 24 days, 22–23 being most common. Six or 7 eggs are laid and the nest is heavily downed with a particularly fine, dark down. They are poorly represented in collections worldwide. American breeders seem to do much better than their European counterparts.

Another African Teal is the pretty Cape Teal (*Anas capensis*). Definitely not shy, Cape Teal are aggressive and renowned for their mighty sexual appetites in captivity. I have seen many interesting hybrids with teal and larger ducks resulting from the Cape Teal.

They are common worldwide in captivity and are a hardy species. They do not have an eclipse plumage and thus gain popularity with many breeders (until their other "habits" are brought to light)! They have a reputation as good parents, both adults tending the young. They lay 7 eggs in a ground box or in cover and incubate for 25 days.

A small teal resembling a Pintail, although with a markedly shorter tail, is the Red-billed Teal (or Pintail) (*Anas erythrorhyncha*). As Delacour suggests, it probably may represent a link between teal and the smaller Pintail like the Bahama. It is a common duck both in the wild and in captivity and is another bird which left no impression on me in terms of personality.

They nest in close cover (sometimes a ground box) where they lay 8 eggs and incubate for 24 days.

Australia and New Zealand have several representatives of

the teal family, some of which are exceedingly rare and have never been kept in captivity outside of their native habitat.

The New Zealand Brown Duck (*Anas aucklandica chlorotis*) is an endangered species. These teal are large and aggressive. They have been known to kill adversaries, relentlessly picking on them and bullying them to death. The only Brown Ducks I ever saw were at the Wildfowl Trust in England where they bred freely for some time. Several females were lost, and the end result was a collection of males only. Brown Ducks have responded well to captive breeding in their native New Zealand, but the recent re-introduction to the wild program has been put on hold. It seems that the numbers released were not sustaining themselves due to continued predation by cats and other predators. It seems quite crazy to me that a re-introduction attempt of any sort would be contemplated while there still existed the feral predators that were responsible for the downfall of the teal in the first place! They normally lay 6 eggs in a nest on the ground (or occasionally in a ground box) and their incubation period is around 26 days.

(The Auckland Island Teal and Campbell Island Teal are flightless birds and are very rare. They have never been recorded in captivity.) Both the Campbell Island Teal and the Auckland Island Teal are essentially flightless, and are virtually unknown to aviculturists outside of New Zealand. The Campbell Island Teal was considered extinct, until its rediscovery in 1975 on Dent Island, a tiny volcanic plug of fifty-seven acres, west of Campbell Island. The original Campbell Island birds were wiped out by introduced rats by 1810, but obviously a few survivors made it to tiny Dent Island, where they remained unnoticed for 165 years! There are currently about thirty birds left in the wild. If I remember rightly, upon their rediscovery in 1975, the then Prime Minister of New Zealand was supposed to have said, "We must ensure that these birds never become extinct again!"

Subsequently, both the Auckland and the Campbell Island races have been bred in captivity in New Zealand, so there may be some hope yet for the survival of these little marine teal.

Two Australian teal that are more numerous are the Chestnut-breasted Teal (*Anas castanea*) and the Australian Grey Teal (*Anas gibberifrons gracilis*) which ranges into New Zealand, and is considered somewhat of a pest.

The Chestnut-breasted Teal is aggressive during the breeding season and is a notorious hybridizer. They are well known in captivity and breed readily. In the wild these teal, like many Australian waterfowl, nest two or three times in a season, depending on rainfall. They are not as numerous as Grey Teal, but are locally common (although thought to be declining now).

They nest in raised boxes in captivity and occasionally on the ground, laying 8 eggs. Incubation is 24 days. They are fairly hardy.

The Australian Grey Teal is also a well known hybridizer and is common in Europe but less so in America.

They use the same nesting facilities as the Chestnut-breasted and clutch size and incubation period are similar. This little teal has close relatives representing isolated populations throughout Celebes and Java: these are the East Indian Grey Teal (*Anas gibberifrons*) and the Rennell Island Grey Teal (*Anas gibberifrons remissa*). The Rennell Island Grey Teal is isolated to the island of its name. Similar to the Australian Grey Teal, it has never been recorded in captivity. The East Indian has only very rarely been imported and probably may have bred being confused with *gracilis*. They have a high-crested head very much like another relative, the rare Bernier's Teal of Madagascar (*Anas bernieri*).

The last relative, almost completely unknown to aviculturists, is the Andaman Teal (*A. g. albogularis*). During my years at the Wildfowl Trust we kept some of these birds, and when I left, one pair was looking as if they might lay. They were first bred in 1905 at the London Zoo but in a short while the stock had died out. They are known cavity nesters, and this was evident when the female mentioned earlier was seen inspecting a raised box on several occasions.

They appeared aggressive during the breeding season. They lay 7 eggs and incubate for 24 days.

19

Torrent Ducks

Waterfowl that evolved on the South American continent needed to adapt to some of the most difficult conditions found anywhere on our planet.

This is certainly true in the case of the 6 races of torrent ducks. As the name suggests, this bird lives among the raging torrents of the glacier-fed Andean rivers, feeding almost solely on stonefly larvae. To combat such a hostile environment this beautiful bird has evolved sleek lines and strong, large, webbed feet to hold itself in the rushing heavy water. It has rather small wings that streamline it further and has large strong claws to grip slippery rock surfaces, plus a broad, stiff tail to act as a rudder. They skitter across the top of a raging torrent using their large feet and wings. Torrent ducks are shy birds by nature and are difficult to locate. Little is known about their habits from field observations, and only recently have wild eggs been hatched and reared for the first time, by the noted British aviculturist Bill Makins. Certainly much has been learned from the youngsters, previously only a handful of adults of the Chilean race had ever been kept in captivity as they require highly specialized conditions.

The difficulty of traveling to their native habitat, getting permits for egg collection and overcoming the political chicanery involved, will ensure that these birds stay virtually isolated from aviculturists for sometime. Coupled with the special facilities they need to keep them properly, the aviculturist is faced with an almost impossible task.

Data relating to nesting is very scarce, but the Chilean variety is known to nest in recesses in cliffs and banks and occasionally under vegetation. It appears that only the female incubates but the male participates in rearing young. The incubation period is quite long at 40 to 44 days.

As of August 1996, the Chilean Torrent Duck has been placed on the endangered species list. An effort is currently being made to collect eggs of this species and of the Bronze-winged Duck in order to establish a breeding program in Chile. Numbers of both species are estimated at only 1,000 birds.

Nesting requirements, clutch size and incubation period is summarized as follows:

TORRENT DUCKS

	Average Clutch Size	Incubation Period (days)
Chilean (*Merganetta armata armata*)	3–4	40–44
Peruvian (*M. a. leucogenis*)	Probably as above	
Turner's (*M. a. turneri*)	Probably as above	
Bolivian (*M. a. garleppi*)	Probably as above	
Berlepsch's (*M. a. berlepschi*)	Probably as above	
Columbian (*M. a. columbiana*)	Probably as above	

20

Whistling Ducks

The 11 types of whistling ducks represent a specially adapted tribe. A glance at any whistler shows that they have unusually long legs, an adaptation to their arboreal life. The distributions of the various whistling ducks are limited with the exception of the more cosmopolitan Fulvous Tree Duck—which has an extraordinarily diverse distribution spanning four continents and smaller islands.

Of the 11 varieties, 6 are either commonly kept and bred or are well represented. As a rule, they are not hardy birds (especially tropical varieties) and greatly benefit from shelter and warmth during winter. Some of the less tropical varieties can tolerate cold weather, but all can suffer from frostbite after prolonged hard weather.

Birds kept full-winged can often escape the crippling or deforming effects of frost by perching off the ground. Pinioned birds should be provided with perches, and if possible, some warmth. Straw is good bedding material as it helps insulate birds, but it must be changed regularly before it gets damp.

Large packing cases (three-sided with a roof) with a perch fitted inside and a heat light or two suspended above are ideal if no indoor quarters are available. Providing a heat bar or other heating device which does not produce light would be best since constant exposure to light throughout winter can cause birds to start molting before breeding. This applies to many birds, the most susceptible being the Arctic varieties. Normal diet should be supplemented with greenery (lettuce, pond weeds, etc.) and a seed mixture, mixed with a vitamin and mineral supplement for the least hardy varieties. This can be fed on the surface. It will be obvious how much these birds love to dabble and sieve away through the surface of the pond.

With one exception, whistling ducks can be kept in groups. Enough pen space should be provided so that pairs can find and set up their own territories. The exception is the Spotted Whistling Duck (*Dendrocygna guttata*).

Established pairs of this variety can be nasty to rivals and should be kept as separate pairs or trios. Delacour describes those he kept at Cleres as unobtrusive and shy when kept with teal. These birds can be hardy, depending greatly on geographic location. In areas where damp, cold and frosty weather is usual, these birds need protection. In drier, colder areas they only suffer when exposed to subzero temperatures. Open water is a must for these and all waterfowl during cold weather.

Whistling ducks will nest on the ground in close cover, but favor a raised box. Ducklings of this family are particularly beautiful and become favorites in collections which are open to the public. Both parents look after young and will attack intruders; if the intruders are too large, they will try to lure it away by feigning a broken wing. Curiously, even half-fledged young display this characteristic if one of their siblings is picked up. As soon as distress whistles are heard, one or two young will run over, wings drooping and flapping and will gape and scream at the offender. I have seen Spotted, White-faced, Fulvous, Cuban, and Red-billed Whistling Ducks do this.

"Spotteds" lay up to 9 chalky, round eggs and incubate for 30 days. They are probably the rarest Whistlers in captivity, while the Javan runs a close second.

One of the most common is the Northern Red-billed or Black-bellied Whistling (or Tree) Duck (*D. autumnalis*). The closely related Southern Red-bill (*D. a. discolor*) is often kept alongside its northern cousin and, as in the wild, hybrids have occurred. In fact, years ago a pure bird of either species was difficult to find, especially in Europe.

They nest on the ground in a ground box or in an elevated box where they lay 14 eggs and incubate for 29 days. Ducklings display striking black and yellow hoop markings. These markings seem to disappear within 2 or 3 days, only the head retaining a stripe and the body markings merging into clearly defined black and yellow patches.

The Fulvous Whistling Duck (*D. bicolor*) is common in collections and has an immense range in the wild, which includes California, Texas, Mexico, Columbia, Brazil, Peru, Paraguay, North Argentina, East Africa, South Africa, Madagascar, India, Ceylon and Burma. Within this vast range there is no discernable change in color pattern.

Despite their subtropical range, Fulvous are among the hardier whistling ducks. Occasionally males are belligerent—especially yearling males that travel in a gang.

They use a variety of boxes, both ground and raised and will also nest in reeds or other cover on the ground. Clutch size is 12 eggs and incubation is 25 days.

The largest whistling or tree duck is the Cuban or Black-billed Whistling Duck (*Dendrocygna arborea*). These ducks are well represented in captivity and are known to have varying temperaments. Some have been known to kill other birds in captivity while others are docile.

Unfortunately they are under mounting pressure in the wild. Although officially protected, these birds are suffering from habitat loss, and other human influences. I have never seen a Cuban use an elevated box, though I am sure they are capable of this. Normally they choose a ground site or box where they lay 9 eggs, and incubation is 30 days.

The Plumed or Eyton's Whistling Duck (*D. eytoni*) is a tropical duck. One of the more attractive "Whistlers," they are rapidly becoming more common in captivity. Once an established pair begins to breed many young can be produced, but they seem slightly difficult to care for over the first few days. Eytons benefit from winter shelter and are not hardy. They use a variety of boxes—I have known them to use natural ground sites, boxes, elevated boxes, Shelduck burrows, even in one case an old nest built by Scarlet Ibis kept in the same aviary was used. Males can be belligerent, but usually only during the breeding season. They lay 10 eggs and incubate for 29 days.

Probably the least hardy, smallest, and to my eyes, most charming of all the Whistlers is the lovely little Javan Whistling Duck (*D. javanica*). They suffer badly from even mild winter conditions (such as in England) and must be sheltered accordingly. They probably have the unlucky status of being the second rarest of this family represented in captivity. Only a few American breeders have had propagational success with the Javan and even fewer British and Europeans.

Todd wonders why these birds should be so difficult to breed. It is baffling, but the only ones I experienced always seemed timid and nervous. I would like to see them fully winged in a group in a large flight aviary with no other Whistlers present. This way they may settle and become tame. On the other hand, maybe the presence of a pair of breeding Fulvous or Red-billed in a neighboring aviary may serve as a spur to production.

Javan use a variety of nesting places in the wild and average 9 eggs and incubate for 27 days.

There are 3 races of Wandering Whistling Ducks; an Australian race (*D. a. australis*), and Lesser Wandering (*D. a. pygmaea*, and East Indian (*D. a. arcuata*). In habit and coloration the Australian and Lesser are essentially the same.

The Lesser and Wandering have a tendency to hybridize with other ducks and as the 2 races are similar it is best to keep them separately. They are not hardy although I have kept specimens outdoors in England through winter without apparent upset. They are only slightly more numerous than Javans in captivity and breed sporadically. Normally *D. a. arcuata* is the more common representative in collections. They lay 8 eggs which are incubated for 28 days.

The last of this group and very popular with aviculturists is the White-faced Whistling Duck (*D. viduata*). These ducks are starting to be bred in large numbers after initially being quite rare. Pairs are very devoted and engage in mutual preening, a trait all Whistlers display, but none so readily as the White-faced. Generally pairs are docile, but small groups with excess males may be quite belligerent, going from fence to fence and annoying occupants of other pens.

They nest on the ground in a ground box and occasionally in an elevated box. Normal clutch size is 10 and incubation is 27 days.

21

Geese

As a group of rather specialized waterfowl, geese can be broken up into four categories; Grey Geese, Snow Geese, Black Geese and a small aberrant group. Only seven of the forty or so members of this family inhabit warm, neotropical climates. These are the Orinoco, Egyptian, Ne-Ne, Magpie, Cereopsis and the two races of Spur-winged Geese.

The majority of true geese are northern species, some nesting above 80° N latitude. Most high Arctic nesters are small, indeed as a general rule, the further north a goose nests, the smaller it is. This is the result of evolution. It enables the birds to take advantage of the sparse edible vegetation in the high tundra and thus competition for food is reduced. Also most of these geese have finely tuned breeding characteristics. In such a hostile environment, the breeding success of these birds is entirely dependent on a normal Arctic summer. A late spring, a cold early autumn, or a cold midsummer kill many young, ruining a breeding season. These geese arrive at their breeding grounds paired and ready to lay. Nests are quickly constructed and eggs laid. Most eggs hatch mid to late June. Again, this is a brilliant adaption to enable newly hatched chicks to feed for most of the 24-hour light cycle, which itself stimulates plant growth. The young goslings need to fledge and be ready to leave with their parents by mid-September at the latest—an incredibly short three-month period. Late-hatched birds perish after being abandoned by their parents, who are eager to leave for their wintering grounds, to avoid being trapped by the approaching winter.

These characteristics, also present in many northern ducks are often reflected in captivity. Some of the hardest to keep and propagate of all waterfowl are the high Arctic breeders. Day length in most collections is nowhere near peak day length in the Arctic and, as was mentioned earlier in the Baikal Teal section, artificial lighting can help in stimulating breeding activity.

Three important factors for successful breeding of Arctic waterfowl seem apparent.

First, lengthening daylight triggers the development of the sexual organs. Second, birds must be fit and not fat in order to breed successfully. In the wild, their long migration back to the breeding grounds achieves this as any fat built up during wintering is quickly lost. As has been mentioned, fat insulates a bird's sexual organs causing a lethargic response (if any) to the oncoming breeding period. This in itself can be a major factor in the production of infertile eggs. The third point is closely linked with the second and is probably more applicable to ducks than geese. For some reason, cold water stimulates breeding activity greatly. Newly arrived birds experience the cold meltwater of spring or the naturally cold sea water, and most collections that are successful at propagating these northern waterfowl tend to have abundant cold water and are located within more northerly latitudes. There seems to have been an alarming decline in the numbers and varieties of geese represented in captivity in America over the last twenty years. Some very common European species are almost unheard of in America. There are virtually no Greylag, Pink-footed, Swan Geese, European Whitefronts or Bean Geese represented in modern-day collections. Many of these varieties have been previously maintained and bred in America, but mysteriously, almost all representatives of these varieties are now gone. What so often happens with a species in captivity is that they become established, easy to breed and numerous. Slowly, a variety will become unattractive because of its ease of breeding and/or its cheap price and by this time the bloodlines of the species have become thoroughly diluted. All of a sudden, people are not rearing the numbers they used to and others are giving away their stock because of its boring familiarity. This seems to be a cyclic event and many species have suffered. The harsh and unrealistic laws governing importation of waterfowl do not foster enthusiasm for help with the re-establishment of a species in the wake of captive population crashes, and so, all aviculture loses.

Grey Geese

Probably the best known of the Grey Geese complex is the Greylag Goose (*Anser anser anser*). Greylags have been in captivity for centuries, and are the ancestors of many domesticated varieties such as the Toulouse, Embden, Sebastapol, Buff, Roman, etc. Certainly the Saxons employed them as "guard dogs" in ancient times. They are the only indigenous goose to Britain breeding in Scotland, the Shetlands and in the Western Isles. Generally they make wonderful parents and are easily maintained and propagated in captivity.

There are 2 races of Greylag, the more common (*A. a. anser*) being known as the Western Greylag while its close cousin is known as the Eastern Greylag (*A. a. rubrirostris*). This bird is larger, lighter colored and has a pink beak as opposed to the darker, smaller and orange-beaked western.

The Eastern variety is currently under some pressure in the wild. It was once quite common in captivity, but many breeders since seemed to have overlooked it (or hybridized it) and consequently they are not particularly well represented in collections in their pure form; some breeders having very questionable stock. It is probably represented better in European than in American collections.

Both of these geese hybridize readily with other birds so it is advised to keep groups on their own.

They lay 5 eggs and incubate for 28 days. Generally nests are well constructed and sometimes very cleverly hidden in loose cover or under bushes. Typically, the incubating female when approached will only leave the nest at the last minute, leaving herself and the nest's protection to the generally vigilant and pugnacious gander. However, if the gander isn't around, the female will lower her conspicuous orange or pink beak until it is tucked close against her neck, and even try and hide it in the nest material. If you walk around her, she will gradually rotate her head to keep the sides of her bright beak from giving her away. Whitefronts do this as well, and it may be that they are aware of their conspicuous facial or beak markings and actively attempt to camouflage themselves. Whether this is a cautious action or simply a "programmed" response is another matter altogether.

Another Grey Goose who is an ancestor of the Chinese and African varieties of domestic waterfowl, is the Swan Goose (*A. cygnoides*). Their incredibly long and straight bills do not serve as a particular adaption for specialized feeding habits but may represent a feature showing how prehistorically unchanged these birds are. Much stock in captivity has been hybridized with domestic varieties especially in America, where there may only be one or two birds of the pure strain left. Many of the best specimens of this goose exist in Europe.

Swan Geese utilize open ground or cover to nest. Unlike their Greylag and Whitefront counterparts, Swan Geese have a black bill, and so sitting females generally try to hide their bills by stretching their necks flat out along the ground and staying motionless.

They lay 5 eggs which are incubated for 28 days.

The Whitefront complex consists of 6 recognized races. Three races are well known to most aviculturists, these being the Pacific, Greenland and Lesser Whitefronts, and the European variety is well known overseas.

Whitefronts (like most geese) are flock birds, only splitting into pairs and establishing territories during the breeding season. Also, like most other geese, whitefronts can be kept in groups in pens large enough for individual pairs to take up breeding areas during the season. Geese need little more than grazing and the appropriate food at the right time of year to be maintained and propagated under captive conditions.

Two other races of Whitefronts which currently may number no more than 4,000 birds in total, are the Gambel's Whitefront

(*A. a. gambelli*) and the Tule Goose (*A. a. elgasi*). Both types are little known to most aviculturists.

I have been fortunate enough to propagate both these varieties and, as Todd also relates in his book, there are quite apparent differences between the two races.

Once you have seen a Tule Goose, you will immediately be struck by its size and darker overall coloring, as compared to its smaller, paler cousin, the Gambel.

Bob Elgas of Big Timber, Montana, was the first to breed both of these geese in captivity and had been fighting for recognition of the two races—originally they were considered the same bird.

It seems that the U.S. Fish and Wildlife Service, and the Alaska Department of Fish and Game is working to establish an appropriate management program for these geese, and because much of the breeding area in Alaska and the overwintering area in California are on state and federally controlled lands, the opportunity for proper control and management is excellent. Barring some unforeseen circumstance and in view of the current interest on their behalf, it would appear that the future of the California/Alaska race of Tule Geese is comparatively secure.

More aviculturists are breeding Tule Geese now, but it is still by no means a well-represented member of the White-front Goose family.

As with all waterfowl, care should be taken in order to maintain purity of species. Don't keep closely related species near each other; hybrids result! Most geese require good grazing and space during the nesting season. Don't crowd geese together in smaller pens, give them space, or keep then in pens in single pairs. Other than grass or greens of some sort, most geese can be successfully maintained on standard waterfowl fare, and most will nest on the ground, preferring to make their own nests, although it is always a good idea to make up a few nest sites incorporating some cover. When doing this, take advantage of natural cover if at all possible. Use logs, or parts of fallen trees, bushes, or build a wigwam (see Nesting Requirements chapter).

Although to my eye unattractive, old truck tires make a good base for a nest too!

	Average Clutch Size	Incubation Period (days)
Lesser *(Anser erythropus)*	6	25
European *(Anser albifrons albifrons)*	5	27
Greenland *(A. a. flavirostris)*	5	26
Pacific *(A. a. frontalis)*	5	25
Gambel's *(A. a. gambelli)*	Probably as above	
Tule *(A. a. elgasi)*	5	25

Another group within the Grey Goose family are the Bean Geese.

Most varieties commonly kept in Europe seldom appear in American collections.

Bean Geese are divided into two groups, those who breed at the Southern extent of their range in wooded habitats (Forest Bean Geese) and the Arctic nesters, known as Tundra Bean Geese.

The Forest group includes the Western, Johansen's and Middendorf's subspecies. The Tundra varieties are the Thick-billed and Russian forms. Visual differences between the races are slight and occur in beak shape and size, and overall body shape, size and color. My own experience with Bean Geese is limited to the Western, Russian, Thick-billed and Middendorf's varieties.

Bean Geese are no more difficult to maintain than any other goose, and the Western, Russian and Thick-billed will breed readily given adequate space and nesting cover. Obviously no one race should be mixed with another (as unfortunately many European strains of Thick-billed, Western and Russians have been) otherwise hybridization will occur.

Bean Geese utilize nesting cover and seem to like to be able to view the surroundings to the nest when incubating. Interestingly, females revert to either of the camouflage tricks mentioned earlier. When approached, they will either stretch their necks out along the ground and lay completely still or try and hide their yellow, patterned beaks in the same fashion as White-fronted Geese.

BEAN GEESE

	Average Clutch Size	Incubation Period (days)
Western *(Anser fabilis fabilis)*	6	28
Russian *(A. f. rossicus)*	5	28
Thick-billed *(A. f. serrirostris)*	5	28
Middendorfs *(A. f. middendorfi)*	Probably as above	
Johansen's *(A. f. johanseni)*	Probably as above	

The Pink-footed Goose (*Anser brachyrhynchus*) at first sight looks rather like a small, miscolored Bean Goose, but it merits its own specific race. Again, Pink-footed Geese are better repre-sented in European than in American collections. Generally they are peaceful birds, but I have come across the odd gander who wasn't impressed by anyone else's size and would be quite sav-age on occasions. Interestingly, a blonde or silver form that occurs in captivity on occasion, is being nurtured (out of pure interest) in England by at least two breeders. Pink-feet utilize a surprising diversity of nesting sites, from totally enclosed, mini-ature sheds to completely open ground surrounded by ½-inch high vegetation.

They average 4 eggs which are incubated for about 26 days.

Snow Geese

Snow Geese are among the more common geese kept in captivity. They are quite spectacular and noisy on the wing and a pure delight to behold when flying—often at great heights. There are three varieties of Snow Goose, the Greater (*Anser caerulescens atlanticus*) which migrate from their Greenland and eastern Ca-nadian Arctic island breeding grounds down along the eastern American seaboard, and the Lesser Snow (*A. c. caerulescens*) that migrates from its Siberian and central Canadian breeding areas to the Mexican Gulf and Louisiana.

The Lesser Snow has a blue phase often called the Blue

Goose. The markings range from blotchy patches of blue-gray feathers over the bird's back, to a completely blue-gray bird, often with white underparts and a white head. Lesser Snows have a slender beak, while the greater has a substantially thick beak especially noticeable in the massive upper mandible. Unfortunately very few of the greater variety in captivity are pure greater snows, having been crossed extensively with Lessers.

Both varieties are ground nesters in captivity—favoring some surrounding cover to their next site. Like the Bean Geese, sitting females seem to like a clear view around the nest. Logs piled and laid in a V-shape make excellent nesting sites as do tree trunks that have rotted in the center leaving a ring. The ganders love to perch up on top, ready to defend their mates. Snow Geese can be very belligerent in captivity and care should be taken not to mix the races. Also, don't include too many other types of geese otherwise countless fights and beatings will take place. Full-winged birds have a great advantage over pinioned ones when fighting so don't mix other geese with flying birds unless you know they can take care of themselves. Snow Geese average 5 eggs and incubate for between 23 and 25 days.

The third member and the smallest of the Snow Geese is the lovely little Ross' Goose (*Anser rossii*). These are favorite geese with many breeders and are best kept in small flocks. They have pleasant personalities and so can suffer from bullying by larger birds. There may be a blue phase but it is possible the specimens observed in the wild are hybrids between Ross' and Blue Geese. Ross' Geese can be difficult to breed but I feel this is probably because of the lack of bloodline outcrossing in the breed, leading to pairs with a lethargic response to breeding and having genetically weak lines. It cannot be stressed too strongly that related birds, after several generations, will be difficult to manage or breed, and their young will not generally be hardy. Unfortunately, very few breeders I know of take pains to segregate individual broods from different parental blood lines. Most "pairs" sold are brother and sister, and a great many small flocks are descendants of one or two original pairs. Care must be taken when buying waterfowl to get as many birds from different strains as is possible. Adults should be color ringed for ease of identification during the breeding season and eggs marked so that resulting young can be reared separately, ensuring that when the young are sold they can honestly be called unrelated. Ross Geese will generally nest in fairly open conditions but occasionally favor cover if provided. They lay an average of 4 eggs which have a short 22-day incubation period.

One of the more maritime species of geese is the Emperor Goose (*Anser canagicus*). Many breeders in Europe and America propagate these birds and they are firm favorites in many collections. Not only do they have an attractive gray-blue plumage, which barred with black and white gives a striking effect, but the white head, pink and black beak and yellow legs make a pleasing contrast in color. They are inquisitive geese and generally quite docile, though well able to defend themselves. Their appearance is stocky and one only has to pick up an Emperor to see how strong they are. Left fully winged, they are magnificent birds in the air, flying with speed, strength and great precision. They are (in the wild) more omnivorous than other geese, consuming shellfish and other marine organisms along with quantities of sea weed and salt grass.

In captivity, Emperors will nest in open conditions but nests built in the same manner as for Snow Geese are readily utilized. They often "dump nest," depositing their curious elongated eggs in other birds' nests. Generally they lay 6 eggs and incubate for 24 days.

The last of the Grey Goose and Snow Goose complex is the Bar-headed Goose (*Anser indicus*).

This is a goose used to high altitudes both in nesting and during its migration flights. They are Asian in origin, and part of their migration flight takes them over the Himalayan mountains. They have been seen at heights in excess of 29,000 feet, and one wonders just how these birds compensate for the lack of oxygen at these heights. Their breeding areas are often over 12,000 feet in elevation and so it can be assumed that goslings must be hardy.

Bar-heads in captivity can be notorious hybridizers, but their general nature is quite inoffensive. Displaying birds can be heard some distance away by their peculiar moaning. Someone once described the sound as resembling a swarm of bees, which is really quite accurate.

Bar-heads are well known to aviculturists and breed freely. Nests are constructed on the ground (although they apparently will nest in trees in the wild) usually in some sort of cover. Six eggs are normal, and incubation lasts 27 days.

Black Geese

This group of geese is comprised of the Canada complex, the Brents, Red-breasted, Barnacle and Ne-Ne.

The largest group by far consists of the 11 varieties of Canada Geese. Many aviculturists keep and breed Canadas and unfortunately many races have become hybridized under captive conditions. In the wild some races overlap and undoubtedly hybrids result. In fact, it would not be too far fetched to speculate that, at some stage, certain races of wild hybrids set up their own group territories and we now know them as definable subspecies. Consider the enormous variation in color in Cackling Geese.

These 11 varieties are probably the most difficult to visually distinguish of all the geese. The largest variety in this group is the Giant Canada (*Branta canadensis maxima*).

A good "giant" should average 15 pounds plus in weight, have a thick, long neck and an elongated body. They should also have proportionately long legs, and a broad white cheek patch extending up behind the eye and in some cases meeting at the back of the head. The most common markings are the white eyebrows found in this race (which actually can also be present in other races), but it does not necessarily mean that you have a good giant just because it has white eyebrows. I have seen many so-called giants which have been made and I doubt whether more than a handful of breeders have pure specimens.

The Atlantic Canada (*B. c. canadensis*) is probably the best-known goose in the world. Since their introduction to Britain and Europe their numbers have rapidly multiplied and in many areas they are now a pest. Slightly smaller and lighter on the breast than the giant, the Atlantic never shows a white neck ring.

It is less stocky in appearance, but even so is a formidable bird when defending its nest or young.

The Moffitt's Canada (*B. c. moffitti*) is about the same size and color (maybe slightly darker on the breast) as the Atlantic but its main distinguishing feature is the long, very slim, almost snakelike neck. Many wild Moffitt's have been interbred with feral Atlantic Canada's and in central and midwestern states quite a few hybrids occur.

The Todd's or Interior Canada (*B. c. interior*) is smaller than the Moffitt's, and has a pronounced uniformity to its coloring. It is grayer in appearance both on its underparts and back, and has a shorter neck.

The Lesser Canada (*B. c. parvipes*) is smaller than the Todd's, and in general resembles a small Atlantic. This race actually varies in color as much as the Cackling Goose but most captive specimens of pure origin seem to be light breasted and display varying degrees of neck ring thickness.

The Dusky Canada (*B. c. occidentalis*) is the easiest of the Canadas to distinguish as it has a overall smokey chestnut color. However, even these birds in captivity display grayer coloring showing their dubious backgrounds. Adults weigh around 9 pounds in weight, and have always struck me as one of the more belligerent races of Canada when in captivity.

The slightly larger and lighter-colored Vancouver Canada (*B. c. fulva*) is becoming a rather rare bird in captivity. Good specimens are almost impossible to find in Europe, although American breeders have one or two good blood lines. Again this is the result of interbreeding between subspecies. I have always believed that hybrids should never be allowed to exist and concerned professional aviculturists should never allow this situation to arise. Closely related species or subspecies that are notorious for their hybridization qualities should be well separated. Even in areas where visiting waterfowl occur in spring, steps can be taken to ensure the visitors don't strike up relations with other stock.

Another rare race of Canadian Goose in captivity is the Taverner's (*B. c. taverneri*). Generally they are smaller and darker

241

than the Lesser and have a more elongated body, with the primaries (when folded), trailing over the tail.

The Richardson's Canada (*B. c. hutchinsii*) is around the same size as the Tavener's, but appreciably lighter on the breast. They generally display a white neck ring, and have the same sort of grayish coloring on the back that the Interior displays. Their necks are rather short and stubby and happily many good examples exist in captivity.

The smallest, and maybe one of the commoner Canadas in captivity is the Cackling Goose (*B. c. minima*). Occasionally they exhibit the same white eyebrows as the giant, and usually display a white neck ring of varying width, although occasionally it may not be present. Their color should be a dark grayish chestnut similar to the Dusky but examples can be found that are as gray on the breast as are the interiors. Groups in captivity can be somewhat disturbing to other small geese as they are incessantly active often dominating other geese such as Ross', Red-breasted and Brents. They also are well known for their hybridization qualities.

The last of the Canadas is to my mind the loveliest of all, the little Aleutian Canada Goose (*B. c. leucopareia*).

They slightly resemble Cackling or Richardson's Geese, being lighter colored, a sort of overall gray-brown. They have the same sort of short neck as the Richardson, but the white cheek patches culminate in a much darker and more expansive black chin area. Always prominent is the white neck ring. Their bills are short (though perhaps not as much so as the Cackling) and always appear more delicate and slightly elongated probably because of the prominent nail at the bill's end.

Their wild breeding range is restricted to no more than two of the Aleutian Island chain (Buldir being the main one) and the population once dropped to 300 in 1963. The most chronic damage was done as a result of the introduction of foxes to their island breeding strongholds—Buldir being the only exception.

Luckily the U.S. Fish and Wildlife Service established breeding groups on the mainland and now are annually rearing hundreds of geese. A quota of these are now being reintroduced. They remain the hardest of the Canadas to propagate, although the 4 or 5 pairs that I have had or seen, bred fairly easily (especially when given artificial lighting during Spring).

Another rare goose in the wild with some affinity to the Canadas is the Hawaiian Goose or Ne-Ne (*Branta sandvicensis*). These geese are believed to be remnants of a landlocked variety of Canadas possibly originating from storm-blown stragglers from a mainland U.S.A. population. Once exceedingly rare (33 in 1953), these birds are now widely kept and bred and very familiar to most aviculturists. They were first bred in captivity in the early 1820s (Lord Derby 1823) but by the beginning of the twentieth century had virtually disappeared in collections. Their plight in the wild was recognized in the 1930s, and by 1951 various bodies such as the Wildfowl Trust started receiving wild caught birds. Their breeding success in captivity was not far short of phenomenal, with the result that introductions back to their former breeding ranges in the Hawaiian Islands have started to become successful.

They are incredibly tame birds by nature, displaying almost suicidal stupidity on occasions.

Their environment in the wild consists of volcanic lava slopes with little standing water, and a look at their feet shows how much their webbing has receded in order to allow them a more terrestrial life. They mate on land or close by water (occasionally in it). This seems to be a feature of land-oriented geese (such as the Cereopsis and Magpie), although most geese are quite capable of mating on land and producing fertile eggs in captivity. Ne-Ne nest very early in the year and must be provided protection from the elements. Eggs should be collected as soon as they are laid in colder climates to avoid freezing.

The Canada family generally are ground nesters and nesting cover helps immeasurably with their successful propagation. Races should be penned separately so hybridization does not occur, and careful inspection of stock before buying is advised. Standard grain and protein pellet diet are ample, combined with good grazing, decreasing in the grain part of the diet toward the breeding season.

	Average Clutch Size	Incubation Period (days)
Giant *(Branta canadensis maxima)*	5	28
Atlantic *(B. c. canadensis)*	5	28
Moffitt's *(B. c. moffitti)*	5	28
Interior *(B. c. interior)*	5	27
Lesser *(B. c. parvipes)*	5	27
Dusky *(B. c. occidentalis)*	5	28
Vancouver *(B. c. fulva)*	5	27
Taverner's *(B. c. taverneri)*	5	27
Richardson's *(B. c. hutchinsii)*	5	26
Cackling *(B. c. minima)*	5	26
Aleutian *(B. c. leucopareia)*	5	25
Ne-Ne *(B. sandvicensis)*	5	29

Barnacle Geese (*Branta leucopsis*) are probably quite closely related to Canada Geese and may represent a European version of an otherwise totally American race. Barnacle Geese have long been propagated under captive conditions and many myths and legends exist in Europe about them. Their breeding range includes Greenland, Spitsbergen and Arctic Russia. Researchers at the Wildfowl Trust have found 3 distinct nesting groups who almost never mix as they winter in 3 geographically separate areas.

In captivity, Barnacle Geese nest colonially, vigorously defending their nesting areas. When kept with other geese make sure that their pen mates are large enough to be able to look after themselves in the face of an attack by an irate Barnacle gander. Normally they lay 5 eggs which are incubated for 25 days.

One of the most sought after and beautiful of all geese is the lovely Red-breasted Goose (*Branta ruficollis*). Incredibly, this bird is still a legal game species over part of its range even though its status is far from safe, there being only some 15,000 to 20,000 birds in the wild. Increasing pressure from oil exploration and subsequent activity within the Red-breasted's breeding range is causing further concern to naturalists.

Their remarkable coloration is actually good camouflage as anyone trying to find a Red-breasted nest in tall grass in captivity can testify. In the barren tundra however they are fairly conspicuous, but here this little goose has another trick. It appears that a close bond exists between nesting peregrine falcons and the Red-breasted Goose. Apparently they both alert each other to danger, the more vigilant geese spotting predators, and the fierce little falcon delaying an oncoming arctic fox with aerial dive bombing giving geese and goslings a chance to flee to safety.

With the use of DDT the decline in the numbers of falcons has resulted in a decline in the numbers of Red-breasted Geese, which underlines the point that many wild animals exist in a more delicate ecosystem than we imagine.

In captivity many strains of Red-breasted, especially in America, remain unproductive—probably due to weak blood lines. European collections fare much better in this respect and at least two breeders in England turn out over 100 young birds each per year. One collection I worked in England had females producing three clutches per year—but only after a lot of experimentation with diets. In fact 4 females produced 42 eggs in 1980, a staggering 10.5 eggs per bird per season! The earliest eggs were laid in mid-May and the last in mid-August.

The usual clutch is 3 to 5 eggs once a year, and incubation is relatively short—around 23 days. These geese do well in small flocks and benefit from being settled and fairly tame. Nests may be situated in long grass or out in the open. It is advisable to allow a pair breeding for the first time to hatch something (perhaps a few Cackling goslings) as it reassures the parents and gives greater confidence for future seasons.

The 3 races of Brent or Brant Geese represent a single very marine species. They spend a lot of their winter foraging along the shoreline and feeding on shellfish, invertebrates and various salty seashore grasses. They are equipped with efficient salt extraction glands as most of their life entails living and feeding on or near salt water.

During hard weather Brents often come inland to graze on stubble fields and in Europe can impose severe damage to early crops such as winter wheat and barley. They have long been a hunted species though why I can't imagine. The only two I ever ate were positively disgusting!

They are highly prized among aviculturists and are extremely difficult to propagate.

Probably the easiest Brents to breed are the Pacific or Black Brent (*Branta bernicula orientalis*), although the term "easy" is a relative fashion. Brents are among the most northerly of all breeding birds. They are easily kept in areas where good grazing is available. They eat grass almost entirely, ignoring conventional diets. This can cause problems as parasitic worms are ingested and birds need regular worming especially in autumn.

The Pacific Brent is a dark-bellied race, with gray/white flanks and a prominent white neck ring. There are many dubious specimens in Europe but a few breeders maintain and breed good lines. It is best to keep Brents in small groups of 15 to 20 birds by themselves or with pen mates that do not bully them. (Ross' Geese make good pen mates).

Pacific Brents lay about 4 eggs and incubate for 22–23 days. Nests are usually out in the open with no surrounding cover. The down produced to line the nest is among the densest and softest of all waterfowl and clings together even better than Eider down. Sitting females display amazing courage (or stupidity), sitting tight and hissing at intruders. Likewise, the gander attacks anything coming near the nest. I once watched a Pacific Brent gander repelling a very large rabbit that decided that the vegetation surrounding the Brent's nest was the best in the pen. The male attacked with flailing wings and ripped beakfuls of fur from the unfortunate rabbit. Eventually the Brent attached its beak to the rabbit's ear and the terrified rabbit simply cowered on the ground squealing and crying until the Brent let go. The male raced back to the female in triumph and a full 5 minutes of cackling terminated the encounter. Interestingly, this pair shared incubation duties. I only allowed them to sit for 10 days on Cackling Goose eggs, the Brent eggs being placed in an incubator. Then I switched the eggs for a chipping clutch and the Brent hatched and reared 4 little Cacklers. As it was their first time breeding I wanted them to rear something, but just as importantly, I didn't want the female Brent sitting for too long. Incubating females lose weight and are prone to predators, especially in such exposed locales and as they are such valuable birds I had no intention of letting this happen.

The Russian or Dark-bellied Brent (*B. b. bernicula*) is hardly represented in American collections and only rarely so even in Europe where it is a common wintering goose.

They have remained the most stubbornly unproductive of all of the Brents but this may simply be a result of the lack of work done with them in captivity. I had a laying female, who had 4 very active male suitors. Although she laid, I doubt whether any of the males copulated with her as she was persistently being bothered by first one and then the others throughout the season.

The Russian race is very dark both on the belly and flanks and the white neck ring rarely meets at the back of the neck, although it can appear to be very broad in the front. Nesting habits are almost identical to the Pacific.

The third race, the Atlantic Brent (*B. b. hrota*) appears at first sight rather similar to the Pacific. However, they normally differ in being very light on the belly and the neck ring is quite narrow and small, often not meeting at the front or back of the neck thus appearing only as a side stripe.

There are far more Atlantic Brent in America than in Europe at present, but they appear to be almost as difficult as the Russian to propagate.

I was fortunate enough to work with a breeding pair while in England with Christopher Marler. This pair had been hand raised from "wild" eggs. They never got along with the other Brent we had, and so as soon as the male started courting a female, I caught them and put them in a large pen on their own. They subsequently laid in typical Brent fashion (out in the middle of nowhere!) and I gave them some Cackling Goose eggs to hatch. Only one egg was infertile (the first egg) the other three turning out to be females. (This pair is currently lodged with a good friend in Northern Ireland along with two other breeding pairs.)

This variety is bred regularly by Eldon Pace in Nova Scotia. His flock of 20 birds nest communally and several trios and one male mated to 3 females occur with all females producing young regularly. They lay 3 to 4 eggs and incubate for 24 days.

Aberrant Geese

Probably the strangest of all geese, and maybe even of waterfowl generally, is the Australian Magpie or Pied Goose (*Anseranas semipalmata*).

No one quite knows to which group of waterfowl this goose belongs. Some have suggested affinities with geese, others with screamers. The latter suggestion is based on feather-protein analysis. I have had the opportunity to work with both Screamers and Magpie Geese, and if an affinity exists anywhere, I think it is between these two.

Magpie Geese are perfectly at home perching in trees. On the wing, they resemble enormous buzzards (as do Screamers), their peculiar round wings and fingerlike primaries giving a bird-of-prey look.

Rather like the Ne-Ne they have only partially webbed feet (less webbing than the Ne-Ne in fact) although they can swim awkwardly in water.

Unlike other waterfowl, these geese molt gradually and so are never left flightless. Other physical peculiarities are the curious knob on the head, and the rather large, naked face, a trait swans possess. They also possess a rather pungent smell which can be detected in the wild at quite some distance.

Males may take 1, 2 or even 3 females and they remain as a breeding group. A large clutch, averaging about 6 eggs, is laid. Both parents share incubation duties for 25–28 days.

Young Magpie Geese are endearing in their ugliness, and again, unlike other waterfowl, are fed initially by their parents (another trait shared with Screamers). Hand-reared young can become incredibly tame.

Adults may attain great ages in captivity even before they breed (18 or 19 not being uncommon) although in the wild, birds probably breed at 4 years old.

The Magpie has never been well represented in captivity. It was first bred in captivity in 1945 at the San Diego Zoological

Park. Subsequently Delacour bred them at Cleres in France, and the Wildfowl Trust produced young from their trio.

They are not particularly hardy and suffer from frost bite unless perches or deep, clean straw is provided. Fully winged birds do better, and should be kept in a large flight aviary. A nesting platform of twigs and grass should be provided, and even if birds are not pinioned a climbing ladder to the nest is advisable. They can be maintained on wheat and protein pellets, although the addition of pond weed and lettuce and some smaller seed matter (canary seeds) is much appreciated.

Another Australian oddity comes in the shape of the Cereopsis Goose (*Cereopsis novae-hollandiae*). Luckily this goose is well known to (and revered by) many breeders. It has connections with both geese and Sheldgeese.

The Cereopsis is a formidable bird in many ways. Armed with a powerful green bill, long and sharp claws and a bony knob at the elbow of the wing, these geese can take care of themselves in a most savage way. Traditionally they are kept in pairs in their own pens and it is advisable to locate the feed bowl close to the front of the pen—going in to feed them can be a painful business!

In the wild, they were persecuted by sheep farmers. Apparently their droppings have a pungent odor which deters sheep from feeding in areas where Cereopsis have been grazing. However, their numbers are quite secure at present.

In captivity they construct a good-sized nest in cover early in the Northern Hemisphere breeding season. Cereopsis may nest as early as January or February so care must be taken to provide adequate shelter for females. Where cold nights are experienced eggs must not be left in the nest for fear of freezing. I would not recommend females be left sitting; in cold northerly climates weight loss is accelerated in cold weather and this can bring on many ailments. (I find it most unfair and callous to treat a bird in this fashion). An average of 5 eggs are laid and while the female alone apparently incubates for 35 days in the wild, I know of at least half a dozen captive pairs that share incubation.

Also it is believed that the adult female "oils" her goslings as they are reputed not to have functional preen glands before

249

they are 2 weeks old. This may be because of their highly terrestrial existence and it is feasible that many wild Cereopsis goslings never swim or bathe until they are this old. However, take a 3-day-old Cereopsis and drop it into a pond for 10 minutes twice a day, and the preen gland functions adequately. Many breeders believe that most waterfowl young seem to be unable to oil themselves. My own findings are that when reared "dry" and not exposed to swimming water this is true, but putting them in water for controlled periods triggers the preen gland to function. This topic is discussed at greater length in the Rearing Section.

The 2 races of Spurwinged Geese, the White Spurwing (*Plectropterus gambensis*) and the Black (*P. g. niger*) are another baffling oddity to the avian student. Some biologists suggest an affinity with Shelduck based on skeletal structure. Others base observations on external physical traits, such as the cranial knob, bald face and bill, very reminiscent of the Magpie goose. When you look at young Spurwings they closely resemble Fulvous Whistling ducklings, both in pattern and physical structure.

Personally, I don't see them as perching ducks, more as an abberant species as is the Magpie and Cereopsis. They are capable of perching but then so are many other waterfowl not placed in the perching duck family although they are physically acceptable for membership.

Spurwings are poorly represented in collections and few pairs breed. They are certainly not the most attractive waterfowl proposition to a lot of breeders both from a cosmetic point of view or from a character standpoint. To many aviculturists they appear as large, powerful, ugly and vicious birds. Personally, they fascinate me. A breeding pair of Black Spurwings I used to look after could amuse me almost any day of the year with their antics. I learned at least 6 distinct vocal patterns in the female to the male's 3. Their seemingly long pre-nesting courtship would start in December the female laying at the very end of February or first two weeks of March. Curiously, the male was never quite ready and generally only managed to fertilize the last 2 eggs. The female would then lay again in June, when the male was sexually very active. This pair were very good around other birds sharing a pen with various species of ducks and geese. Only when we purchased another pair which were housed 2 pens away did the male become vicious. He climbed a 6-foot dividing fence with an overhang at the top and killed the other male. Spurwings have enormous wing spurs up to 2 inches in length, and this male put one of these lethal instruments straight through the head of the other male. The female was very long pinioned and could fly quite well. She would often fly down to the river (some 2 miles away) and rob surprised fishermen of their maggots! She would also fly from her favorite pen right down the length of the collection (400 yds.) to nest. The male would follow her climbing all the pen fences in between! I never once saw either of them perching either on fallen logs or even on gate tops.

They were hardy birds, but I still provided them with deep straw under bushes in winter as their long legs are susceptible to frostbite.

The female would nest either in an old barrel or under a large pampas grass clump. She became amazingly adept at creeping away from the nest without my seeing her. She was also difficult to spot before she laid, as the rather copious wing coverts disguised the characteristic bulge at the vent indicating her imminent condition. She averaged 9 eggs which were very reminiscent of Whistling Duck eggs, round and hard, and incubated for 32 days. The young resembled Fulvous Whistling Ducklings and quickly became my favorite goslings. Interestingly these goslings seemed loathe to feed until I hand-fed them. This may or may not be a Spurwing peculiarity as Mike Lubbock told me he had no such problems with his White Spurwing goslings.

The adults were maintained on wheat and protein pellets with canary seeds and occasionally brown bread and dog chow. I advise separate pens for Spurwings unless you know they are a gentle pair.

The White Spurwing acts in much the same way, and can be maintained like the Black. Their nesting habits are essentially the same. (The Egyptian, Andean, Kelp, Ashy-headed, Ruddy-headed, Greater and Lesser Magellan, Orinoco and Abyssinian Blue-wing are included at the end of the sheldgeese section).

22

Shelducks

As a family, shelduck represent a rather large, aggressive and intermediately developed group of waterfowl with distinct marine tendencies.

They possibly represent a link between sheldgeese and ducks proper, and as a family have the same characteristics in size and weight and the same nesting tendencies.

The smallest and nonmarine of the family Tadornini, are the two races of Radjah Shelduck, the Australian or Red-backed (*Tadorna radjah rufitergum*) and the Moluccan or Black-backed (*Tadorna radjah*). Not only are they smaller in stature but they tend to choose tree cavities or elevated boxes in which to nest.

Once they start breeding they produce prodigious numbers of young. Normally they are kept in their own pens as they can be aggressive to other ducks. They benefit from winter shelters and perches on which they can sleep and escape the frost. Most shelduck are omnivorous and Radjahs are no exception. Normal fare is wheat and pellets, however they take to dog chow well and floating seeds such as millet. I have seen them eat small minnows on occasion, and if this diet trait can be fostered and catered for, it would likely be an excellent additional food item.

Radjahs lay about 9 eggs and their incubation period is 30 days.

Of the 6 races of shelduck in the world, one of the most aggressive is the Australian (*Tadorna tadornoides*). Probably not quite as well represented in collections worldwide as the others of this family, they are by no means rare.

A very marine shelduck, the female will often take her newly hatched brood to sea, and quite often the sea will be in no mood to receive them. I have seen film of day-old shelducklings leaping 30 feet from a cliff ledge into a very choppy sea—the mother encouraging them all the time a little distance away.

If the quickest way from nest site to the feeding area is found to be by land, she will take them this way, but if it is quicker by sea then she chooses this often perilous path.

I have not seen enough pairs with young to observe whether the male participates in brood care. Certainly on film I have seen males guarding and driving off intruders, but never being let too close to the brood by the mother. I once saw a pair in captivity with a brood, and the male was definitely not being barred from brood protection—the keeper even telling me he once saw the male brooding the young. However, these are casual observations and so no special interest ought to be attached to this behavior. The females will form creches of young and depart to feed with their still sexually active mates.

In the wild, Australian Shelduck utilize an old rabbit burrow or cave where they lay 9 eggs and incubate for 30 days. In captivity, one of the best nesting boxes is a large square ground box dug into a bank and provided with a large pipe for an entrance thus mimicking a rabbit burrow (see nest boxes).

Sitting females emit a loud "hissing" noise when disturbed at the nest, presumably searing off the intruder by making it think there is a large reptile present in the darkness of the nest burrow.

They are hardy birds, and must be given their own pen or aviary because of their pugnacious behavior. In a full-winged state they are skilled perchers, an ability which undoubtedly saves their feet from frost damage although shelducks as a group, are not as susceptible to this malady as are Whistling Ducks for example. A diet of wheat and pellets is sufficient, but like Radjahs, if dog chow is available they do seem to enjoy it.

Wheat and dog chow fed in a pan of salt water is beneficial in keeping their salt extraction glands operating correctly. They often feed in heavily salted pools in the wild, and are seen with their beaks encrusted in dried salt.

The other 4 races of shelduck are very common in collections and because their behavior and breeding habits have been documented many times previously I will not spend too much time on them. Suffice to say they can be maintained in exactly the same fashion as the Australian with the possible exception of the European variety (*Tadorna*). Due to their smaller size and less vicious attitude they can be kept alongside other ducks.

The other family members are the New Zealand or Paradise Shelduck (*Tadorna variegata*), the Ruddy Shelduck (*Tadorna ferruginea*) and the Cape Shelduck (*Tadorna cana*). Average clutch size and incubation periods are as follows:

SHELDUCKS

	Average Clutch Size	Incubation Period (days)
European *(Tadorna tadorna)*	8	30
Cape *(T. cana)*	9	30
Paradise *(T. variegata)*	10	30
Ruddy *(T. ferruginea)*	9	28
Australian *(T. tadornoides)*	9	30
Red-backed Radjah *(T. radjah rufitergum)*	9	30
Black-backed Radjah *(T. radjah)*	9	30

23

Crested Ducks

The 2 races of crested ducks represent a midway development between shelducks and dabbling ducks. They have some behavioral characteristics and anatomical similarities to both parties. They may even have some close relatives currently classified within the dabbling duck family. Certainly the Marbled Teal resembles the Crested Ducks, being an almost identical scaled down replica, even having the same sort of display as the Crested Duck. Another duck, the Bronze-wing could well be classified alongside them.

The 2 races of crested ducks are the Patagonian (*Lophonetta specularioides specularioides*) and the Andean (*L. s. alticola*). The chief differences are that the Patagonian is larger, darker and has a red eye, whereas its smaller, lighter Andean cousin has a yellow-orange eye.

Unfortunately, some stock has been hybridized, so care should be taken when buying a pair. Both varieties nest on the ground, in cover or occasionally in a box where they lay 6 eggs and incubate for 30 days. Like shelduck they are very aggressive and so should be given their own pen. They are quite hardy but prolonged subzero temperatures can cause them much discomfort so shelter should be provided in northern locations. If anything, I have found the Andean marginally more hardy than the Patagonian. This may just be a reflection of the slightly different wild locations they inhabit. The Patagonian is more marine. The Andean is only occasionally observed along the seashore and favors the lakes of the "alti-plano"—the high plateau.

24

Sheldgeese

Sheldgeese represent a rather specialized and highly terrestrial family of waterfowl. Their representatives come from southern South America, with closely affiliated relatives in Africa (the Abyssinian Blue-winged Goose and Egyptian Goose). Another relative, the Orinoco Goose is more of a specialized tropical sheldgoose.

Most sheldgeese are extremely territorial in the breeding season, and become quite savage to other birds. Most are grazers, consuming large quantities of grass and in mild, wet climates need to be watched for parasitic worm build-up.

Probably the most marine of all this family is the Kelp Goose (*Chloephaga hybrida*) which is currently recognized in two forms, the birds from the Falkland Islands (*C. h. malvinarum*) being larger, and in the female, having more pronounced barring than their Patagonian cousins (*C. h. hybrida*).

Kelp Geese have only rarely been kept, and currently there are none in captivity. They have proved very delicate, being especially susceptible to respiratory infections. The San Diego Zoo managed to keep a pair for many years, and Christopher Marler in England kept a pair in very good health for 7 years. Interestingly, the mild, wet climate in England should have been a much harder climate to keep these geese in, but for Christopher Marler, one essential diet provision kept them so well. This was the way in which Christopher fed greens, such as lettuce or cabbage in iodized salt water. Here again, it appears that these delicate marine species can be kept successfully if fed with the addition of salt—especially iodized salt—as a lot of sea vegetation has high amounts of iodine present in its make up.

At the Wildfowl Trust in England, we received some eggs from the Falkland Islands and hatched and reared some young. They were not especially difficult, and were reared mainly on a hard floor. This may not have been necessary but sadly we never found out for certain as a fox managed to get into their aviary and kill them all just as they were fledging.

Unfortunately these geese will probably stay a virtual nonexistent commodity in collections until some sort of sanity is injected into laws governing egg and adult importation.

In the wild, Kelp Geese nest on cliff ledges or tussock grass close to the high tide line and lay an average of 5 eggs which have a 30-day incubation period.

Another member of this group is the high-altitude-dwelling Andean Goose (*Chloephaga melanoptera*) of South America. In the wild, they can readily be found living above 10,000 foot elevation, which would seem to suggest that they are hardy creatures. However, I have seen adults become quite distressed even in the relatively mild winter climate of England. I can only imagine that, like a lot of animals that live in high altitude, or cooler, drier climates, the addition of moisture to the cold will only make them more uncomfortable.

In captivity, they can be downright vicious to other birds, and their own species. All sheldgeese can be belligerent to a point, but the Andean seems to be in a class of its own. I would recommend that all sheldgeese have their own pens, especially the Andean goose. They lay 5 to 10 eggs in a nest that can either be on the ground or in cover, or sometimes they will take advantage of a ground located barrel or some similar structure that affords a little cover. (I have heard of pairs using a large box that was a foot or two off the ground, but this is not normal.) The female incubates alone for 30 days.

Two of the larger and most aggressive of the South American

sheldgeese are the two types of Magellan Geese—The Greater Magellan (*C. picta leucoptera*) and the Lesser Magellan (*C. p. picta*). They are both quite well known to waterfowl breeders.

Interestingly, there are two distinct color forms (on mainland South America) of the Lesser. Some birds are completely barred all the way from flank to flank including the belly, whereas others have white bellies, and barred sides, resembling the Greater, although, of course, smaller in size.

Some writers are of the opinion that the two mainland forms constitute two races with the Greater Magellan of the Falkland Islands being a larger variant of the mainland white bellied form. Others are of the opinion that all mainland birds are Lessers, and those on the Falklands (and the few introduced to South Georgia) are Greaters.

In captivity, both varieties have been interbred but young males from crosses of Greaters and Lessers seem to resemble the mainland light form of the Lesser.

Both varieties are good grazers and are easily maintained being very hardy birds. They tend to nest quite early in the year, March to May being normal.

Usually, they are kept in their own pens because of their pugnacious behavior toward other birds, although, like some swans, some pairs seem quite docile.

They favor a sheltered nest site, many breeders provide a large kennel or barrel for the female to lay in.

Clutches are normally around 5 to 8 eggs, and incubation about 30 days.

They have been ruthlessly persecuted on mainland South America by sheep owners as they are thought to compete for grazing. However, it seems more likely that the short-cropped grass the sheep leave behind, is more palatable to the birds. Undoubtedly some of the Greaters on the Falklands have also been shot, but nothing like the amount destroyed on the mainland. Consequently, the Lessers are becoming slightly more restricted to certain areas—but within these strongholds populations do not seem to be in any danger. Like most sheldgeese they do not need a large expanse of water—a simple

259

washing pool being quite sufficient.

The Ashy-headed Goose (*Chloephaga poliocephala*) and the Ruddy-headed Goose (*C. rubidiceps*) are superficially similar with a difference in head color and an overall chestnut gray barring in the Ruddy-head, rather than the white belly and chestnut breast of the Ashy-head.

The Ashy-head is probably better represented in captivity than is the Ruddy-head, who in the wild is severely threatened on mainland South America. The Falkland Island population fares much better and even the *tete-a-tete* between the British and Argentineans does not seem to have taken any toll.

Basically, the Ashy-head represents a more interior land dweller, the Ruddy-head being more coastal in distribution.

In captivity both can be aggressive but essentially their breeding styles are the same.

Both types like cover around a nest, and the sort of tepee described in the nest requirements chapter serves as an admirable nest site.

Six eggs are laid, and the incubation period is 30 days.

The Orinoco Goose (*Neochen jubata*) is currently regarded as a link between sheldgeese and shelducks. It is essentially a jungle dweller of the Orinoco River area.

In captivity they are not so dangerous to other birds as are sheldgeese and are popular with aviculturists even though they are not widely established. There are probably more in America than in Europe. It can be difficult to breed them in captivity, but once started they normally lay well. In colder climates, these birds need winter protection. They are not hardy, especially in colder, wetter areas. Some Orinocos display remarkable behavior in captivity. One breeding female I had seemed fascinated by the box-nesting Hooded Mergansers, Buffleheads and Smew in her aviary. She paid absolutely no attention to these birds at all most of the year. However, during the breeding season, the female Orinoco would wander around locating all the raised boxes and stick her head into them looking for the ducks. Generally the ducks would fend her off, but I saw her one morning, pulling a Hooded Merganser from a nest box. She and her mate were immediately removed from the aviary. The season before I housed the pair in this aviary, I had had odd occurrences happening, such as reliable sitting Smew and Hooded, mysteriously deserting their eggs during incubation. As I hadn't seen the Orinoco behaving in this fashion previously, I had no clue what she was up to. Needless to say, upon her departure from the aviary, things got back to normal. Now, the Orinoco was to surprise me again, by locating the nests of ground-nesting ducks, and rolling out the eggs in their nests! I had to get rid of the pair. I often wondered if she was intentionally cleaning house, making sure nobody else was nesting in "her" territory before she did, as she was clearly and intentionally looking for nesting birds.

Another interesting trait both birds had, was their love of live fish. They would try desperately to catch some of the live minnows I fed as treats to my sea ducks. Of course, they were too slow to compete with the mergansers, Smew and Buffleheads (even my fish eating Pygmy Geese could catch fish quicker), so I would stun the odd fish and throw it to them. I often wondered if part of their natural diet in the wild involved fish and/or fish or meat carrion?

A raised barrel, or kennel-type nesting facility is preferred for these cavity nesters where an average 6 eggs are incubated for 30 days.

The 2 African sheldgoose relatives are the Egyptian Goose (*Alopochen aegyptiacus*) and the Abyssinian Blue-winged Goose (*Cyanochen cyanopterus*).

The Abyssinian may be, as Frank Todd speculates, the nearest relative of the Andean Goose and they certainly have a similar display and superficially similar voices, although when actually displaying the Blue-wing whistles continually, whereas the Andean produces a sort of belching whistle-grunt. Likesheldgeese they can be very aggressive. In captivity they are fairly well represented. They utilize a similar sort of tepee or wigwam as the Ruddy-headed, and average 5 eggs and a 32-day incubation period.

The Egyptian Goose is the other sheldgoose in the African connection. This bird is well represented in captivity despite its vicious nature. There is a white form developed in captivity, and an intermediate blonde form.

In the wild, Egyptian Geese utilize the tree nests of other birds, or nest on cliff ledges, old buildings or nest on the ground in cover. In captivity a large kennel or barrel is used and these geese can produce prodigious numbers of eggs, 4 clutches being fairly usual. Clutches are sizable, averaging 8 eggs and their incubation period is about 30 days.

All sheldgeese can be sustained on wheat and pellets. However, I find they respond well to the addition of a multivitamin supplement and greens. Some of these geese, depending on their individual personalities, can be trusted with smaller ducks in their pens—but pairs will have to be watched carefully for a period to determine whether or not there will be a problem.

25

Swans

Swans are among the largest and longest-lived of birds. Maintained in captivity for centuries, one species, the Mute Swan has even been afforded the honor of "Royal Swan" in England. Undeniably they are graceful and noble birds, but on occasion as wasteful and bad tempered as their regal human counterparts.

Swans are also among the heaviest of flying birds, the immense Trumpeter Swan weighing as much as 38 or 40 pounds.

Swans and mankind have shared an affinity through the passage of time. They have been idolized, eaten and utilized for their down, feathers (for arrows and pens) and eggs. Myths and legends are recorded concerning their life styles and even about their supposed death song or "swan song." Most of these stories are, quite simply, the product of inventive imaginations.

The best known of all the swans is probably the Mute Swan (*Cygnus olor*) which is nearly as heavy as the Trumpeter. All swans under captive conditions should be kept in their own pens as they are famed for their savagery to other animals and even humans!

Mutes (as all swans) make very good parents and most pairs could be trusted to rear their own young. However, it must be remembered that a young cygnet cannot scale the same gradients of bankside that their parents can. Make sure that ponds have gently sloping sides or at least 2 or 3 exit points for birds with young. Also make certain that young get fed properly and are being cared for during bad weather.

Swans are well known for their devotion to each other but they will mate again should one of the pair perish. Unfortunately they are prone to collision with power lines and death through dredging up lead fishing weights, hooks and discarded nylon. Also they are occasionally shot as pests by farmers. However in Europe at least, the development of old gravel pits as water sport areas means that bird sanctuaries are set aside and so the Mute will never really be under pressure.

Most swans construct huge nests if enough material is available. I like to make nests for swans giving them 2 or 3 within their pen. Make the nests tall (they will settle in time) and leave lots of bits and pieces around each site as swans like to finish off a nest themselves (see nesting requirements chapter). Mute Swans lay around 6 eggs which are incubated for 35 to 36 days.

Another well-known swan in captivity is the Black Swan (*Cygnus atratus*). Many hundreds are reared annually. Again a quite savage swan, they are nevertheless much sought after, being the only totally black swan.

They can, in mild climates, lay through every month of the year. Colonies can also be established by starting a group of young birds together in a pen. They average 6 eggs and incubate for 35 to 38 days.

The Black-necked Swan (*Cygnus melanocoryphus*) is one of the two South American Swans. Again, they are well known in captivity and breed quite early in the season.

They carry their young on their backs and probably are more aquatically adapted (if that is possible) than any other swan species. I have seen Mutes, Black, Coscoroba and once a Trumpeter carry young, but none do it as readily as the Black-necked. They are devoted parents and males can be just as savage as any other variety. As Black-necked Swans are early season nesters and are particularly clumsy on land, it would be advisable to locate their nest site for them, as close as possible to the water, if not actually on it, as in the stifftail nesting raft form. The sitting female will benefit from a cover of sorts over the nest to protect her from the wind, rain or snow.

The Coscoroba Swan (*Coscoroba coscoroba*) is a puzzling bird. It is not a swan-like bird at all at first glance. It has a fully feathered face, long legs, and a suspiciously ducklike bill. Their young are patterned and resemble enormous whistling ducklings. They also produce far more down than any of the other swans. It is probable that they represent a link between swans, geese and ducks and thus are a sole survivor of a very old type of waterfowl. In the wild, Coscoroba Swans can be found on both fresh and salt water. Those that live along shore lines ingest more animal material than most other swans and maybe this is why they need their extraordinary ducklike bills. Might it be possible that their long legs are better suited to scrambling around on tide pool rocks? Frank Todd told me once that he had seen a Coscoroba Swan many miles out at sea, so they might be good travelers, too. They are numerous in captivity but not quite so easy to breed as Black Swans or Mutes. They lay 5 to 6 eggs and incubate for 35 days.

The last group of swans could almost be termed the Arctic Swans. The Whistling or Tundra Swan (*Cygnus columbianus columbianus*) is a well-known North American swan and is better represented in American collections than in Europe. They were bred first in Canada then possibly in America before two pairs in Europe (C. Marler and The Wildfowl Trust) laid simultaneously in the same year. Chris Marler's hatched first and so technically were the first of these swans bred in Europe. Chris also holds the distinction of being one of the few people who have bred Trumpeters, Whistlers, Bewick's and Whoopers all in one season—and it wasn't a "one-off" occurrence. In fact, while I was lucky enough to be his curator for 3 years we even had the Jankowski's Swans laying, although no young were produced. (This pair is now in America.)

Whistling Swans are among the smaller swans, marginally larger than the Bewick's, the smallest of the swans. They show tremendous variation in the extent of yellow on the beak, varying, from a large patch to none at all.

It seems one way to get reluctant pairs to nest is to place them in a pen next to an established pair of Whistling Swans, or Trumpeters. The constant threatening of the established pair seems to resurrect protective feelings in the reluctant pair and often the pair bond strengthens considerably. If you try this, make sure that birds cannot reach over the wire, and screen the fence up to the bird's wing height, otherwise they will try to thrash each other through the wire and tear wings and toenails badly. Whistlers lay 4 to 5 eggs and incubate for 32 days.

In the beautiful little Bewick's Swan (*Cygnus columbianus bewickii*), the eastern variety has been designated as Jankowski's Swan (*Cygnus c. jankowski*) by some enthusiasts.

There is much argument as to whether there is any credibility in bisecting the subspecies. My own opinion is that there could well be grounds for splitting them. I have been lucky enough to have worked with both Bewick's and Jankowski's for some 10 years and the true Jankowski's is a thick-beaked bird and has more bill color than the Western. It also migrates through China to Japan, whereas its Western cousin goes to Europe, the British Isles and Ireland to winter.

The Bewick's has been kept in Europe for some time and was apparently bred in captivity before 1915. When I left Christopher Marler in 1982 to come to America, he was the only person breeding Bewick's swans. The Wildfowl Trust's old female (Mrs. Noah as she was known!) had become too old. Even Chris' female was 22 years old at that time. Some of the young that we produced as Chris' were sent to America, and at the time of going to press, I am unable to ascertain whether or not any Bewick's still exist in American collections, or for that matter in European collections, let alone if any are being bred. It is a great shame that these pretty and very likable little swans are not better repre- sented in collections, but at the same time, I feel especially privileged to have been able to have worked with Bewick's and Jankowski's at Mr. Marler's Flamingo Park and Zoological Gar- dens in England.

Bewick's lay 3 to 5 eggs (4 being normal) which are incu- bated for 32 days.

The Whooper Swan (*Cygnus cygnus*) has an enormous circum-tundra range. From Iceland going east, it ranges through Northern Europe and Russia even occasionally nesting in Alaska. This is a midrange swan in terms of size, not as large as the Trumpeter or Mute but sizably larger than either the Whistler or Bewick's.

They can be savage birds. The largest bruise I ever saw on a man was the work of a supposedly tame and docile male Whooper. Most pairs are extremely vocal especially during spring and their incessant vocalizing can quickly become an annoyance to neighbors.

They like to construct enormous nests in which the female lays 5 eggs and incubates for 34 days.

The final member of the Arctic Swan group is the massive and very regal Trumpeter Swan (*Cygnus buccinator*). These swans have 2 distinct wild populations, one group nesting in Alaska and a much smaller and virtually nonmigratory group residing in the Red Rock Lakes area of Montana. There are nesting pairs in the Yellowstone National Park and one wonders if these birds are as prone to rearing failure as are the Red Rock birds. It appears that certain optimum conditions need to exist in any one breeding season if any young are to be reared at all. The Red Rock population was about 60 birds at one stage and their recent recovery in numbers means that a lot of these birds must be suffering from sibling genetic links.

Trumpeters do well in captivity and are fairly well represented in American and European collections. Because of their size and power they can do considerable damage, but like all swans they are individuals. I've known pairs of these swans to be very docile and timid while others would score 11 on a rating of 1 to 10 for aggression!

Like the Whooper, they build massive nests and so the same facilities for nest sites mentioned earlier ought to be employed. Make sure (for all your swans) that the water is deep enough in their pond so that they can copulate properly or you'll end up with infertile eggs. A depth of 2 feet or more is advisable.

Trumpeters lay around 5 eggs and incubate for about 35 days.

Epilogue

This then has been a resume of the waterfowl of the world and their habits. I must reiterate that the vast majority of my work with waterfowl has been in the captive environment as opposed to the wild, and what little experience I have had observing wild ducks, geese and swans, has been of great importance to me. Because I was almost always employed by other people to care for their birds on a full-time basis, it became a full-time job for me, and therefore what little free time I had was not necessarily devoted to watching the creatures I looked after at work. I always loved to talk with the people I knew who had time to go to the wilder places on earth, and study or collect waterfowl and their young or eggs. Frank Todd, Mike Lubbock, Chris Marler, Bill Makins, Butch Allen, Bob Elgas, Walt Sturgeon and countless others, all gave me ideas from their observations of birds in the wild. When I did have the time to watch birds for myself, I was always asking myself why an individual was doing this or that, trying to pick out clues that might benefit their counterparts in my care back home.

When I finally did get to build my own aviaries and keep my own birds, all this accumulated knowledge was vital to me, and in this book, I have tried to lay out a little of the more important things I have learned in more than 20 years of dealing with the ducks, geese and swans of the world.

Probably the MOST important thing I learned was to take the time to observe what my birds were doing, to see how they behaved and interacted. Secondly, I would guess that because I took the time to talk to people about what they had seen of the wild birds and their habits, and because I took the trouble to find out HOW waterfowl work (internally and mentally), I got a quicker and larger grasp of the world they live in.

There are hundreds of well-known breeders of waterfowl in America and Europe today, all equally successful in their own right. When I first got into the waterfowl business, there were few, and secrets to breeding this or that species in captivity were closely guarded. If waterfowl are to survive in all their many and varied forms in the wild and in captivity for the benefit of generations to come, it seemed senseless to me to simply hoard this knowledge for personal gain, and hence, the reason for this book.

Not everyone reading this book will agree with my methods or conclusions, and that in itself is a good thing. In my experience, discussion and trial and error are the cornerstones to successful waterfowl propagation. You learn the most from your mistakes. If we never made any, not much of significance would ever be learned, and I can guarantee you that the major names in the business of waterfowl propagation today have probably made more mistakes than most. The difference between success and failure in this business is the ability to LEARN from each occurrence, and make sure it never happens again.

You don't become proficient in waterfowl breeding overnight, or by reading books. It is a time consuming affair and requires dedication and, sometimes, quite a lot of money. My hope is that in reading this book, you may acquire the former and save yourself the latter.

Sometime in the future, a field biologist, searching for the last remaining specimens of some race of waterfowl may cry, "How was this allowed to happen, and how come we don't know anything about them?"

Hopefully, somewhere, a private breeder will be able to raise a hand and say, "Actually, some of us do. We have hundreds still alive."

Index
Common and Scientific Names

In the following listing, bold numbers refer to pictures.

272

C

Cackling Goose 242
Cairina hartlaubi 187
C. moschata 186
C. scutulata 186
Call Duck 73–74
Calonetta leucophrys 189
Campbell Island Teal **148**, 222
Canvasback 178
Cape Shelduck 254
Cape Shoveler 173
Cape Teal 221
Cereopsis Goose **9**, 45, 62, 93, 122, 249–50
Cereopsis novae-hollandiae 249
Chenonetta jubata 190
Chestnut-breasted Teal 223
Chilean Pintail 170
Chilean Teal 220
Chilean Torrent Duck **149**, 225
Chiloe Wigeon 169
China Goose 73
Chinese Merganser 184
Chinese Spotbill 163
Chloephaga hybrida 257
C. h. hybrida 257
C. h. malvinarum 257
C. melanoptera 258
C. picta leucoptera 259
C. p. picta 259
C. poliocephala 260
C. rubidiceps 260
Cinnamon Teal 37, 161, 171–73
Clangula hyemalis 201
Columbian Ruddy Duck 216
Columbian Torrent Duck 225
Comb Ducks 192–93
Common Black Scoter 207, 208
Common White-eye 180
Coscoroba coscoroba 265
Coscoroba Swan 63, **130**, 265
Crested Duck 255–56
Crozet Island Pintail 171

Cuban Whistling Duck **133**, 227, 228
Cyanochen cyanopterus 261
Cygnus atratus 264
C. buccinator 267
C. columbianus bewickii 266
C. c. columbianus 265
C. c. jankowski 266
C. cygnus 267
C. melanocoryphus 264
C. olor 263

D

Dendrocygna arborea 228
D. arcuata arcuata 229
D. a. australis 229
D. a. pygmaea 229
D. autumnalis 227
D. a. discolor 227
D. bicolor 228
D. eytoni 228
D. guttata 227
D. javanica 229
D. viduata 229
Dusky Canada Goose 241, 244

E

East Indian Grey Teal 223
East Indian Wandering Whistling Duck 229
Eastern Greylag 233
Egyptian Goose 45, 261–62
Eider 66, 98, 194–99, 205
Emperor Goose 52, 62, 66, 239
European Eider 194
European Goldeneye 204
European Goosander 184
European Greater Scaup 179
European Green-wing Teal 217, 218
European Pochard 177
European Shelduck **135**, 254
European Shoveler 173

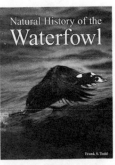

Fine Books Available From Hancock House

Altai Snowcock

Birds of Africa, Vol I

Birds of Africa, Vol II

Birds of Africa, Vol III

Birds of Africa, Vol IV

Buffalo Cookbook

Chameleons

Cheng and the Golden Pheasant

City Peregrines

Compleat Falconer

Cranes

Emu Farmer's Handbook, Vol. 1

Emu Farmer's Handbook, Vol. 2

Encyclopedia of Fishes

Falconry Manual

Game Bird Breeders Handbook

Great White Sharks

Hawking Ground Quarry

Hawking with Golden Eagles

Hedgehogs

Hornbills

Hunting Falcon

Intro. to Ornamental Pheasants

Intro. to Squirrel Hunting

A Life with Birds (Ronald Stevens)

Megapodes

Monster! Monster!

Natural History of the Waterfowl

Naturalized Fishes of the World

Penguins

Pheasant Jungles

Pheasants of the World

Pheasants of the World, Ltd. Ed.

Photo Guide to N. A. Raptors

Pirate of the Plains

Practical Incubation

Rumors of Existence

Softbills

Some Time w/ Eagles and Falcons

Stewart the Skyscraper Falcon

Understanding the Bird of Prey

Waterfowl

Order From:

Hancock Wildlife Research Center

Order Desk: (800) 938-1114 fax: (800) 983-2262

(604) 538-1114 fax: (604) 538-2262

email: hancock@uniserve.com